TOLSTOY'S *THE DEATH OF IVAN IL'ICH*

A Critical Companion

TOLSTOY'S *THE DEATH OF IVAN IL'ICH*

A Critical Companion

Edited by Gary R. Jahn

Northwestern University Press

The American Association of Teachers of

Slavic and East European Languages

Northwestern University Press

Evanston, Illinois 60208-4210

Copyright © 1999 by Northwestern University Press. Published 1999. All rights reserved.

Printed in the United States of America

ISBN 0-8101-1406-2

Library of Congress Cataloging-in-Publication Data

Tolstoy's The death of Ivan Il'ich : a critical companion / edited by Gary R. Jahn.

    p. cm.—(Northwestern/AATSEEL critical companions to Russian literature)

    Includes bibliographical references.

    ISBN 0-8101-1406-2 (paper)

    1. Tolstoy, Leo, graf, 1828–1910. Smert' Ivana Il'icha.

  I. Jahn, Gary R. II. Series.

PG3365.S63D4   1999

891.73'3—dc21   98–43613

                                        CIP

Contents

Prefatory Note on References and Acknowledgments

The authoritative, scholarly edition of the works of Leo Tolstoy in Russian is *Polnoe sobranie sochinenii v devianosto tomakh* (Moscow and Leningrad: Gosudarstvennoe Izdatel'stvo Khudozhestvennoi Literatury, 1928–1958). This edition, which contains more than thirty thousand pages of text and commentary in its ninety volumes, is the most complete single collection of Tolstoy's works (published and unpublished) and private papers. It is often referred to as the "Jubilee edition" because its publication commenced on the hundredth anniversary of Tolstoy's birth. The text of *The Death of Ivan Il'ich* is printed in volume 26 of this edition. I am indebted to the editors of this volume for the information provided in their commentary on the novel; I have made free use of that information in this book.

I have selected the translation of *The Death of Ivan Il'ich* by Louise and Aylmer Maude as the English text of the novel. Of the various editions of this translation currently in print I would steer the reader toward a recently published anthology of Tolstoy's short fiction: *Tolstoy's Short Fiction*, edited and with revised translations by Michael R. Katz (New York: Norton, 1991). The annotations to the novel supplied in part 3 of this book are keyed to the translated text of *The Death of Ivan Il'ich* as published in this edition, which also provides the texts of several of Tolstoy's other shorter works of fiction, including another major work from the same period as *The Death of Ivan Il'ich*, the short novel *Master and Man*. In addition, the collection is supplemented by a number of scholarly studies of Tolstoy's shorter fiction, including several directly relevant to *The Death of Ivan Il'ich*. I selected the Maudes' translation of the novel rather than any of several others because they were Tolstoy's contemporaries, indeed were close friends of his, and were very much attuned to the spirit of his works, particularly his later writings.

Parenthetical references to the text of *The Death of Ivan Il'ich* in part 1 of this book give the page number(s) of the English text first and then those of the Russian text (e.g., 123 [26:61]). The methods of displaying page references adopted by the authors of the five scholarly studies presented in part 2 are explained by each author. All translations of Russian language material other than the text of the novel itself are my own or those of the contributing scholars whose works are printed here. Some of the material in this book has appeared in previous publications. I am grateful to the copyright holders for their permission to use portions, revised for this publication, of my earlier study, *The Death of Ivan Il'ich: An Interpretation* (New York: Twayne, 1993), © 1993 by Twayne Publishers; all rights reserved. Of the scholarly studies printed here, two (those by Professor Turner and Professor Rancour-Laferriere) were newly written for this collection. The other three contributions have all appeared previously and are reprinted here with thanks. Professor Gutsche's "Moral Fiction: Tolstoy's *Death of Ivan Il'ich*" first appeared in his book *Moral Apostasy in Russian Literature* (DeKalb: Northern Illinois University Press, 1986). Professor Salys's "Signs on the Road of Life: *The Death of Ivan Il'ich*" first appeared in *The Slavic and East European Journal* 30 (1986): 18–28. Professor Rogers's "Scrooge on the Neva: Dickens and Tolstoy's *Death of Ivan Il'ich*" was published in *Comparative Literature* 40 (1998): 193–218.

Note on Transliteration

Russian words, names, and phrases are transcribed according to the Library of Congress system of transliteration in the case of all bibliographical references and linguistic citations. In most other contexts, a less formal system is in place: the traditional spelling of a name like Tolstoy is retained.

I  INTRODUCTION

The Importance of the Work

GARY R. JAHN

Every passing year brings fresh proof of the continuing vitality of Tolstoy's *Death of Ivan Il'ich*. Indeed, the untimely death of Tolstoy's hero seems almost to have been compensated by the longevity of the story memorializing him. What is it that accounts for the continued vitality of this short novel?

Nearly everything Leo Tolstoy wrote is of considerable interest, since he is one of the giants of Russian literature. *The Death of Ivan Il'ich*, however, is regarded as one of his great masterpieces; many would say that it is the chef d'oeuvre of the second half of his literary career. Written in 1886, it was the first major fictional work published by Tolstoy after his crisis and conversion of the late 1870s. For a considerable period after 1878 Tolstoy had turned away from literature altogether in favor of his biblical and theological writings. Thus it was with considerable interest that the reading public of the mid-1880s learned of the publication of a new novel from the pen of the author of *War and Peace* and *Anna Karenina*. The novel they read in the pages of the twelfth (and last) volume of Tolstoy's *Collected Works* (1886), subtitled *Works of Recent Years*, surprised many of Tolstoy's admirers and disappointed others.

The reasons for disappointment were largely ideological. I will discuss the initial reaction to the novel's publication in the next section. Here suffice it to say that it was not long before the novel came to be universally regarded as one of the greatest works of a very great writer. *The Death of Ivan Il'ich* can be and has been variously interpreted, but it possesses certain basic qualities that must be accounted for in any cogent reading of the novel. It is a devastatingly satirical account of the life of the well-to-do professional class of late-nineteenth-century Russia. In representing the life of a member of this class, Tolstoy shows a masterful (and occasionally uncanny) ability to seize on the apt situation or detail. The novel is a remarkable example of realism, but at the same time it contains many anticipations of the symbolist art that would shortly (during the 1890s and the first decade of the twentieth century) begin to predominate in Russian literature. Finally, the novel is exemplary of Tolstoy's postconversion philosophical concerns and revised understanding of the mission of art and of the artist.

These qualities, however, could hardly account, by themselves, for the continuing power of *The Death of Ivan Il'ich* to seize and hold the imagination of its readers. The English poet and critic Matthew Arnold once said of Tolstoy (referring to the novel *Anna Karenina*) that "he created not art, but life itself."[1] Tolstoy was a master of representation and verisimilitude. His characters, and the situations in which they find themselves, come so alive that readers often feel as though they know Tolstoy's characters as well as or better than some actual acquaintances. In addition, the particular dimension of life Tolstoy addresses in *The Death of Ivan Il'ich* is one of inescapable interest to all readers. His basic subject is the inevitable confrontation of a human being with her or his own mortality, the coming to grips with the certainty that our lives will end. It is one of Tolstoy's major contentions in the novel that people are, in general, adept at hiding this ultimate truth from themselves, and he spares no effort in his determination to "remove the coverings" with which we attempt to mask the figure of death in our consciousness.

The importance of the novel for the general reader, then, is that it provides a keenly observed and unsparingly realistic account of a moment in life we shall all experience; as the character Gerasim says in chapter 1 of the novel, "We will all come to it one day." Aside, then, from the elegance of its structure, the apparent simplicity and directness of its style, and the authenticity and acuity of its observation of a form of life that seems still rather familiar in the 1990s, the novel impresses the reader with the seriousness of its purpose and its moral earnestness, and above all with the evident applicability of the life and death of its protagonist to each reader individually.

Historical and Biographical Background

The accession of Tsar Alexander II to the throne of the Russian Empire in 1855 followed, by three years, the appearance of Leo Tolstoy's first published work and had been celebrated with hopes for a more liberal, more European future for the political life of the nation. These hopes were realized at least in part as Alexander carried through a number of basic reforms in the first half of the 1860s, most notably the emancipation of the serfs (1861). As often happens, a taste of reform became a hunger for reform, a hunger that Alexander, in the late 1860s and 1870s, was increasingly unwilling to satisfy. Disaffection from the "Tsar-Liberator" culminated in 1881 with his assassination on the streets of St. Petersburg during a royal procession.

Alexander III, who succeeded his murdered father, determined not to meet a similar fate. Whereas his father had been educated by the gentle poet Zhukovsky, Alexander III had been tutored by Konstantin Pobedonostsev, a theoretician of arch-conservatism, who would become one of the new tsar's main advisers and the chief architect of Russia's final renunciation of the liberal promise of the early reign of Alexander II. Many repressive measures were adopted by the government of Alexander III: some university departments were closed for "free thinking," the censorship of printed materials was strengthened, school curricula were impoverished. Tolstoy's younger contemporary, Anton Chekhov, chronicled the effects of these changes in such stories as "Sergeant Prishibeev" and "The Man in a Shell." He portrays a public life in which the main rule of action is "what is not expressly permitted is forbidden."

Tolstoy brought himself to the unfavorable attention of the new tsar almost at once by writing him an open letter in which he urged Alexander III to set a radically new example for his nation and the world by pardoning his father's murderers. The tsar refused to grant Tolstoy's request, and, in the years that followed, the tsar's censors refused to permit publication of any of Tolstoy's works that detailed the beliefs which had inspired his dramatic plea for royal clemency.

These works occupied Tolstoy's attention almost exclusively in the late 1870s and early 1880s, and not one of Tolstoy's fictional works written in the 1880s or later (including *The Death of Ivan Il'ich* [Smert' Ivana Il'icha, 1886]) can be fully understood in isolation from the ideas he presented in those works. Tolstoy was by no means the first to hold the ideas of brotherly love, mutual support, and Christian charity that became so precious to him in the second half of his life; in fact, he came to believe that they were none other than the central tenets of a perennially fresh philosophy of life to which the great sages throughout history and in every corner of the earth, from Socrates to Schopenhauer, had subscribed.

No other representative of the "perennial philosophy,"[2] however, has left so clear and vivid an account of the spiritual and psychological travail amid which his new convictions were born. In *A Confession (Ispoved')*, written mainly in 1879–80 but not completed until 1882, Tolstoy wrote that the factor, before all others, that prompted the psychological crisis he endured in the mid-1870s (which is reflected in the character of Konstantin Levin in *Anna Karenina*) was his inability to find an acceptable meaning in human life. Every formulation of life's meaning with which he experimented was wrecked by his long-standing and by now almost overwhelming sense of the dreadful inevitability of death. He writes in *A Confession*: "My life came to a standstill. I could breathe, eat, drink, and sleep, and I could not help doing these things; but there was no life, for there were no wishes, the fulfillment of which I could consider reasonable."[3] Tolstoy describes several attempts he made to shake off the feelings of depression and despair from which he had increasingly suffered since his first experience, in 1868, of what he called the "Arzamas terror"[4] (vividly described in his unfinished short story "The Notes of a Madman"). His reading of the great philosophers of the past only confirmed the apparent meaninglessness of life that so troubled him. Turning from his library to his friends and acquaintances for help was also of no avail; either his contemporaries did not concern themselves at all with the questions he found so perplexing or their answers were no more comforting than those of the philosophers.

Finally, he turned for help to the broad masses of the Russian people, the peasants. It seemed to him that these illiterate and uneducated folk nevertheless possessed a definite conception of the meaning of life. He wrote in *A Confession* that "it became clear that mankind as a whole had a kind of knowledge, unacknowledged and scorned by me, of the meaning of life. . . . They find this meaning in irrational knowledge. And this irrational knowledge is faith, the very same faith [that is, the theology and cult practices of the Russian Orthodox Church] which I could not but reject" (23:32–33). He saw that the faith of the Russian peasants gave meaning to their lives and protected them from the despair from which he suffered; their faith itself, however, both in its dogma and its cult, had long been abhorrent to him.[5] He seemed to face a choice between a saving but irrational faith and the meaningless despair his reason showed him. In the end he reconciled himself to the irrational. "Faith still remained for me as irrational as it was before, but I could not but admit that it alone gives people a reply to the questions of life, and that consequently it makes life possible" (23:35).

He first attempted to renew his connection with the church of his childhood. For a time he carefully and conscientiously observed all the Orthodox rites, but the superstition he detected in that faith, especially as practiced by the peasants whose life he declared otherwise so admirable, soon proved fatal to his resolve. He abandoned the attempt to find a place for himself within the existing system of religion and determined to develop a system of his own. This task occupied him intensively for about four years (1878–82) and resulted in the preparation of four works which Tolstoy thereafter considered his most important achievement. After *A Confession*, which is a brief account and interpretation of his life and moral struggle through the mid-1870s, he wrote *A Critique of Dogmatic Theology (Issledovanie dogmaticheskogo bogosloviia); A Harmony and Translation of the Four Gospels (Soedinenie i perevod chetyrekh evangelii)* and *What I Believe (V chem moia vera*). Once completed, these works formed the conscious intellectual center of his thought and action for his remaining thirty years of life.

The central, indeed the only article of Tolstoy's faith was a belief in the existence of a creator God:

> But here I examined myself, examined what was taking place within me; and I recalled all those hundreds of dyings and quickenings which had taken place within me. I recalled that I lived only when I believed in God. As before, so now, I said to myself: "I need only to know about God, and I live; I need only forget, disbelieve in God, and I die." I am alive, really alive, only when I sense God and search for God. "Then for what should I look further?" cried a voice within me. "That is God. God is that without which it is impossible to live. To know God and to live are one and the same. God is life." (23:45–46)

Tolstoy's ideas may be seen as one aspect of the turning away in Russian intellectual life from the materialism that had dominated the late 1850s and 1860s toward a renewed emphasis on spiritual and religious values. The old materialism, however, continued to be philosophically viable, whereas the renewed spiritualism was sharply fractionated, particularly between proponents of the traditional religious values and practices of the Orthodox faith and those who, like Tolstoy, rebelled against the teachings of the church. The movement away from realism in art and literature was particularly sharp. The leading trend in literature from about 1890 is called *modernism*, a catchall term that subsumes the work of the so-called decadents, the symbolists, and a variety of other groups, which, despite their diversity, shared a distaste for traditional realism. It is interesting that although Tolstoy bitterly attacked the artistic practices of the modernists in his *What Is Art? (Chto takoe iskusstvo?* [1898]), *The Death of Ivan Il'ich* is profoundly symbolic and may be seen as a harbinger of the symbolist art that followed in the 1890s and later.

Criticism of the Novel

INITIAL CRITICAL RECEPTION

The critical reaction that greeted the appearance of *The Death of Ivan Il'ich*, strange as it may seem given the novel's title, paid little attention to the theme of death. Contemporary critics were more concerned with matters of style and ideology. Thus the populist critic N. K. Mikhailovsky, while noting that the novel was a "fine story," also declared that it was "not of the first rank in artistic beauty, in strength or clarity of thought, or finally in the fearless realism of the writing."[6] The response of a certain Lisovsky was more positive – "the story is without parallel in Russian literature and should be acknowledged a triumph of realism and truth in poetry" – but was still confined to generalities.[7]

The various camps in Russian literary criticism and appreciation had been arrayed in ideologically adversarial groups at least since the time of V. G. Belinsky (the founder of modern Russian literary criticism) in the 1840s. Works of literature were generally presumed to have an ideological or at least broadly educational function, and much of the literary comment of the time consisted of estimates of the degree to which a given author or a given work had succeeded in the fictional or poetic promotion of one or another ideological agenda. Once Tolstoy's fame had spread to Europe, stimulated there by the high praise accorded to his work in *Le Roman Russe* (*The Russian Novel*) by Vicomte Melchior de Vogué,[8] one finds occasional responses to the novel there also. Again, however, these tend toward evaluative generalities. The early history of the novel's reception makes it quite clear that Tolstoy's contemporaries were much struck by the novel; by and large the novel was read as an unflattering commentary on the moral shortcomings of the lifestyle of the privileged classes rather than as a reflection on the common mortality of all people.

MODERN CRITICISM AND SCHOLARSHIP

Modern critics and scholars of *The Death of Ivan Il'ich*, for the most part, no longer consider themselves obliged to deal with the question of the novel's literary value.[9] Considering that the question of value has been settled, commentators have devoted themselves to the consideration of specific aspects of the novel's themes and ideas, on the one hand, and its organization and artistic strategies, on the other.

Themes and Ideas of the Novel

SOCIAL ISSUES

An early avenue of approach to the novel was to consider it an attack on the empty and valueless life of its protagonist and the privileged society of which he was a part. This was a main theme within Soviet criticism, which, generally speaking, venerated Tolstoy as an exemplary practitioner of "critical realism." This term denotes a style in literature that, while perhaps not informed by a "proper" (i.e., Marxist) understanding of the human universe, was at least capable of arriving at "correct" (i.e., negative) judgments on precommunist forms of social organization. It was mainly used to describe the practices of such giants of nineteenth-century Russian literature as Gogol, Turgenev, and (certain aspects of) Dostoevsky, besides Tolstoy. From such a point of view *The Death of Ivan Il'ich* is without doubt an exemplary text. The life of the protagonist is that of an educated, relatively prosperous, and, above all, ordinary member of the privileged classes of the latter part of the nineteenth century, and the entire direction of the narrative is toward the display of the falseness, insincerity, insensitivity, and consequent spiritual inadequacy of that life. The *History of Russian Literature in Three Volumes*, published by the Soviet Academy of Sciences in 1964, puts it this way: "With profound artistry Tolstoy brands the petty, selfish motives, the insincerity and lies that form the basis of the 'pleasant and decent' life of the privileged members of the gentry and the state bureaucracy"; or, again, "Leo Tolstoy's merciless satire manifests itself in all its power in *The Death of Ivan Il'ich*. Ivan Il'ich's friends, even at his graveside, continue to lie and to pretend. . . . The author pitilessly tears the masks from [the faces of his characters], revealing what they really think and feel."[10] It certainly cannot be cogently maintained that the novel does not do these things; one may well wonder, however, whether the novel does these things in order to reveal the inadequacy of the social structure implicated in the narrative or whether that inadequacy is revealed as part of some other, larger literary enterprise.

Non-Soviet readers, too, have often drawn attention to the novel's critique of society. The materialism of nineteenth-century bourgeois society, or its twentieth-century counterpart, has been found either responsible for or productive of Ivan Il'ich's malaise and alienation. His physiological sickness is read as an indicator of the diseased quality of his life in society and/or of that society itself.[11] The novel has also been taken as a revelation of the manner in which society or "the social" acts as a hindrance to the discovery of the truths every person requires as an individual. In this reading, the novel is the narrative of the individual's inevitable separation from the social as the "truth" perceived by the dying protagonist becomes ever more opaque to those surrounding him.[12]

PSYCHOLOGICAL ISSUES

Most commentators on the novel have declared that Tolstoy is a masterful observer of human psychology; their admiration has been particularly occasioned by such scenes as the conversation among the deceased's colleagues or that between Ivan's wife and Peter Ivanovich. In both these passages from chapter 1 of the novel the true motives and feelings of the participants are revealed as Tolstoy strips away the masks of sympathy and condolence that they wear. The text provides such an abundance of similar examples that it may well be taken as a revelation of the psychological masking and hypocrisy characteristic of Ivan and his associates' layer of society. In this sense, Tolstoy's talent for psychological observation is understood to be employed in the furtherance of the social criticism discussed earlier.

Some scholars have understood the psychological dimension of the novel to be of primary, rather than ancillary, importance. Thus

Boris Sorokin draws our attention to Ivan's habit of psychological "encapsulization," that is, Ivan's habit of retreating from the unpleasantness of life, principally, of course, from death. The protagonist's retreats from actual reality into a controlled, internal, purely psychological (but, of course, false) reality, which he gradually establishes for himself as he ages, result, in the end, in his isolation from actuality (Sorokin, 295). William Edgerton sees the life of Ivan Il'ich becoming a form of death from this isolation.[13] This view of psychology in the novel accounts for the behavior of Ivan Il'ich on general, human grounds rather than as a psychopathy occasioned by a particular social environment.

A third approach to psychology in the novel has been along medical or quasi-medical lines. There was at one time (around the turn of the century) some interest in attempting a diagnosis of the illness from which Ivan suffers and eventually dies,[14] despite it being rather clear in the novel that the exact nature of Ivan's physiological disease is beside the point; his spiritual well-being is the main issue. Yet the basis of this early "medical" criticism, wherein the fictional account is viewed as an actual clinical record, has persisted in certain psychological studies of the novel. James Bartell, for example, applies the theories of Otto Rank and Arthur Janov to the case of Ivan Il'ich. He finds the material of the novel suitable for his purposes both on the grounds of its general fit with Rank's and Janov's explanation of the origins of neurosis in the fear of separation/rejection (one manifestation of which is the fear of death) and on the grounds of the presence in the text of the lengthy retrospective analysis of his own life, which Ivan undertakes and which leads to his ultimate escape from "that which was oppressing him." Bartell understands this as a clear anticipation of the therapy suggested by Rank and Janov.[15] Y. J. Dayananda's work on the novel shares the same sort of concern with the material, but he focuses his attention on Ivan's story as an anticipation (and corroboration) of modern research on the psychological stages involved in death and dying. He discovers analogues in the novel to each of the five stages isolated by Elisabeth Kübler-Ross in her *On Death and Dying:* (1) denial and isolation; (2) anger; (3) bargaining; (4) depression; and (5) acceptance.[16] Such interpretations as these clearly indicate that Tolstoy's powers of psychological observation were acute to the point of creating a flawless illusion of reality in the presentation of the thoughts, feelings, and behavior of the main characters. A new analysis of this type is offered in the present volume, Daniel Rancour-Laferriere's "Narcissism, Masochism, and Denial in *The Death of Ivan Il'ich.*"

George Gutsche's analysis of the novel, included in this volume, also has a psychological emphasis, but it proceeds from an entirely different assumption; the hero's story is not seen as material for psychological analysis, but rather a psychological viewpoint is adopted because it seems to offer insight into the novel. Gutsche claims, very cogently, that Ivan Il'ich's story is that of a man who comes gradually, and painfully, to the awareness that his perception of the world (his moral and psychological foundations, as it were) has been in error. Tolstoy's novel traces the arduous path the protagonist follows in his progress toward rectification of these errors of perception. At the same time "Moral Fiction: Tolstoy's *Death of Ivan Il'ich*" also explores the moral dimensions of the life and death of the protagonist, and thus Gutsche's work also has an important place in the next section.

PHILOSOPHICAL ISSUES

It is entirely in accord with Tolstoy's own interest in philosophy, religion, and ethics or morality that much of the criticism on the novel can be included under this heading. Furthermore, there can be no strict separation between the social criticism (discussed earlier) offered by the novel and the ethical teachings it seems to offer. Tolstoy's main concern in philosophy was undoubtedly with ethics and morality: the distinction between right and wrong (good and evil) actions. Many commentators direct our attention to the novel as an account of a life wrongly lived and of the protagonist's ultimate realization of its wrongness. This is one of the main points urged by Professor Gutsche, and there is much precedent for this point of view. Philip Rahv compares the life of Ivan Il'ich to that of Joseph K.

of Franz Kafka's *The Trial.* In both works it is the protagonists' certainty that their lives have been well lived that is the root of their inability to deal with the situations in which they find themselves. Sorokin (500) and Charles Glicksberg[17] both suggest that a major cause for the wrongness of the manner of Ivan Il'ich's life is his misapprehension of the nature of his life. Ivan overlooks the spiritual dimension of his life and the need for faith, and these are shown to be the only antidotes for the oppressive fear of death. Ivan's incorrect understanding of the nature of the moral situation in which he finds himself leads him further and further into a state of unreality; thus his striving for a life of illusory material reality is at the expense of his life of genuine spiritual reality (Sorokin, 487–88).

The same theme of the irreality of the life of Ivan Il'ich is taken up by Geoffrey Clive in his discussion of the "inauthentic." Although his attention is focused on moral questions, Clive, like some of the psychologically oriented critics mentioned earlier, in effect identifies the novel as being concerned mainly with social criticism. He depicts Ivan Il'ich's inauthentic life as the product of the inauthentic (by which is meant insincere) behavior that is characteristic of Ivan Il'ich's social milieu.[18] The constant practice of inauthentic behavior toward others results, at last, in a lack of truthfulness to the self and a futile attempt to conceal from oneself the significance of life's major occasions, especially death (Clive, 114–17). To this James Olney adds that what Clive would call "authentic" behavior is modeled in the story in the character of the servant Gerasim.[19] Associated with Clive's ideas, but along a different axis of development from that selected by Olney, are the several studies that delineate the roots of existential thought in the novel. Ivan's situation in life is seen as featureless and deprived of meaning and he himself as subject to a steadily increasing sense of alienation. Lev Shestov (now regarded as one of the founders of existential thought) commented at length on the novel (Shestov, 116–27). William Barrett, who regards the novel as "a basic scripture of existentialist thought" (Barrett, 143), has indicated points of comparison between the novel and the writings of both Kierkegaard and Nietzsche (Barrett, 144). Irving Halperin has developed the connection with Kierkegaard, especially with the Danish philosopher's *Sickness unto Death*.[20]

John Donnelly's article on *The Death of Ivan Il'ich* bespeaks the concerns of the philosopher more than those of the literary scholar. His work is primarily a discussion of his own view of morality and is more an occasion for his own reflections than an attempt to illuminate the novel. Mainly at issue is what Donnelly regards as the inappropriately (because unrealistically) absolute moral tone of the novel.[21] In a certain sense, Donnelly's essay is akin in spirit to those by Dayananda and Bartell, which also, in their own way, regard the novel more as a source of exemplary matter than as a text in need of interpretation. *The Death of Ivan Il'ich* has often been used in this way also by linguists (e.g., the various studies of Barlas) on the grounds that it offers a conveniently sized specimen of the conversational language of educated speakers of the period. The purpose of such studies is, however, openly linguistic, and it is made quite clear that the intention is to use rather than comment on the text of the novel.[22]

With the exception of Professor Gutsche's detailed analysis, not as much as one might expect has been made of Tolstoy's religious views as a background to the understanding of *The Death of Ivan Il'ich*.[23] Glicksberg (83) explains Tolstoy's failure to "develop to the full" the awful irony of death as a function of his belief in "redemption." In terms of Tolstoy's religious beliefs redemption would refer to the individual's freedom to select and his or her actually selecting the spiritual dimension of life as superior to the physiological. Richard Gustafson's recent book *Leo Tolstoy: Resident and Stranger* considers the novel in the context of the theological teaching of the Russian Orthodox Church concerning suffering and sin. He suggests that here, as elsewhere, Tolstoy was closer to church teaching than his many militant statements to the contrary would suggest. Thus suffering is portrayed as the way to self-understanding, almost as a divine kindness to the lost soul of Ivan Il'ich. Ivan's illness is discussed as a metaphor for his misapprehension of the nature of human life, or "sin," to use Gustafson's term.[24] Gustafson's treatment of the novel is informed by a comprehensive knowledge of the contents of Tolstoy's religious writings and by a preference for what these writings may suggest as opposed to what they seem to say. A more straightforward link between Tolstoy's religious writings and *The Death of Ivan Il'ich* has been suggested by W. R. Hirschberg, who has drawn attention especially to the treatise *On Life* (especially chapter 9), which Tolstoy wrote immediately after *The Death of Ivan Il'ich*. This connection has been explored in detail by Jahn.[25]

Structure and Style of the Novel

The general artistic organization of the novel, its artistic structure, has occasioned considerable critical comment. Halperin was one of the first to point out the steady narrowing of narrative focus in the text. He associates this feature with the portion of the text that recounts Ivan's life after his fall from the ladder. The narrative focus becomes most concentrated at the very end of the novel (Halperin, 337–39). The disproportion of space assigned to Ivan's life before he became ill (about one-fourth of the text) and his illness and death (about three-fourths of the text) has been noted by Olney, who explains this feature as an indication that Ivan's death is much more significant than his life (Olney, 108–9).

In considering the artistic organization of the story, considerable interest has been taken in the question of the placement of the material contained in the first chapter of the novel. Put simply, it has been seen as somewhat problematical that while the vast majority of the text is devoted to a chronological account of the life and death of the protagonist, the material in chapter 1 pertains to the period after Ivan's death. In terms of the primarily chronological narrative, this material seems to belong at the end of the novel rather than at the beginning. C. J. G. Turner has suggested that the placement of the material in the first chapter may be explained by the history of the novel's creation: Tolstoy's original plan had been to tell the story through the device of Ivan's personal diary account of his experiences. The first chapter was to offer an opportunity for this diary to come into the hands of one of the characters (the one who later became Ivan's friend and colleague, Peter Ivanovich) and thence to the reader. Turner also notes that the linguistic structure of chapter 1 is similar to that of chapter 2, which in fact follows it, but would be in strident contrast to that of chapter 12, which would precede it if the material in chapter 1 were placed chronologically.[26] Gunter Schaarschmidt commented extensively on the placement of the first chapter in his analysis of the language of the novel. Professor Turner's newly written contribution to the present volume revisits this theme and presents a further analysis of word clusters and semantic groups in the novel.

The placement of the material in the first chapter is one of a number of questions that have to do with what we may call the "narrative strategy" of the novel. Edward Wasiolek has commented on this topic at some length. He has suggested that the placement of Ivan's death at the beginning of the text alienates the reader's sympathies from the very outset by providing a sharply critical portrait of those who survive Ivan Il'ich and, by implication, of the sort of life that the decedent had lived (Wasiolek, 324).

Wasiolek, however, is mainly concerned to address a primary criticism of the novel, namely, that its narrative is arbitrary and its narrator intrusive. Wasiolek points out that the basis of such a criticism is in what he calls the "Jamesian fictional imperative." By this is meant that the unfriendly critic has invoked criteria that may be very appropriate to a consideration of the work of Henry James (who is on record as being no admirer of Tolstoy) but very inappropriate to a consideration of a work by Tolstoy (Wasiolek, 318). Wasiolek admits that by the Jamesian standard the narrative strategy of the novel seems arbitrary or "arranged"; it is clear that Tolstoy is intent on interpreting as well as telling the events portrayed in the novel. Authorial intrusion is part of Tolstoy's narrative stance; if the novel is approached with a prejudice against such a strategy, naturally only an unfavorable judgment of the work is possible (Wasiolek, 317). Wasiolek describes Tolstoy's technique as a "clear and unambiguous control of the meaning he intends" (Wasiolek, 319). This acknowledgment of the importance of considering the author's intentions, at least with an author like Tolstoy, is a most important concept in dealing with *The Death of Ivan Il'ich*. Jahn's *Death of Ivan Il'ich: An Interpretation* is an attempt to discuss the novel largely from this point of view and from within the context of Tolstoy's own writings. Although attempting to pay attention to the author's intentions in the interpretation of a work of literature has a long history and the support of substantial theoretical argument (see especially E. D. Hirsch, *Validity in Interpretation* [New Haven: Yale University Press, 1967]),[27] it has also been noted the exclusive allegiance to this method of work may lead to an inappropriate narrowing of the interpreter's horizon. Certainly such an approach as that taken by Daniel Rancour-Laferriere in his contribution to this volume cannot be said to be anchored in the conscious intentions of the author, but its helpfulness to readers grappling with the significance of the novel may be no less for that.

The undisguised presence of Tolstoy the author as an interpreting and guiding force in the narrative has been confirmed by the discovery of a variety of subtexts within the novel. A subtext may take various forms, most commonly that of a pattern of allusions to some other text (either by the same or another author) or a pattern within the narrative that seems to be at odds with the pattern on the surface of the narrative. Chapter 9 of Jahn (1993) contains the most complete discussion of subtext in the second meaning suggested here. The first sort of subtext (which has also been called "intertext") has occasioned frequent comment in the context of Tolstoy's many attempts to deal with the theme of death in his writings. David Matual has considered one particular example at length: the intertextual relationship between *The Death of Ivan Il'ich* and Tolstoy's *A Confession*, written some half-dozen years earlier. Matual has displayed numerous parallels between the situation of Tolstoy as described in *A Confession*, and that of Ivan Il'ich, as described in the novel.[28] The effect of the discoveries of such subtexts are, of course, that readings of Ivan's physiological illness as symbolic of underlying spiritual malaise become easier to defend and seem more likely to be appropriate.

Related to the notions of subtext and intertext is the connection between *The Death of Ivan Il'ich* and the works of other writers. Philip Rogers, for example, has produced a magisterial discussion of the connections between Tolstoy and the English novelist Charles Dickens, with particular reference to *The Death of Ivan Il'ich*. That study is reprinted in the present volume.

As we conclude this brief survey of critical comment on the novel, let us turn to the question of the use of image, symbol, metaphor, and other literary figures in the text. It was mentioned earlier that Tolstoy was very much at odds with the symbolist writers of the 1890s and early 1900s on the grounds that their art was exclusive and unconcerned with the ethical questions Tolstoy considered so important. It is a curious irony that Tolstoy's works, to some extent, prefigure, in their use of symbol and metaphor, some of the aesthetic devices of those later writers whom he would soon be so roundly denouncing. To prevent any misunderstanding, however, it needs to be said that Tolstoy's symbolism is of what we might call a metonymic sort: it is based in the use of one report of experience to comment on, reflect, foreshadow, or explain another experience. Characteristic of the symbolists, however, is a metaphorical (or even metaphysical) symbolism, wherein a report of experience on one plane of existence is taken to reflect, explain, etc., experience on a different plane.[29]

Already in *Anna Karenina* (from the mid-1870s) Tolstoy had written a book that many have found to contain profoundly symbolic (in the metonymic sense) elements. The chapter describing the horse race in which Vronsky competes or the scene of Levin mowing hay with the peasants come immediately to mind. In *The Death of Ivan Il'ich* this tendency is much intensified. Situations, details, even turns of phrase seem full of meaning and suggestiveness for the reader's understanding of the life and death of the protagonist. Various critics have explained the symbolism of the card game that Ivan is so fond of playing, of his interest in the furnishing of his apartment, of the ladder from which he falls, and of the position he adopts on the couch in his study. Rimgaila Salys's "Signs on the Road of Life: *The*

Death of Ivan Il'ich," reprinted in this volume, has a thorough discussion of such usages in the novel.[30] George Gutsche's is the best general summary account of the artistry of Tolstoy's use of language, especially of the patterned repetition of key words and phrases and of the play with prefixes, roots, and suffixes in the text. Jahn has advanced the notion that it is characteristic of *The Death of Ivan Il'ich* that what is metaphorical on one level of the text must often be taken literally on another (as when, on the physiological plane, a friend says that Ivan Il'ich is so ill that he seems to have become a corpse, while on the spiritual plane this proves to be already true).

By far the greatest amount of attention has been paid to the image of the "black bag" or "black hole," which plays so prominent a role in the last four chapters of the novel. Matual has pointed out that this key image is one of the connections between *the Death of Ivan Il'ich* and *A Confession*, in which the image first appeared as a "black spot" (Matual, 126). In the main, critics have regarded this image as suggestive of the uterus and as part of the symbolic depiction of Ivan's rebirth (Halperin; Olney). However, Sorokin has elaborated a solid case for the idea that the symbolic referent of the black bag is the bowel, especially in the many textual references to the cecum (the "blind gut," the appendix). In either case, the reader's attention is drawn to the conclusion that the entire account of Ivan Il'ich's life and death is symbolically referential, that his physiological life symbolizes his spiritual life. The conclusion has been drawn by Edgerton that Ivan's death is a door to genuine life and that his life had been a form of death (300).

In this chapter I have introduced the main trends in the scholarship and criticism of *The Death of Ivan Il'ich*. Many of the ideas mentioned here will reappear in the studies that follow, and I have indicated briefly the particular avenues of scholarship in which each of them is to be found. The history of the scholarship and criticism of a notable work of literature is rather like a lengthy discussion. In order to understand any new contribution to such a history one needs to be aware of the context in which it is offered and to which it responds, just as one needs to know in a discussion what the participants have talked about so far if one is to assess the meaning and significance of any new contribution. In this section, then, we have been orienting ourselves to the main themes that have emerged in the discussion of *The Death of Ivan Il'ich*. In part 2 we will present five examples of contributions to this discussion. First, however, some specific background to the writing of the text.

Background of the Novel

The Death of Ivan Il'ich was the product of a time in Tolstoy's life full of hope and anxiety. The years 1885 and 1886 brought death into Tolstoy's house and serious illness to Tolstoy. In December 1885 he wrote (although he never sent the letter) to his friend and disciple, V. G. Chertkov: "I am living through what are perhaps the final hours of my life, and living badly – mournful and irritated with those around me. I am doing something that is not as God would have it; I try to find out what it is, but it eludes me. And always there is this constant anxiety, mournfulness, and worst of all, irritation and the desire for death" (85:294). If the essence of Tolstoy's conversion in the 1870s had been the elaboration of an answer to the question posed by the ineluctable and nullifying power of death, these re-marks of the mid-1880s suggest that that answer, which had until then "made life possible" for Tolstoy, was losing its power to per-suade. Despite this, or perhaps because of it, these years also saw the creation of many of Tolstoy's most affirmative fictions (the majority of his "Stories for the People" were written in 1885 and 1886) as well as *On Life*, his most detailed statement of his views on the positive potential of human existence.

The surface of Tolstoy's story about the life and death of Ivan Il'ich seems to reflect more clearly the anxious rather than the hope-ful side of the author as he was in the years 1885 and 1886. A full appreciation of the novel requires the reader to bear in mind both Tolstoy's conscious conviction of having arrived at a satisfying expla-nation of death and its significance and his more hidden but still persisting and still powerful anxiety over it. The purpose of the remainder of this introduction, however, is to describe how it was that the novel came to be written, to provide background information concerning Tolstoy's conception of art and of the artist's mission, and to offer preliminary observations on the organization of the text.

Composition of the Novel

Tolstoy worked intensively on the novel from August 1885 to March 1886. In a letter to his friend D. Urusov (22 August 1885) Tolstoy refers to "an account of the simple death of a simple man, told from his own point of view" (26:681). Tolstoy's active interest in this subject can be traced back to July or August 1881, when he first heard of the recent (2 July 1881) death of a certain Ivan Il'ich Mechnikov, a prosecutor in the regional court of Tula government (the major subsidiary regions in the administrative organization of Russia were called "governments"; these, in turn, were subdivided into "districts"). Tolstoy knew and liked Mechnikov, about whose death he learned from the deceased's brother, Il'ia Il'ich. Mechnikov, who was known as a kindly and benevolent man, served as the partial prototype of Ivan Il'ich Golovin, the protagonist of *The Death of Ivan Il'ich*. Tolstoy's sister-in-law, Tatyana Kuzminskaya, states in her memoirs that she repeated to Tolstoy what had been confided to her by the deceased's widow, that Mechnikov's dying thoughts had been of the "uselessness of the life he had lived."

Tolstoy took no immediate action on the impressions aroused by Mechnikov's death. He seems to have left them to develop without conscious supervision in some quiet corner of his reflecting mind; in the period between his first knowledge of the incident and August 1885 only twice is he known to have mentioned a continuing interest in the topic (in April and December 1884).

Once Tolstoy had actively set to work on the novel, however, he involved himself in it intensely. He completed a finished draft of the story in January 1886 and sent it to the publisher late in that month or early in February; the proof sheets were returned to him for correction in mid-February; Tolstoy heavily revised these and submitted what was essentially a new version of the novel in early March. He further revised the new set of proofs, which he received in mid-March. These corrected proofs, the novel's final revision, were returned to the publisher on 25 March. The novel was first published in volume 12 (the final volume) of *The Works of Count L. N. Tolstoy* (edited by Mrs. Tolstoy) later in 1886.

Tolstoy on Art and as Artist

In defining artistic unity Tolstoy paid scant attention to the traditional methods of linkage for which his critics were perhaps looking. In his "Preface to the Works of Guy de Maupassant" ("Predislovie k sochineniiam Giui de Mopassana," 1894) he wrote:

> People who have little artistic sensibility often think that the unity of a work of art depends on its portraying the actions of a single set of characters or being organized around a single set of complicating circumstances or describing the life of a single person. This is incorrect. . . . The cement that joins any work of art into a unified whole and thus produces the illusion of life is not the unity of characters and situations but rather the unity of the author's own moral relationship to his subject. . . . Therefore, a writer who lacks a clear, definite, and original view of the world . . . cannot produce a work of art. (30:18–19)

As is so often the case, this pronouncement of the old Tolstoy has roots in his youth. Already in 1853 he had written:

> In reading a composition, especially a purely literary one, the main interest is the author's character as revealed in the composition. There are compositions in which the author makes an affectation of his view or changes it several times. The best are those wherein the author tries, as it were, to conceal his personal view while always remaining true to it wherever it shows through. The most colorless are those in which the view is so inconsistent as virtually to be lost. (46:182)

The "character of the author," his "view," is his understanding of reality. It is this understanding that determines his moral relationship to his subject. For Tolstoy, art was primarily a means of communicating the author's understanding of the nature of reality. The author devises the "reality" in which the characters live and act to reflect his own understanding of the nature of the reality in which he lives and acts. The unifying effect of the author's consistency in applying his insight to the separate fates of the diverse creations of his imagination is the basis of the wholeness of the literary work of art; matters of organizational technique and artistic device are of secondary importance. In part 5 of the novel *Anna Karenina*, the heroine, Anna, and her lover, Vronsky, call on the painter Mikhailov in his studio. A true artist, Mikhailov echoes Tolstoy's impatience with questions of technique and is compared very favorably with the dilettante Vronsky, who is a master of such matters. Mikhailov's portrait of Anna displays her as she really is by "removing the covers" that obscure her true nature (19:42). This suggests that the mission of art, for Tolstoy, is to express reality as it has been revealed to the artist. The substance of Tolstoy's remarks about the unity of a work of literary art, then, is that it is to be found on the thematic level. Its form will be that of an underlying conception of the nature of reality, and its function will be to unite the diverse and occasionally contradictory fates of the characters as they participate in that reality.

It would be shortsighted, however, to ignore other factors that contribute to the work's unity. To say that Mikhailov, in the example from *Anna Karenina* just given, attaches minimal value to technique in art is not to say that his work lacks (or that the work of a genuine artist may lack) technical mastery. A brilliant example of Tolstoy's technical skill in the organization of an artistic text is the novel *Anna Karenina* itself.[31]

Organization of the Text

The text of *The Death of Ivan Il'ich* runs to about fifteen thousand words and is divided into twelve chapters that may be grouped into three parts. The text is apportioned among these as follows.

GROUP 1		GROUP 2		GROUP 3	
Chapter	Lines of Type	Chapter	Lines of Type	Chapter	Lines of Type
1	301	5	139	9	93
2	290	6	102	10	72
3	253	7	153	11	96
4	255	8	234	12	73

Roughly speaking, the chapters are organized in a pattern of decreasing length, and, without putting too fine a point on it, one may speak of chapters that are long (250–300 lines), medium (140–150 lines), and short (70–95 lines). Besides the general pattern of decreasing length, then, the visual appearance of the text also suggests a division into three parts: chapters 1 through 4, which are all "long" chapters; 5 through 8, of which 5 and 7 are "medium" chapters, 6 a long "short" chapter, and 8 a short "long" chapter; and 9 through 12, which are all "short" chapters.

These data take on added significance when considered in the light of the chapters' contents. Following the introductory material provided in chapter 1, chapters 2 through 4 give an account of the life of Ivan Il'ich from his childhood, through the development of his career in government service and his marriage, to the onset of his illness: a period of more than forty years. Chapters 5 through 8 present the development of the illness, Ivan's further attempts to deal with it, and his growing awareness of the approach of death: a period of several months. The last four chapters recount the hero's final decline and agonized death: a period of a bit more than four weeks. Thus the decreasing size of the chapters is matched by a parallel decrease in their time frame: from years to months to weeks. The last chapter makes this gradual focusing still more apparent by shrinking the temporal framework from weeks to days, then to hours, and finally brings the flow of time to a stop altogether in the "one changeless instant" in which Ivan finds himself following his illumination.

There is a parallel decrease in the spatial dimensions of the story. Chapters 2 through 4 present the protagonist in the broad context of his official peregrinations from town to town and conclude by localizing him in the city to which his final promotion sends him and in the stylish apartment that he engages there. Chapters 5 through 8 curtail this spatial mobility, and Ivan is ultimately confined to his study. The process is completed in chapters 9 through 12 as the comparative freedom of the study is reduced to the limits of the sofa (chapter 10) on which he dies. Thus the temporal and spatial stages of the narrative coincide with the three groups of chapters. The gradual contraction of time and space around Ivan Il'ich leads logically to the story's time line reaching time-zero and its space line reaching space-zero at the moment of his death.

This brief analysis of the story's textual surface indicates the basis for a common criticism of the novel. On the one hand, the text prepares the reader to accept time-zero and space-zero as points of termination. On the other hand, when time- and space-zero are finally reached in chapter 12, they are, apparently unexpectedly, revealed to be a new beginning, as is shown by Ivan's sense of relief and well-being, his overcoming of time, and his escape from the confines of the "black hole" into a space that contains no dimensions at all, only light.

The linearity and gradually increasing tempo of the text prepare the reader for a conclusion very like that which Ivan Il'ich imagines when he describes his life as "a series of increasing sufferings" that "flies faster and faster toward its end, the most terrible suffering" (163 [26:109]). The astonishing, last-minute reversal that the reader is offered instead has struck some readers as incredible or artistically unjustified. This is not so much a matter of religious convictions as of artistic consistency, and it represents one of the main questions that have moved scholars and critics to undertake specialized studies of the novel. The papers by Gutsche and Rancour-Laferriere devote close attention to this question.

In this introduction I have tried to provide a general and abbreviated account of the historical, biographical, and philosophical context in which the novel was produced and a summary of the main points of view from which scholars and critics, readers like the rest of us, have sought to understand and appreciate Tolstoy's novel. Their main concerns have centered on the moral implications of the novel, its structure and organization (particularly the placement of the material presented in the first chapter), the psychology of the central character as he confronts his imminent demise, the strange mixture of the literal and the symbolic in the text, and the relationship between *The Death of Ivan Il'ich* and Tolstoy's other works or between the novel and the works of other writers. The various studies that form the substance of the next part of this book were chosen because of the masterful way in which they involve themselves in these central questions of the appreciation and understanding of Tolstoy's great short novel. With this background in mind, and with a reading (or rereading) of the work freshly accomplished, we may now proceed to the consideration of these specialized studies. Each of them brings something particular to our individual and collective understanding of Tolstoy's short novel and helps to define further its place within our intellectual landscape.

NOTES

1. Matthew Arnold, "Count Leo Tolstoy," *Fortnightly Review* (December 1887). Reprinted in A. V. Knowles, ed., *Tolstoy: The Critical Heritage* (London: Routledge and Kegan Paul, 1978), 353.

2. I use this term, apparently first coined by the philosopher Gottfried Leibniz, following the example of Guy de Mallac, who has been kind enough to share with me his unpublished monograph on Tolstoy's philosophy.

3. Lev Tolstoi, *Polnoe sobranie sochinenii* (Moscow: Gosudarstvennoe Izdatel'stvo Khudozhestvennoi Literatury, 1928–58), vol. 23, 32. References to the Russian originals of Tolstoy's works, including letters, are to those works as published in this, the "Jubilee edition" of Tolstoy's complete collected works. All translations from the Russian are my own, except those from the text of *The Death of Ivan Il'ich*. Hereafter all references to the Russian originals of Tolstoy's works will be given parenthetically in the text in the form "volume number:page number"; thus the present reference would be "23:32."

4. On a business trip in that year to the small town of Arzamas, Tolstoy was obliged to pass the night in a hotel and was there, in the wee hours of the morning, overcome for the first time by a personal sense of the futility of life and the dreadful inevitability of death.

5. As early as the middle of the 1850s Tolstoy had expressed the belief that Christianity would provide a viable philosophy of life were it relieved of the insupportable weight of its theology and dogma. Still earlier, as he later recalled, he had dramatically thrown away the icon that the Orthodox commonly wore on their necks in favor of a medallion engraved with the face of Jean-Jacques Rousseau.

6. N. K. Mikhailovskii, *Sobranie sochinenii*, vol. 6 (St. Petersburg, 1897), 382. Cited in L. D. Opul'skaia, *Lev Nikolaevich Tolstoy: Materialy k biografii s 1886 po 1892 god* (Moscow: Izdatel'stvo "Nauka," 1979), 14; hereafter cited as Opul'skaia.

7. Lisovsky's remarks appeared in the journal *Russkoe bogatstvo*, no. 1 (1888): 182. Cited in Opul'skaia, 15.

8. This book, published in France in the mid-1880s, was a crucial factor in the European intellectuals' dawning awareness of the excellence of the Russian literary culture.

9. One exception that should be noted is Edward Wasiolek, "Tolstoy's *The Death of Ivan Ilyich* and Jamesian Fictional Imperatives," *Modern Fiction Studies* 6 (1960): 314–24; hereafter cited in text as Wasiolek. This essay disputes the validity of criticism directed at the novel's overtly moralizing tone. Wasiolek finds the basis of this criticism in the assumptions and presuppositions of a Jamesian aesthetic of indirection and suggests a rejoinder along the lines of taking Tolstoy on his own, rather than another's, aesthetic terms.

10. D. D. Blagoi et al., eds., *Istoriia russkoi literatury v trekh tomakh*, vol. 3 (Moscow: Izdatel'stvo "Nauka," 1964), 575.

11. See especially Boris Sorokin, "Ivan Il'ich as Jonah: A Cruel Joke," *Canadian Slavic Studies* 5 (1971): 487–88, 490 (hereafter cited in text as Sorokin); Philip Rahv, "The Death of Ivan Illych and Joseph K.," in *Image and Idea: Twenty Essays on Literary Themes* (Norfolk, Conn.: New Directions, 1957), 135; and William Barrett, "Existentialism as a Symptom of Man's Contemporary Crisis," in *Spiritual Problems in Contemporary Literature*, ed. Stanley Hopper (New York: Harper, 1952), 143.

12. Lev Shestov, "The Last Judgment: Tolstoy's Last Works," in *In Job's*

Balances: On the Sources of the Eternal Truths (Athens: Ohio University Press, 1957), 117; hereafter cited in text as Shestov.

13. William B. Edgerton, "Tolstoy, Immortality, and Twentieth-Century Physics," *Canadian Slavonic Papers* 21 (1979): 300; hereafter cited in text as Edgerton.

14. A number of studies of this type appeared; they generally concluded that some form of cancer was the proper diagnosis.

15. James Bartell, "The Trauma of Birth in *The Death of Ivan Ilych:* A Therapeutic Reading," *Psychological Review* 2 (1978): 106–11.

16. Y. J. Dayananda, "*Death of Ivan Ilych:* A Psychological Study on Death and Dying," *Literature and Psychology* 22 (1972): 192–97.

17. Charles L. Glicksberg, "Tolstoy and *The Death of Ivan Illyitch*," in *The Ironic Vision in Modern Literature* (Hague: Martinus Nijhoff, 1969): 82–83; hereafter cited in text as Glicksberg.

18. Geoffrey Clive, "Tolstoy and the Varieties of the Inauthentic," in *The Broken Icon: Intuitive Existentialism in Classical Russian Fiction* (New York: Macmillan, 1970), 108–12; hereafter cited in text as Clive.

19. James Olney, "Experience, Metaphor, and Meaning: *The Death of Ivan Ilych*," *Journal of Aesthetics and Art Criticism* 31 (1972): 113; hereafter cited in text as Olney.

20. Irving Halperin, "The Structural Integrity of *The Death of Ivan Il'ich*," *Slavic and East European Journal* 5 (1961): 337; hereafter cited in the text as Halperin.

21. John Donnelly, "Death and Ivan Ilych," in *Language, Metaphysics, and Death*, ed. John Donnelly (New York: Fordham University Press, 1978), 118.

22. A notable exception is Gunter Schaarschmidt's study of the syntax of the novel, which, though written by a linguist, suggests important conclusions on the artistic structure of the work ("Theme and Discourse Structure in *The Death of Ivan Il'ich*," *Canadian Slavonic Papers* 21 (1979): 356–66; hereafter cited in text as Schaarschmidt).

23. Gutsche, in fact, devotes a major part of his chapter on *The Death of Ivan Il'ich* to exploring the extent of the relevance of Tolstoy's formal religious ideas, as well as those associated with traditional dogmas of institutionalized Christianity, for an interpretation of the novel (*Moral Apostasy in Russian Literature* [DeKalb: Northern Illinois University Press, 1986]).

24. Richard F. Gustafson, *Leo Tolstoy: Resident and Stranger* (Princeton, N.J.: Princeton University Press, 1986), 155–60.

25. Concern with the author's intention is central to Gary R. Jahn, *The Death of Ivan Il'ich: An Interpretation* (New York: Twayne, 1993); see especially 84–103.

26. C. J. G. Turner, "The Language of Fiction: Word Cluster in Tolstoy's *The Death of Ivan Ilych*," *Modern Language Review* 65 (1970): 121; hereafter cited in text as Turner.

27. See note 25, above.

28. David Matual, "The Confession as Subtext in *The Death of Ivan Ilich*," *International Fiction Review* 8 (1981): 125–28; hereafter cited in text as Matual.

29. Art, for the symbolists, involved the portrayal of "realia" (the real) in the interest of leading our attention to "realiora" (the more real, the essence of existence).

30. Rimgaila Salys, "Signs on the Road of Life: *The Death of Ivan Il'ich*," *Slavic and East European Journal* 30 (1986): 18–28.

31. See Gary R. Jahn, "The Unity of *Anna Karenina*," *Russian Review* 41 (1982): 144–58.

II 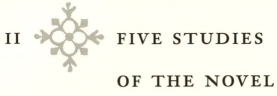 FIVE STUDIES

OF THE NOVEL

Why Do People Write Such Studies, Anyway?

GARY R. JAHN

Readers familiar with Russian literature may recognize the title of the first subdivision of this part of the companion as a paraphrase of a famous line from the last page of "The Nose," a celebrated story by Tolstoy's literary predecessor Nikolai Gogol. Having offered his readers a story about a minor government official who awakened one morning to find that his nose had absconded from the middle of his face, leaving behind only an "empty space, flat and smooth as a pancake," and who later on encountered his nose, dressed in the uniform of a high-ranking official, at prayer in church, and whose nose was finally returned to him by the police, who had seized it in the act of attempting an illegal flight over the border into Lithuania, we may, like Gogol's narrator himself, find it difficult to understand why "authors might take up such subjects as these."

> I confess that this is quite beyond my grasp, this is precisely . . . but no, no, I just don't understand at all. In the first place, there is no benefit at all to our fatherland in such things, and in the second place . . . well, in the second place there isn't any benefit either. I simply don't know what to make of it.

So, too, may readers of the scholarly or critical writings of specialists be puzzled as to the point or purpose of such work. But just as there really *is* a point to Gogol's story after all, so, too, is there value in the various scholars' work presented in the pages that follow. Each work has important points to demonstrate and significant contributions to make to our understanding and appreciation of Tolstoy's novel. Before turning to the studies themselves, however, it may be well to

discuss, even briefly, some of the general presuppositions that under-
lie traditional literary scholarship. In so doing I hope to help readers
understand the value and benefit, if not to our fatherland then
at least to ourselves, in considering such studies as appear in this
volume.

Whatever else a work of literature may be, and already there is an
enormous and ever-increasing menu of proposed definitions of the
literary work, it is always a potential occasion for interaction between an author and reader. In fact any interaction of this type
implies the presence of at least three elements: an author, a text, a
reader. The relative weight and significance of these elements may,
and do, vary from one occasion of interaction to another. Thus, for
example, one reader may find a text important as a means of communication with the ideas of the author who produced that text. For
another reader, the author's ideas and intentions may be entirely
irrelevant, and the text may function as no more than an occasion for
the reader to reflect on his or her own ideas and intentions. For a
third reader, the text may seem to be disconnected from both the
author's and the reader's concerns and have a purely literary or artistic value, or perhaps to function as an imaginative surrogate for
another reality. My purpose here is not to attempt to legislate appropriate parameters for the interactions among authors, readers, and
texts but only to point out that these parameters may and do vary
widely from one occasion to another and from reader to reader. It is
entirely appropriate in fact, and even to be anticipated, that the
interaction will differ, perhaps widely, for the *same* reader on different occasions.

Despite the great variety of interactions that can occur between
readers and texts, any particular interaction will be marked, either
consciously or by implication, with some particular intention on the
reader's part; that is, the reader will think or feel that he or she is
interacting with or using a particular text and author in a certain way
or for a certain purpose. For example, one reader may use a text (let
us say Tolstoy's novel *War and Peace*) with the intention of learning
something about the Napoleonic invasion of Russia in 1812, whereas

another may use it as a source of psychological insight into human behavior; a third may use the novel as a means of gauging or analyzing Tolstoy's own psychological condition, and a fourth may be fascinated with the novel's creation of a lifelike and vivid portrait of Russian society at a certain period. Most readers, I fancy, will find their interactions with this novel a rather motley collection of several different uses and intentions that are organized and given coherence by the fact that all of them coexist within the psyche of a single reader. To other readers our experience of, and interaction with, particular texts may, and often will, seem hopelessly jumbled, confusing, even contradictory. Our interactions with texts, however, are no less important to us because they are complex and not obviously coherent. Most often we ourselves and our experience in general are far from simple and easily understood, so how can we expect our literary experiences to be any different?

So long as our experience of a text remains a matter private to ourselves, that it is diverse, vague, incompletely understood, and irreducible (though of course no less powerful for all this) is of no particular significance. If, however, we wish to share with other readers our interaction with a text, then we need to bring our experience of the text into sharper focus. This is most often done by isolating one particular dimension or aspect of our experience of the text and abstracting it from our experience as a whole; that is, we may, like most everyone else, be in the grip of a multidimensional and possibly even confused understanding of the text but be willing, in the interest of sharing at least a portion of our experience, to reduce the complexity and uniqueness of our total experience to a discussion of one of its parts. Such a discussion would have the general form: "If I were to confine myself to looking at this text from this particular point of view, then I would offer the following relatively clear and precise discussion of the text as seen from this point of view." You may fill in the spaces to suit yourself. For example, if the text in question were that same story by Gogol, "The Nose," with which I began this discussion, I might want to limit myself to a discussion of the story as a satire of the social conventions arising from the exaggerated importance of the system of ranks within the Russian civil service. On the other hand, I might want to discuss the text as a symbolic representation of the psyche of the author who produced it or of the characters represented in it. Again, the story might be examined from the point of view of a general popular fascination with noses, which is known to have existed in the mid-1830s, when the story was written.

As it happens, each of these suppositions has actually been produced, and of course there are many more. The point I wish to make about these discussions is twofold. First, those who produced them need not be thought of as having attempted to reduce the text, or their experience of it, to the single dimension they have chosen for discussion. Their concentration on the one aspect they have brought to our attention should by no means suggest that they think this one thing is all there is to the text, or even to their own interaction with that text, and certainly not to the highly varied experiences of other readers. Second, what these discussions should be taken to mean is that within a relatively narrow field of consideration, as defined in the discussion itself, one or a few particular aspects of that reader's interaction with the text may be set forth clearly and coherently, and may be seen to be demonstrated effectively as one particular form of experience that may emerge from an interaction with the text. In brief, these discussions of a text should be seen as consciously and conscientiously limited attempts to provide a clear explanation and demonstration of a particular aspect of a particular reader's experience of a particular text.

In effect, the foregoing remarks are a paraphrase of the formulations of the noted literary scholar R. S. Crane who, in his *Languages of Criticism and the Structure of Poetry* (1953), explained that a work of literary criticism or scholarship should not be expected to do more than provide a reasoned and verifiable answer to a conscientiously defined question when using a stipulated standard of procedure and known rules of evidence. Even if one agrees that this is a reasonable way to look at the offerings of the commentators whose works appear in this collection, and even if one understands these writers' desire to express answers to particular questions that most interest them, one may still wonder why one reader's questions and answers should be of any interest to any other reader. From a certain point of view, of course, it may be said that there is no comprehensive and universally compelling reason why such discussions should interest us as readers of the text being discussed. There is also no generally persuasive reason why we should even be interested in the text discussed. But if we ourselves have read the text, and if it has made an impression on us – either strong and definite or mild and confused – then indeed we may very much want to hear clearly reasoned and convincingly argued opinions of other readers. Perhaps these discussions will alleviate our own confusion or help us to focus our own ideas or suggest ways to look at or interact with the text that seem intriguing, even though we hadn't considered them previously.

At least that is my hope, as well as the hope of the other writers whose works are presented here. The studies in this volume have been selected to represent the various prominent threads of discussion of *The Death of Ivan Il'ich* that have developed over the century and more since the novel's publication. The authors' keen awareness of these reflections on the novel for one another's views and interpretations is powerful testimony to the concept of literary scholarship as a shared and cooperative venture. Professor Turner focuses on the basic dimensions of the verbal construction of the text, its artistry as revealed in its use and combination of words and phrases. Professor Gutsche, on the other hand, is concerned with certain moral and philosophical questions the novel presents, questions that are of particular interest to him as these touch on the feelings, thoughts, and perceptions of one facing a situation like that besetting the novel's protagonist. His work also provides a model of the placement of one's own insight into the context of the diverse and continuing discussion of a great work of literature. Professor Salys has written an elegant account of the symbolic and multileveled nature of *The Death of Ivan Il'ich*, a discussion that helps us appreciate the interrelationship of the physical and spiritual planes of the protagonist's existence as these are presented in the novel. Professor

Rancour-Laferriere, whose main interest is in human psychology from the perspective of psychoanalysis and psychoanalytic theory, has found much to discuss in the novel from that point of view. At the same time he has made an important and challenging contribution to the religious/Christian interpretation of the novel. Professor Rogers's study will be of particular interest to those who are fascinated by the connections between writers. His paper is also a masterful example of how the discussion of one text and its elements can be greatly enriched by comparison with those of another text, regardless of whether a claim is made that one text or author exerted influence on another.

The Death of Ivan Il'ich has been recognized over several generations and many decades as one of the greatest literary works by one of Russia's greatest writers. It deals with an aspect of life we all will face one day and one that many of us anticipate daily. If we find the story personally important from a particular point of view, the discussions offered here may well clarify, perhaps even intensify, the significance the novel has for us.

Ivan Il'ich – Resident and Stranger

C. J. G. TURNER

The nonconformist is obviously alienated from his society, but perhaps those who conform are alienated from themselves.
—Walter Kaufmann

You are like everyone else . . . that is, like very many of them; only you ought not to be like everyone else – that's the point.
—Alesha Karamazov

When I was writing my first academic article on Russian literature,[1] I had been reading a number of essays by Russian formalist critics and had been impressed by their use of statistical data, especially with respect to verse but also in their criticism of literary prose. This unusually scientific approach had in fact been pioneered in Russia by some of the symbolists, such as Belyi and Briusov; but their work was often stigmatized by the formalists as merely the exposition of subjective impressions backed up by examples. Tomashevskii, for example, calls an article by Briusov "a brilliant example of where the study of rhythm can lead us when it completely lacks method."[2] By implication, a more objective and scientific method is used to apply statistical data in his own concurrent work on Pushkin's iambic tetrameter.[3] Tomashevskii later applied his methods to the prose of Pushkin's *Queen of Spades;* but for a more wide-ranging application of statistical techniques to prose one should look at something like Belyi's posthumously published book about Gogol, in which, for example, the preponderance of different color-epithets is examined.[4] Moreover, at the time I was writing, David Lodge had recently pleaded for a more rigorous verbal analysis in the criticism of the English novel and had illustrated what he meant with a series of essays emphasizing features like recurrent imagery in the novel.[5]

My article, then, attempted to apply a statistical technique to Tolstoy's *Death of Ivan Il'ich*. It was conceived as the result of a problem and an observation. The problem was chapter 1: given that it is set after the death of Ivan Il'ich, why does it exist at all in a story devoted to the life and death of Ivan Il'ich? And if it had to exist at all, why is it placed at the beginning of the story rather than at the end where it belongs chronologically? The observation was one that must have been made by practically every reader of the story, namely that Tolstoy tirelessly repeats expressions from two word clusters in particular: on the one hand, pleasant/proper/decorous and cognate or related terms occur with notable frequency in chapters 2 and 3; on the other hand, falsehood/lies/deceit and cognate or related terms occur with increasing frequency in the subsequent chapters.[6] Furthermore, it was observed that both sets of terms usually refer to one and the same thing, namely, the accepted norms of social life; and this fact is symbolized at one point in chapter 8 where words from both groups come together with the same referent: "They all became afraid that the proper deception would be destroyed and the truth become plain to all" (104/159).[7]

My feelings, as I look back at my earlier article, tend to underline some of the strengths and some of the weaknesses of the statistical technique. Its main strength and attraction, on the one hand, is its claim to a degree of objectivity that can only be enhanced by the development and use of computers. Its main weakness, on the other hand, is that total objectivity is vitiated by the inevitable interference of subjectivity in at least two respects: someone has somehow to decide which features to search for and collate and how to define and distinguish them, and someone has somehow to decide what is the significance of the data observed. The rhythm of a poem or sentence length in a novel may be compared with those of casual discourse with a fair degree of objectivity; but the conclusions to be drawn from their deviations (or nondeviations) from that or any other norm tend either toward subjectivity or insignificance or both.

Repetition, whether of meter or rhyme in verse or of words or images in prose, seems to be a significant and, as propagandists and advertisers well know, a persuasive rhetorical device. One job of the statistically minded critic is therefore to pursue features in a literary work that are repeated markedly beyond what one should expect (and, of course, the definition of the reader's horizon of expectation can be a moot point), to indicate and make explicit how they create an impression, and to attempt to define that impression as an integral part of the aesthetic effect of the whole work. In a longer work one can also plot patterns of repetitions that occur in one part of the work but not in another, although their significance may remain questionable: in a biographical novel, for instance, it is unlikely to be significant that motifs of youth should be recurrent in the early chapters and of old age in the later chapters. In my article, however, I found that the patterns formed by statistical data of the occurrence of words from two word clusters tended to confirm what others have maintained on other grounds, namely, that the first chapter of *The Death of Ivan Il'ich* belongs where Tolstoy in fact places it, with the early, "pleasant" part of Ivan Il'ich's life story, and hence that the prime function of the chapter as it stands in the published text is one of "generalizing."[8] Half a dozen occurrences of words such as *pleasant* or *proper* (as against only two of *pretense*) suggested that the dominance of the social norms of Ivan Il'ich's life before the onset of his illness is extended by chapter 1 both spatially (i.e., beyond Ivan Il'ich to the narrator and Petr Ivanovich, whose point of view pervades the chapter) and also chronologically (i.e., beyond the lifetime of Ivan Il'ich). It is, however, not a total dominance: there is some awareness of pretense, and the judgments of Petr Ivanovich, in whom Tolstoy resisted the temptation to duplicate the conversion of Ivan Il'ich that had been indicated in an earlier draft of the story,[9] remain ambivalent.

The application to the norms of social behavior of two apparently contradictory sets of terms (implying value judgments made, for the most part, by the same person, namely Ivan Il'ich, although not at the same time) is just one of a number of paradoxes that have been identified in *The Death of Ivan Il'ich*, beginning with the identification of life with death and of death with life that is hinted at in the title and is sustained by the moral gist of the whole story. Another such contradiction is that between, on the one hand, the impulse toward generalization that is inherent in any piece of writing intended to carry a universal message (Ivan Il'ich as Everyman) and, on the other hand, the impulse toward individualization that is inherent in realistic fiction (Ivan Il'ich "was not Caius, not man in the abstract," 93/149). And a third contradiction is that between the desperate loneliness of the dying Ivan Il'ich and his constant concern to run with the herd. This last paradox is what I wish to consider here with some use of statistical data.

Several critics, especially those of an existentialist bent, have emphasized the loneliness, solitude, or isolation of Ivan Il'ich. This is expressed most strongly by Shestov, who couples him with Brekhunov (of *Master and Man*) as "dying in complete solitude": Tolstoy deliberately "cuts them off from everyone, from every kind of 'doing' and from all the sources from which we usually draw our vital forces."[10] Occasionally some qualification is made to this view. Jahn, for instance, sees Ivan Il'ich's contact with Gerasim (who at one point addresses him in the intimate second-person singular, 98/154) as beginning to reverse the process of isolation;[11] it is a contact that involves the physical just as the contact he finally establishes with his son begins with the physical. And George Gutsche contends that, in Tolstoy's view at least, Ivan Il'ich's actual death was not "lonely."[12] But normally it is almost axiomatic that we are born alone, that we die alone (Lidiia Gromova-Opul'skaia cites Tolstoy's fondness for the aphorism that *il faudra mourir seul* [one will have to die alone]),[13] and that we make any significant or existential decision alone, including the experience of conversion as Tolstoy interprets it. In *War and Peace* he had portrayed Prince Andrei as dying in the company of those he loves and who love him and yet as, in the process of dying, already distancing himself from them; similarly, Pierre finds himself naturally distanced from the dying Karataev. At about the time he was finishing *War and Peace* Tolstoy began to read Schopenhauer, and found himself in accord with the latter's assertion that the "principle of individuation" belongs to the phenomenal world and is thus illusory or, at best, temporary: to put it briefly, at death one does not cease to be but one does cease to be one. After his own spiritual crisis Tolstoy depicts Ivan Il'ich, like Brekhunov, as not only dying on his own but also undergoing a conversion on his own.

Ivan Il'ich's isolation is, however, not only required, so to speak, by the theory of the story; it was also emphasized and perhaps exaggerated in the text. In chapter 1 Ivan Il'ich is segregated from others by having died, having been silenced and confined to his coffin; but this physical segregation symbolizes a moral segregation that is expressed when Petr Ivanovich is consoled by "the customary reflection . . . that this had happened to Ivan Il'ich and not to him, and that it should not and could not happen to him" (67/128). In chapter 2, which summarizes most of Ivan Il'ich's career, we see how his isolation grew and how he was himself responsible for most of its growth: together with the rest of his family he had shunned his younger brother as a failure; in his work for the Ministry of Justice he had been careful to preserve the formalities and to "exclude completely his personal opinion" at the same time as deliberately choosing to cultivate "the best circle" of friends (72/132); and, most markedly, when his wife made demands on him during pregnancy and child rearing, he would withdraw into his work, a tactic that, while it was the sole excuse his wife could accept, led only to alienation and increasingly frequent quarrels.[14] In chapter 3 relations with his wife remain uneasy at best, as Ivan Il'ich goes through some critical points of his career. When he is passed over for promotion he "felt himself abandoned by everyone" (76/136); but he decides, on his own, what to do about it and succeeds in triumphing over his enemies by transferring to a good position where he "maintains the semblance of friendly human relations" (81/139). For most of this time a "truce" (one of two martial metaphors in one paragraph on page 78/137) is observed with his wife, with whom some disagreements continue but only one big quarrel is recorded in this chapter; and at the end of the chapter, they are in accord in selecting socially acceptable friends and deterring the approaches made by "various shabby friends and relations" (82/140) after their move to the big city.

Tolstoy has shown Ivan Il'ich as not only failing to make any deep human relationships but as having deliberately avoided doing so; from chapter 4, when he becomes ill, this works against him. Quarrels with his wife become more frequent, he reacts with malevolence, and twice (in later chapters) he is said to hate her. When he consults a doctor he is made to feel as lonely as a prisoner in the dock. "He alone was aware of what was happening, while all those about him did not understand or would not understand it" (87/144). By the end of the chapter "Ivan Il'ich was left alone with the consciousness that . . . he had to live thus all alone on the brink of destruction, without a single person who understood him or pitied him" (88–89/146). The following chapters maintain Ivan Il'ich's malevolent reaction to the failure of others to understand and hence to pity him. He recalls his own emotional inability to accept reference to himself of the syllogism about Caius on the grounds that "he had always been a creature quite, quite distinct from all others" (93/149). It is noticeable, on the other hand, that almost no references to his loneliness are made in chapter 7 in which Gerasim figures largely. In chapter 8, however, Ivan Il'ich dreads being left alone; in chapter 9 he weeps "about his terrible loneliness . . . and the absence of God" and complains to God but without expecting an answer (105–6/160); and in chapter 10, when he is confined to his divan, we are told he experiences a "loneliness in the midst of a populous town, surrounded by numerous acquaintances and relations, but that could not have been more complete anywhere, either at the bottom of the sea or under the earth" (108/162). In chapter 11, after receiving communion, he drives everyone away, telling them to leave him alone. In the twelfth and final chapter he undergoes his Tolstoyan conversion; that is, he attains a consciousness that is at once intellectual (that he had not lived right), which has to be done alone, and emotional (that he must pity others),[15] which cannot be done alone. Hence, it seems to me, a certain confusion is inevitable about his loneliness at the very end.

Tolstoy has made his point, and he has made it with characteristic force and, at times, irony. But he has made it partly, as Speirs points out,[16] by deliberately excluding matter from his story. If one compares it with Tolstoy's life – and almost all his fiction, especially that depicting a conversion, is to some degree autobiographical – or if one compares it with his novels, then one begins to appreciate how much has been simply left out. What, in the light of these comparisons, has been excluded is chiefly three things: the abundance of social and especially family relationships, meaningful dialogue, and a variety of points of view. On the social level, fewer lines are given to Ivan Il'ich's dance evening than there are pages devoted to the ball scenes in *War and Peace* and *Anna Karenina*. In his family there have been at least five[17] children, of whom three die, but, for all that we are told, none impinges on him until the end of his life. He has a father, two brothers, and a sister (his mother presumably, like Tolstoy's, has died early), yet after he is launched on his career, there are, apart from his memories, only two slight references to his father and his sister (at least in the drafts the old man had the decency to fall ill and die, leaving money and furniture to Ivan Il'ich, 513–14). Even as regards marriage, unlike Prince Andrei and Pierre, let alone Levin, Ivan Il'ich can scarcely be said to woo and propose to Praskov'ia Fedorovna – he just gets married.

One social activity present in *The Death of Ivan Il'ich* is bridge; but, as Tolstoy observed in his first attempt at fiction, *A History of Yesterday*,[18] conversation is not required for card playing. This could be a minor reason for the relative paucity of dialogue in *The Death of Ivan Il'ich*, at least after chapter 1. It would appear, from what Tolstoy is prepared to give us, that Ivan Il'ich's conversation with Gerasim in chapter 7 is longer than any conversation with his wife; while the conversation he has with his wife, his daughter and her fiancé, and his son at the end of the following chapter, when they are about to leave for the theater, is conspicuous for its vacuity. It is not so much a question of the amount of dialogue but rather of its meaninglessness, which is one symptom of the almost total lack (again, after chapter 1) of the point of view of any character other than Ivan Il'ich. We are seldom given their words and thoughts firsthand; almost always it is at secondhand (i.e., as interpreted by the narrator: "Everything she did for him was entirely for her own sake; she told him that she was doing for herself what she actually was doing for herself as if that were so incredible that he had to understand the opposite," 102/157) or at thirdhand (i.e., as interpreted by Ivan Il'ich as interpreted by the narrator: " 'I'm doing this for my own sake' . . . He felt that he was surrounded and involved in such a mesh of falsity that it was hard to unravel anything," ibid.). And in most cases the interpretation is done with a degree of malevolence that can only have been exacerbated by the use of painkilling drugs, although the same technique, but with benevolence, is used with reference to Gerasim:[19] "He saw that no one would pity him because no one even wished to understand his position. Only Gerasim understood it and pitied him. . . . Only Gerasim did not lie; everything showed that he alone understood what was the matter," 98/154). This aspect of the story is clearly indebted to Tolstoy's original version in which the story of Ivan Il'ich's life was told through his own diary notes, that is, with little dialogue and from only one point of view.

Many critics have observed that a major strength in Tolstoy is his depiction of scenes replete with dialogue and peopled with fully drawn characters.[20] In *The Death of Ivan Il'ich* the scenes are foreshortened, the dialogues bear little significance, and the characters (after chapter 1 and apart from Ivan Il'ich himself) are fragmentary. There are, of course, compensating strengths in the story, but we need to realize how much has been excluded. The focus has been narrowed, and one effect of this is to emphasize and exaggerate Ivan Il'ich's loneliness precisely by reducing the sense of the presence of other people and his contact with them.

Even so, there is plenty of evidence in the text that Ivan Il'ich cultivated and enjoyed a wide circle of friends. We are told, for instance, with the authority of the narrator, that he was "sociable," and not only at the School of Law but throughout his life (69/130); similarly, while Ivan Il'ich's claim that "everybody in Petersburg had liked him very much" (78/137) gains little credence, there is no reason to question the narrator's statement on the very first page (61/123) that "he was liked by them all." It is at this point that I revert to statistics, since at least some of our impressions are gained through the frequency and distribution of terms for friendship, as well as the choice of terms used. Russian has four main terms that may be translated "friend." In rising order of intensity these are (with notes on their definition and distinctions according to a *Dictionary of Synonyms*):[21] *znakomyi* (acquaintance) is someone one knows, with whom one has been in contact; *tovarishch* (colleague, comrade) is someone close to one in activity, occupation, or circumstances of life and with whom one is linked by common or friendly relations; *priiatel'* is someone with whom one has a good, simple, but not very close relationship; and *drug* is someone close to one in spirit or connections on whom one can rely. Thus the gentlemen gathered at the beginning of the story are described as Ivan Il'ich's "intimate acquaintances [*znakomyi*], his so-called friends [*drug*]" (62/124). In considering the occurrence of these terms in *The Death of Ivan Il'ich* I shall be omitting not only some related expressions ("liked/was close to") but also the more technical expression *tovarishch prokurora* (Assistant Public Prosecutor) and a few occurrences of *znakomyi* as an adjective referring to things (familiar); although it will be recognized that if we are to talk solely about impressions, these, too, are not wholly irrelevant.

The statistics of the occurrence of these four terms (including most cognates) in *The Death of Ivan Il'ich* may be stated briefly. *Znakomyi* occurs seven times in chapter 1, six times in chapters 2–4, and thereafter only once in chapter 10. *Tovarishch* occurs three times in chapter 1, five times in chapters 2–4, and thereafter only once in each of chapters 6 and 7. *Priiatel'* occurs not at all in chapter 1, five times in chapters 2–4, and thereafter only four times in swift succession in chapter 5 (the "friend of a friend," i.e., only twice with reference to Ivan Il'ich). *Drug* occurs twice in chapter 1, twelve times in chapters 2–4, and thereafter only twice in chapter 6 and once in chapter 9. While it must be borne in mind that after chapter 4 the chapters are generally much shorter than are the opening chapters, two things are immediately clear from these figures: (1) the most intense degree of friendship, represented by the word *drug*, occurs predominantly in chapters 2–4 (two-thirds of its total occurrences, and twice as often as any other of our terms); and (2) after chapter 4 the total occurrence of any words designating friendship falls off drastically (eight occurrences in chapters 5–8, only two in chapters 9–12). Both of these findings at once suggest and reflect the stark contrast between the sociable friendships of the early stages of Ivan Il'ich's career and his existential loneliness after he falls ill.

One needs, perhaps, to be more guarded about drawing further conclusions from these figures. It may, for example, be significant that the second most common of these terms is the weakest of them, *znakomyi*, which could suggest that much of the friendship represented here is at a low level. On the other hand, half its occurrences come in chapter 1 where most of them refer to the acquaintances of Petr Ivanovich. But then again Petr Ivanovich in many ways doubles Ivan Il'ich, and the social atmosphere of chapter 1, including its norms of friendship, is meant to introduce the atmosphere in which Ivan Il'ich had lived his life; so that this conclusion, too, has some validity and relevance for Ivan Il'ich. More corrosive, in fact, for any conclusions about friendship in *The Death of Ivan Il'ich* is Tolstoy's persistent irony. For instance, both occurrences of *drug* in chapter 1 (Ivan Il'ich's "intimate acquaintances, his so-called friends" [62/124], and Praskov'ia Fedorovna's words to Petr Ivanovich: "I know that you were a true friend to Ivan Il'ich" [65/126]) indicate that the term is to be taken with an appreciable pinch of salt. Later we learn, in effect, from Ivan Il'ich's example, that friendly relations can be a form of condescension to one's subordinates or inferiors and are to be cultivated only with one's social superiors. Furthermore, it is presumably largely the same colleagues that Ivan Il'ich usually thinks of as friends but that, when his career falters, he thinks of as "enemies" (78/137). In short, as we have already had cause to quote, Ivan Il'ich was an expert at "maintaining the semblance of friendly human relations" (81/139) and knew no better. Nevertheless, it does not seem unfair to contend that Ivan Il'ich had known genuine, if not deep, friendship in his early years (the last two references to him of *drug* are in his memories of his youth). It is when he becomes ill that the concept of friendship is lost to view, and this reversal is evident in the lexical statistics of the story.

There is a parallel ambivalence about Ivan Il'ich's relationship with his wife. Tolstoy provides two motives for his marrying her, only one of which is love; thereby he weakens but does not deny his love for her at the same time as we are told, without qualification, that she had fallen in love with him (73/133). She is called a "good match" (*partiia*, ibid.), a word that in this story refers usually to a game of bridge and once to a virtuoso musical "part" (81/139), suggesting that his marriage, too, is something that is played out more or less on the level of these activities. We are allowed to see Praskov'ia Fedorovna, as has been pointed out, for the most part only through his eyes, eyes that look at her at first with an ambiguous affection but later, when he is sick, only with hatred (92/149, 102/157).[22] But what are we to make of her weeping at the piteous look on his face (103/158)? Perhaps Tolstoy meant, by writing that she "even" wept, to imply that her motivation was complex and her tears were really for herself; but, on this occasion at least, he does not quite say that.

In two draft manuscripts (523–25) Tolstoy had had Ivan Il'ich, not long before his death, declare to a friend that he was happy, that he was not afraid of death, and that he saw no cause to abandon his metaphysical agnosticism. This kind of talk would be out of place in the final version, where Ivan Il'ich speaks neither at such length nor on such a serious subject. His relationships with his wife, his other relatives, and friends are shown as shallow, and shallow by his own choice and decision. He had deliberately fenced himself off from everything that threatened his own comfort and material well-being. From marriage he had demanded the comforts of "dinner at home, housewife, and bed" (74/134) while himself evading the demands it made on him. Yet, in a sense, this was not his choice and decision but simply the result of having let his life run in the grooves laid down by his father and everyone else, of running with the herd. As every animal in the herd looks to its leaders and assumes they have a goal in view, so Ivan Il'ich "from his early youth had, as a fly is drawn to the light, been attracted to people of high station in society, adopting their ways and views of life and establishing friendly relations with them" (69/130). He had "strictly fulfilled what he considered to be his duty; and he considered his duty what was so considered by the most highly placed people" (ibid.). It was their approval that sanctioned actions, when he was at the School of Law, which previously had disgusted him, and that provided the second motive for his marriage. When he moved to the home where he was to die he decorated and furnished it in such a way that "in reality it was just the same as in the houses of all those people of moderate means who want to be like the rich and therefore succeed only in resembling one another" (79/138). There, too, his "pleasures were little dinners to which he invited [not friends but] men and women of good social position" (81/140). Only at the end of his life does he begin to think that "his scarcely perceptible impulses to struggle against what was considered good by the most highly placed people . . . might have been the real thing" (110/164).

It was, I suspect, partly because of his innate aristocratism as well as because of his personal eccentricity that Tolstoy regularly reacted against the herd instinct (which, in *War and Peace*, is capable of persuading men to commit atrocities that none of them would commit as individuals), against imitation (notably in art), against conformism.[23] So, too, Ivan Il'ich is at his worst when he is conforming, imitating, and generally running with the herd. What pulls him up short is when he falls mortally ill, thereby ceases to conform, and sees that this "awful, terrible act of his dying is reduced by those around him to the level of a casual, unpleasant, almost indecorous incident (like the way someone is treated who, on entering a drawing room, gives off a bad odor)" (98/154). The sociable Ivan Il'ich, whom everyone liked, who had plenty of friends, who had made a good marriage, and who was clearly far from slow in making new friends after his final move to the city which in the drafts is identified as Moscow,[24] felt himself completely and utterly alone. He is only made to feel lonely by his friends: by the lighthearted teasing of his colleagues, by Shvarts's balance between playfulness and propriety that reminded him of his earlier self, and by the continuing games of bridge that brook no serious conversation (88/145–46).

There are two aspects to the contradiction that I have sought to define with respect to *The Death of Ivan Il'ich*, and that, perhaps, is best summed up by the subtitle I have gratefully borrowed from Richard Gustafson's recent book *Leo Tolstoy: Resident and Stranger*, in the opening pages of which it is perceptively discussed. Is it possible, in the first place, to reconcile the picture of Ivan Il'ich as "resident" in a society of family and friends with the picture of Ivan Il'ich as a "stranger" to them all? The most obvious answer is to point to the onset of his illness as a turning point which changes Ivan Il'ich from resident to stranger. Thus Edward Wasiolek writes of his pain as "bringing him to isolation and to confrontation with that isolation."[25] But, on further consideration, we find that this is only half true. Just as Tolstoy himself was simultaneously resident and stranger, so he wants us to see that Ivan Il'ich always had been isolated even in the midst of family and friends: the pain had not itself brought him to isolation but had exposed an isolation that was already there. When Ivan Il'ich is sick, he recalls as model the friendship of his early years that I have described as "genuine, if not very deep"; this, I think, is the nature of our childhood friendships. Depth, in this sense, involves serious concerns and demands that test whether a friend is such as "can be relied on." Hence one has to qualify as "shallow" both his relationship with colleagues, which never rises above the level of office gossip and card playing, and his relationship with his wife, whose natural demands he prefers to evade. At the same time one has to recognize that this shallowness is created by fiat of Tolstoy and to serve his parabolic purpose.

The second aspect to this contradiction concerns precisely its underpinnings in Tolstoyan ideology. *The Death of Ivan Il'ich* poses with utter clarity the problem of our fundamental loneliness; but it also clearly rejects as counterfeit (to borrow a term from Tolstoy's theory of art) the answer to the problem offered by human friendship and familial relations. The parabolic nature of the story requires not only that this answer should be depicted as less adequate than it normally is in human life but also that a genuine answer should be at least adumbrated. Like Solzhenitsyn's imprisonment, Ivan Il'ich's pain can be seen as a blessing because the prospect of death confronts him with his isolation and forces him to seek a more adequate answer to it. The answer he finds, it has been suggested above, is twofold: first, a consciousness that life required of him more than the shallow, self-serving relationships he had cultivated; and, second, a sense of pity for or empathy with others that potentially breaks down our isolation, creates profound bonds, and prepares us to meet death. Whether this message owes more to Christ or to Schopenhauer is doubtful; but perhaps its greatest relevance for today is in challenging us to overcome our fear of deep, personal involvement and commitment.

NOTES

1. "The Language of Fiction: Word Clusters in Tolstoy's *The Death of Ivan Il'ich*," *Modern Language Review* 65 (1970): 116–21.

2. B. V. Tomashevskii, "Stikhotvornaia tekhnika Pushkina," *Pushkin i ego sovremenniki* 29–30 (1918): 131–43 (142).

3. "Ritmika chetyrekhstopnogo iamba po nabliudeniiam nad stikhom *Evgeniia Onegina*," ibid., 144–87. This is reprinted together with an essay on Pushkin's iambic pentameter in B. V. Tomashevskii, *O stikhe* (Leningrad, 1929).

4. B. V. Tomashevskii, "Ritm prozy (po *Pikovoi Dame*)," in Tomashevskii, *O stikhe*, 254–318; A. Belyi, *Masterstvo Gogolia* (Moscow-Leningrad, 1934).

5. David Lodge, *Language of Fiction: Essays in Criticism and Verbal Analysis of the English Novel* (London, 1966).

6. At one point in chapter 7 the word for "falsehood" (*lozh'*) occurs seven times in the course of ten lines, plus one occurrence of its verbal form (*lgat'*), and it remains frequent until the end of chapter 8. It is perhaps not entirely coincidental that the syllable *lozh* occurs in at least six diverse words on pages 98–104; such puns in Tolstoy are pointed out passim by R. F. Gustafson, *Leo Tolstoy: Resident and Stranger* (Princeton, 1986).

7. Page references to vol. 26 of L. N. Tolstoi, *Polnoe sobranie sochinenii*

(Moscow-Leningrad, 1928–58) will be given in the text; where a second page reference is given after a slash, it is to the English version by Michael R. Katz in the Norton Critical Edition of *Tolstoy's Short Fiction* (New York, 1991).

8. See R. Russell, "From Individual to Universal: Tolstoy's *Smert' Ivana Il'icha*," *Modern Language Review* 76 (1981): 629–42.

9. " . . . it was precisely here, in this room with its pink cretonne, that I received what completely changed my view of death and life" (508).

10. L. Shestov, *Na vesakh Iova* (Paris, 1929), 122.

11. G. R. Jahn, *The Death of Ivan Il'ich: An Interpretation* (New York, 1993), 60–61.

12. G. J. Gutsche, *Moral Apostasy in Russian Literature* (DeKalb, Ill., 1986), 165 n. 16.

13. L. D. Opul'skaia, *Lev Nikolaevich Tolstoy: Materialy k biografii s 1886 po 1892 god* (Moscow, 1979), 8.

14. Quite how much this reflects Tolstoy's own life and his relations with his wife (who, like Praskov'ia Fedorovna, respected especially her husband's career) it is impossible to tell. Opul'skaia thinks that some of the changes from the drafts of the story may have been made in order to deter suggestions of an autobiographical reference (ibid., n. 11).

15. This, too, accords with Schopenhauer's ethics of sympathy or compassion. See S. McLaughlin, "Some Aspects of Tolstoy's Intellectual Development: Tolstoy and Schopenhauer," *California Slavic Studies* 5 (1970): 187–245, especially 223–33; see also my comments in A. Donskov and J. Woodsworth, eds., *Lev Tolstoy and the Concept of Brotherhood* (Ottawa, 1996), 129–30, 140.

16. L. Speirs, "Tolstoy and Chekhov: *The Death of Ivan Il'ich* and *A Dreary Story*," *Oxford Review* 8 (1968): 81–93 (83).

17. Since Liza is called their "eldest [or older] daughter" (76/135) when we otherwise know only of a son, Vasia, perhaps we should assume that at least one more daughter was surviving, unless we are to identify her with the "one more child" that (we are told in the same sentence) died.

18. Tolstoi, *Polnoe sobranie sochinenii*, vol. 1, 280.

19. Cf. D. Shepherd, "Conversion, Reversion and Subversion in Tolstoi's *The Death of Ivan Il'ich*," *Slavonic and East European Review* 71 (1993): 401–16, especially 406–8.

20. E.g., P. Lubbock, *The Craft of Fiction* (London, 1965), 236–39.

21. A. P. Evgen'eva, ed., *Slovar' sinonimov russkogo iazyka* (Leningrad, 1970–71).

22. The first of these passages connects his hatred with her kiss and the second with her touch. Both passages add that he hated her "with all the force of his soul," which John Bayley finds scarcely credible (*Tolstoy and the Novel* [London, 1966], 90).

23. This is to be distinguished from "swarm-life" in which people (with Tolstoy's approval) are moved by instinct. Tolstoy's most succinct fulmination against conformism comes in a private letter of 1889: "The first general rule is: do not do what the majority does" (Tolstoi, *Polnoe sobranie sochinenii*, vol. 64, 224).

24. In fact the rapidity with which their social network develops during the five months before he dies is quite remarkable.

25. E. Wasiolek, *Tolstoy's Major Fiction* (Chicago, 1978), 173.

Moral Fiction:

Tolstoy's *Death of Ivan Il'ich*

GEORGE J. GUTSCHE

"So that's it!" he suddenly pronounced aloud. "What joy!"

Tolstoy is a towering figure in Russian literature and culture. Much of his prominence derives from the moral passion and earnestness of his search for the "right" way to live and from his efforts to convince others after he had found it. It is hard to discuss any of his writings without referring to moral issues, for his constant grappling with problems of right and wrong was reflected in everything he wrote. Not all readers find his obsessive concern with morality and his uncompromising directness in treating moral problems palatable.[1] Nor has the worldview he constructed, promoted, and embedded in his fiction achieved any kind of lasting appeal and influence on the world of ideas. People have come to view Tolstoy the moralist with a combination of mild praise for his strong position against violence and bemused indifference toward his vegetarianism, cult of simplicity, and prohibitions against sex.

Tolstoy's moral presence, though often felt in his pre-1880 short stories and novelistic masterpieces, *War and Peace* and *Anna Karenina*, was felt even more sharply in writings after his spiritual crisis of the late 1870s. Largely as a result of this crisis and his perception that most art was morally tainted, he devoted most of his energy in the years following *Anna Karenina* to nonfiction, to study of the world's major religions, to exegesis and translation of the Gospels, and to the exposition of his religious and moral views. Fiction, presumably revalued for its moral potential, returned to his arsenal to play an important role in the mid-1880s; from this time until his death in 1910 he wrote numerous enduring works, which include short stories, plays, and one more large novel, *Resurrection*.

Much of what has been written about Tolstoy is flawed in two ways: first, by a failure to appreciate how important it was for actions to have their source in a morality that was "natural" to a person, not imposed from the outside; and second, by a failure to appreciate how critical Tolstoy was of Christian dogma. It is curious but true that many of the readings of *The Death of Ivan Il'ich* rely on concepts Tolstoy explicitly rejects in his nonfiction and, it will be argued, implicitly rejects in the story as well.[2] There is, however, something in this fiction that attracts explications that utilize a conventional Christian perspective, applied with appropriate concepts and terminology.

This article offers a reading of the story designed to cohere with Tolstoy's views on religion as expressed in his other works. In addition, it will establish a context for discussing so-called Christian interpretations of the story; this context may help in accounting for the story's perplexing capacity to attract a wide variety of readings. *The Death of Ivan Il'ich* will be shown to illustrate very clearly the genesis of a quintessentially moral – but hardly Christian, except in an extended sense – vision: the hero's experience of dying leads to disorienting experiences culminating in a final vision. And this vision offers a new way of understanding life and an unconventional way of attaining immortality.

Tolstoyism

Tolstoy's religious views in later years were controversial, offensive not just to official Russian Orthodoxy but also to those who believed in virtually any conventional Christian doctrines. It cannot be, and was not then, easy for Christians to appreciate the seriousness and intensity of Tolstoy's moral convictions and at the same time maintain equanimity in the face of his vitriolic attack on conventional Christian doctrine and those who spoke in its behalf. Religion (which Tolstoy defined in a particular way) represented, in its usual forms, a pernicious threat to the purity of childhood and the integrity of conscience:

From a very early age – when children are most susceptible to suggestion, when those who bring up children cannot be sufficiently careful about what they communicate to them – children are hypnotized with the absurd, immoral dogmas of the so-called Christian religion, incompatible with our reason and knowledge. Children are taught the dogma of the Trinity, which a healthy reason cannot hold; the coming of one of these three Gods to earth for the redemption of the human race, and his resurrection and ascent into heaven; they are taught to expect a second coming, and punishment with eternal torments for disbelief in these dogmas; and they are taught to pray for their needs; and many other things ("What Is Religion and What Is Its Essence?" 35:187–88).[3]

He follows this list of Christian doctrines and practices with a strong accusation: the Trinity, the Resurrection, and hell as a punishment for those who do not believe what the church teaches are corrupting impositions on susceptible children who will grow up spiritually distorted, no longer believing in their own conscience, having yielded it to the authority of the church. If people only would learn to trust their own reason and conscience, Tolstoy argues, they could distinguish right from wrong and truth from lies. The established church perverts the spiritual life, robbing people of the ability to make moral choices on their own (35:188).

It is no wonder Russian religious philosophers have reacted so strongly in condemning this religion that does not have the customary trappings of mystery, sensing behind it an anarchism and distortion of holy writ and ridiculing Tolstoy's mundane obsession with rules of behavior. Although it is quite true that rules against violence, anger, lust, and taking oaths are important components of Tolstoyism, his religious views consist of more than rules. Underlying his views is a belief in the power of reason to direct one's moral life and, more important, a belief that all people have within them a moral sense that can easily be distorted by conventional religious education. And in addition to these beliefs, there is throughout his late writings a deep concern for the right relationship between behavior and attitudes, for actions in harmony with reason and conscience, and for behavior that is engendered spontaneously by the proper attitudes toward life.

To Tolstoy, striving for goodness, truth, and universal brotherhood has no moral validity unless such striving is deeply rooted, unreflective, and untainted by self-consciousness and abstractness.[4] What is important is being oneself, finding the God within, understanding within oneself the meaning of life. "Repentance" (in a quite particular sense, "realizing the right way to life") is possible through self-understanding; brotherhood is a natural result of serving oneself and the God within.

By living truly for oneself, one will be naturally in the right relation to others. In *The Death of Ivan Il'ich* the central figure's realization of this truth comes suddenly, and he does not subject it to deep analysis. He simply becomes compassionate; for compassion, self-sacrificing love for one's neighbor, is what Tolstoy believes people will discover as the meaning of life if they use their conscience as a guide. Ivan's compassion is not a product of abstract reasoning or of judging that one code of conduct or set of rules is more reasonable than another. Because it is not abstract and mechanical, the altruism that flows from this compassion has the right psychological basis: it is firmly rooted within him.

Moral Fiction

The Death of Ivan Il'ich (1886) was Tolstoy's first major fictional work in his post-1880 period. Long regarded as a classic of short fiction, it has stimulated numerous and varied readings. The story's moral dimension is readily apparent: Tolstoy indicts society's reigning values, personal pleasure and propriety, and advocates compassion and love as the best foundation for living. However, the moral and religious context in which the simple message of compassion and moral authenticity is expressed may not be so apparent to readers. Although it is easy to see that Tolstoy advances compassion as one of the highest of human virtues, the moral framework in which we are to see this conventional Christian virtue is, on close reading, far from clear. Tolstoy is usually accused of being heavy-handed in his manipulation of his readers[5] – and heavy-handedness is usually associated with the unequivocal expression of moral imperatives. But, paradoxically, this work has occasioned a variety of interpretations, suggesting that it is not possible to derive a simple, universally and univocally appreciated and understood moral.

As his first major fictional work in ten years, the story represents Tolstoy's recognition of and return to art as a means for illustrating his moral and religious views. On the basis of the rigorous demands Tolstoy made on his art after 1880, those features he ascribed to true art in his later treatise *What Is Art?* (1898), one might well expect in such a story a simple thesis that would lend itself to virtually uniform readings. In his treatise on art, he would argue for an art accessible to and understandable by everyone, an art with universal situations and a clearly moral function, which was to persuade people that they are all brothers and sisters, that they all have within them manifestations of the same spirit (his notion of "God").[6]

One value clearly offered in *The Death of Ivan Il'ich* is compassion, and there is no doubt that the moral advocacy of compassion for the suffering of others exemplified in this story is what Tolstoy later urged in his essay. The fact remains, however, that the advocacy of compassion is part of a very complex context that is susceptible to readings of a diverse and even contradictory character. These readings concern, in the end, the origins, place, and implications of the compassion Ivan, in his last moments, identifies as the meaning of life. The language and the settings surrounding Ivan's discovery suggest the Resurrection. Tolstoy is hardly paying his respects to conventional Christian dogma here. It can be argued, however, that the Christian suggestiveness is designed both to demonstrate Tolstoy's understanding of Christianity and to give solemnity and significance to the deathbed realizations of an ordinary man. Thus traditional Christianity becomes part of a strategy serving a higher purpose: the advancement of Tolstoy's own, radically revised Christianity. It is important to understand how this revised Christianity differs from other forms.

Tolstoy did not hide his skepticism about prevailing views of salvation and redemption. He was painfully blunt in numerous works: *Harmonization and Translation of the Four Gospels* (1880–81), "What I Believe" ("*V chem moia vera?*") (1882–84), "On Life," (1886–87), "Investigation of Dogmatic Theology" (1881–82), and "The Kingdom of God Is Within You" (1890–93). In the latter, for example, he condemned the "idolatry" of Russian Orthodoxy, its venerations of icons, and its reliance on church rites, on salvation, on redemption, and on prayer; he also pointed to the incompatibility of the Sermon on the Mount and the creed; the lack of attention (by the church and by believers) to the former; the distorting effects of believing in personal salvation, redemption, or the sacraments; and the total disregard of the moral teachings of Christ listed in the Sermon on the Mount. Orthodoxy, he maintained, was a form of idolatry that excluded the teachings of Christ (28:60–61).

This strong rejection of the authority of official representatives of religion and morality – and repeated insistence on the validity of the individual's unmediated sense of religious and moral truth – is combined with a carefully elaborated alternative religious doctrine. Tolstoy is usually seen as a moralist with rules of behavior, as a religious thinker deriving his philosophy from Matthew and the Sermon on the Mount rather than from the Book of John, with its revelatory concept of being born again that so impressed Dostoevsky. This distinction is acceptable so long as one realizes that Tolstoy views rules as living parts of a person: they inhere in demeanor and are reflected in behavior that is moral not because it is consciously in accordance with rules but because it derives from the proper attitudes toward the world – one characterized by love for others. Behavior is then manifested naturally, in harmony with rules. As Tolstoy's many religious writings demonstrate, it was more than recognition of universal brotherhood and sisterhood that he wanted. His religion was a religion of actions in this world, together with the proper attitudes and feelings; he promoted love and compassion, and, especially, avoidance of any kind of violence, whether the coercive activities of the state, the church, or other individuals. Compassion was not compassion, however, unless it was sincere and deeply rooted in the distinctive relationship an individual had with the world. This relationship was, Tolstoy insisted, attainable by all who would use their own reason and conscience.

The notion of morality as something instinctive and spontaneous, a guide to action that is accessible to all people without external guidance, finds a suitable niche in Tolstoy's aesthetics as well. Tolstoy believed art should strive "to make that feeling of brotherhood and love of one's neighbor, now attained only by the best members of society, the customary feeling and instinct of all men. By evoking under imaginary conditions the feeling of brotherhood and love, religious art will train men to experience those same feelings under similar circumstances in actual life; it will lay in the souls of men the rails along which the actions of those whom art thus educates will naturally pass."

Art as moral training "in the realm of feeling," as "laying the rails" for the proper feeling that serves as the basis for the proper actions in life, is what *The Death of Ivan Il'ich* should exemplify if it is to live up to Tolstoy's demanding criteria. And these feelings should help to establish that relationship between people and the world that Tolstoy labeled "religion."

The Story

A proper balance between artistic verity and moral explicitness is an obvious desideratum of moral fiction. Ivan is not a superficial vehicle for moral truth, a sacrifice to moral clarity. Nonetheless, there is a strong aura of the ordinary about Ivan that comes dangerously close to depriving him of the fullness we expect in a fictional character. He is given a particularized but unexceptional life as a child, youth, and adult; he is, by design, to be perceived as a very ordinary person; he is an obvious consequence of Tolstoy's effort to generalize and represent a way of life familiar to everyone – and a death everyone will someday face. Only as he comes to grips with death does he become truly individualized, and as he yields to the impersonal force he finds within, even more individualized.

After a conventional childhood and schooling, Ivan makes a career choice, law, that is also unremarkable. Climbing the professional ladder, Ivan became a judge whose work involves condemning or absolving others from guilt and deciding legal right and wrong. Appropriately respectful of his elders and social betters, he makes no waves and observes all society's conventions, living "comme il faut," developing "stability" when it is expected of him, and acquiring a wife and family at the appropriate junctures. He masters and internalizes the appropriate responses, so that he knows exactly the kind of wife appropriate for him and the kind of living quarters that would suit his status. Maintaining propriety and avoiding unpleasantness are the ruling principles of his life and those of the people around him.

Living by the law of society, expressed in the twin terms *pleasantness* and *properness* (*priiatnost'* and *prilichie*), leads him progressively to higher and more prestigious positions; it also channels him (because, in a Tolstoyan world, doing what society desires takes one further and further from meaningful life) into increasingly formalized relations with his family and colleagues. He reaches the very top of the metaphorical ladder: a judgeship and new living quarters. And in these very quarters, at the pinnacle of his career, at the height of his success, he accidentally tumbles from a real ladder, injures his side, and slowly dies. What seemed to be a simple bruise turns out to be more serious; an accident trivial in its origins has profound consequences.

Having judged and condemned the behavior of others, Ivan is suddenly condemned himself and must now ponder the rightness of his life. This abrupt and ironic turnabout from health to disease is the first in a series of disorienting experiences for Ivan: he will fall from success to failure, experience hope and despair during the course of his illness, deteriorate while imagining he is getting better (chapter 9), change his values (between chapters 6 and 7), and, in the end, find his suffering replaced by joy.[7] During his decline, suffering physically and morally, he is himself "formalized" as something unpleasant by former friends, his doctors, his daughter, and his wife. He is pitied only by his son, Vasya, and his peasant servant, Gerasim. After intense suffering, Ivan finally comes to understand the falseness of his past life and the nature of real life; feeling that pain and death have been vanquished, he dies. A veritable paradigm in its vivid illustration of the genesis of moral revelation "on the edge of the abyss," the story dramatizes a mythic conversion.[8] Failing in his flight from the ultimate horror, Ivan must confront it, and this confrontation leads to moral clarity and victory over the fear of death.

Peter Ivanovich

Critics have explored the sophisticated structural patterns Tolstoy employed to undercut the values by which Ivan lived before his illness, paying particular attention to the first of the twelve chapters, Ivan's funeral – chronologically the end of the story.[9] Here we are given an intimate view of the hypocrisy of Ivan's society, the falseness of conventional relations between people, and the various ways in which they avoid thinking about what is truly important. Tolstoy's moral strategy is transparent: he first presents the values Ivan himself lived by most of his life – and these are the values by which his society continues to live after his death – and later shows, through Ivan's example, that those values are inadequate, indeed base. Readers who share the narrator's scorn for the hypocrisy most of the people at the funeral exhibit are presumably then sympathetically disposed toward Ivan's final revelations. Throughout most of the narrative, while Ivan struggles to discover what went wrong with his life, Tolstoy sustains a critical tone. When Ivan dies, no one, except possibly his son, shows any awareness that the kind of life society promotes is based on delusions designed to protect people from unpleasant realities. No one seriously thinks about the most unpleasant of these realities, death; but the story, from the title to the end, keeps this unpleasant reality always in close view.

Earlier drafts indicate that originally Tolstoy had a different strategy. Ivan himself and a friend, not an omniscient narrator, told the story; in the final version the friend, Peter Ivanovich, receives Ivan's diary from his widow, reads it, and then articulates the main message for all to hear:

> "It is impossible, impossible, impossible to live as I have lived and as we all have been living." This is what Ivan Il'ich's death and his notes disclosed to me. I shall describe how I regarded life and death before this event; and I shall relate his notes as they come to me, supplementing them only with those details I learned from his domestics.[10]

Tolstoy's decision not to illustrate, through Peter Ivanovitch, the desired effect of Ivan's story (renunciation of one's previous way of life) but to imply it through Ivan's example alone marked a clear gain in the story's persuasive power. Although the presence of a converted friend of Ivan would be consonant with Tolstoy's didactic aim – it might underscore the thesis that ordinary human life is false and immoral – it would also tend to blunt the effect of the ending, the manner in which Ivan comes to realize that ordinary life is immoral. The newly converted friend is too explicitly moralistic and too easily converted into a critic of society. Moreover, there is a problem of balance: the friend's critique gives too much weight to the negative thesis and not enough to the right way to live, which Ivan discovered only at the end. With the diary narrative, rendering Ivan's last inner thoughts and revelations would present difficulties.

In the early version, the negative moral – the shallowness of conventional life – is succinctly summarized and the persuasive model laid bare: the story of Ivan's life has had a strong effect on his friend, the one we may assume Tolstoy wished us to feel as well. The story is designed to make us question the way we have been living and, ultimately, to renounce it. But, in the end, Tolstoy elected not to model the effect of Ivan's personal story in the verbal response of another character. He chose instead to present the story through the eyes of a narrator who was separate from the events but who had access to thoughts and feelings of all the characters. Tolstoy also fashioned the events so that only Ivan undergoes a radical change in perspective.

The result is a clearer focus on Ivan and the model of "right" living he becomes in the end, a model unobscured by demonstrating the effects of the example on others. Such blurring in focus and its attendant possible violation of verity could very well have undermined the evocation of feelings for which Tolstoy strove. Replication of the appropriate response is too strong a requirement to place on moral art if it is to differ from homily. Laying the rails is part of a program of education and training that can hardly be expected to obtain immediate results.

When Tolstoy recast the story in the third person, Peter Ivanovich was given a different role. We learn that neither he, one of Ivan's best friends, nor Praskov'ia Fedorovna, Ivan's wife, is ultimately converted or affected by Ivan's example, a fact that considerably reduces the optimism engendered by Ivan's joyful revelations. Tolstoy was only too aware of the power of his society's modes of living and thinking, and of course he harbored few illusions about the human capacity for self-delusion.[11] People in Ivan's world are dedicated to the pursuit of pleasure and comfort and to the avoidance of what is discomforting: they cannot imagine their own deaths.

Nevertheless the narrator shows considerable interest in portraying Peter's thoughts and discomfort at the funeral. Three times in the first chapter Peter is given a chance to comprehend the significance of Ivan's death, and thus the meaning of life. In the old days they had been close, they had gone to school together, and in maturity they played cards together. And Peter, more sensitive than other friends of Ivan, had recognized early that Ivan was dying (26:62). The first chance Peter has to step out of society's perspective, which conceals what is really important, is when, looking at the corpse of his friend, he sees that Ivan's face seems more handsome and significant in death than in life. And his expression indicates that "what had to be done was done, and done right." This sense of "fitness" reflects Ivan's achievement of what he had been striving all through his illness to discover, the "right" way of life. "Right" here and through-out the story (Ivan several times will say that his life was *"ne to"* [the wrong thing] which he lived "the wrong way") is not necessarily a moral category but an assessment of aptness or congruence with some standard or set of standards. Also, within Ivan's expression was a "reproach" or "reminder to the living." Something in what he saw was unpleasant to Peter; so he crosses himself, turns, and leaves, in the kind of pain one feels on recognizing a truth one is conditioned to avoid.

The second moment causing Peter discomfort occurs when he hears from Praskov'ia how much Ivan suffered in his final days (26:66) – it "horrified" him, and he feels "fearful" because Ivan has lived an ordinary life: one would not expect it to end with extraordi-nary suffering. His reference to the unfairness of suffering under-lines an important issue in the story: why does such an ordinary man have to suffer so much? One answer relates to Tolstoy's strategy: Ivan's suffering has a shock value;[12] Peter is disoriented enough to begin to think death and suffering could happen to him (26:67). "It is horrible" – "*Strashno*" – is repeated. What restores his calm is the socially conditioned reflex. "The customary thought came" (*prishla obychnaiia mysl'*) that it happened to Ivan, not him, and he believes it could not happen to him. This, of course, mirrors Ivan's reaction in the early stages of his illness, when he would become concerned about his recovery and resist thinking that he, too, could die. Like Ivan, Peter evaded thoughts of his own death.

But there is another possible explanation for the incongruity be-tween Ivan's suffering and the quality of his life. One part of the "picture" of life Tolstoy attacks is the notion that there is a link between sin and suffering. Though Ivan has lived superficially and falsely, he was no monster; and his sins have hardly been commensu-rate with his suffering and illness. Although pain and the fear of death may have connections with one's view of life, this relationship has nothing to do with legalistic balancing of the scales, in which the pain of punishment is directly related to the immorality of one's life. Tolstoy expressed, through Ivan's final vision, a different view: someone with the right understanding of life is "really" immune to physical pain (although others may think the pain extreme) and need not be concerned about mental and moral suffering.

Before he leaves the funeral, Peter see Ivan's two children – the daughter, Liza, looking "gloomy" and "angry," and the tearful Vasya; in the hall he has a brief conversation with Ivan's servant, Gerasim. Peter's suggestion that Ivan's death was a pity elicits Gerasim's reply that it was God's will and that all will end up that way (26:68). The word *pity* (expressed with the impersonal adverb *zhalko*) will recur as a leitmotiv, losing, as the story progresses, its conventional meaning and strengthening its connections with authentic compassion.[13]

Although it is clear in the story that Peter has not seen the truth, he is obviously more receptive to it than others at the funeral, especially associates and fellow card players like Shvarts (whose very name suggests the absence of the "light" of truth); he is also clearly more open to the truth than is Ivan's wife. Even though in this version he is no longer idealized as in Tolstoy's early draft, Peter, obviously sensitive to the deeper meaning of Ivan's death, retains a limited susceptibility to understanding the error of his own ways.[14] Perhaps since his patronymic makes him the son of Ivan, he will some day see the light and carry the message, as did his biblical namesake (who, like Peter Ivanovich, had earlier missed three opportunities to admit the truth); for that matter, Ivan also has a symbolic biblical lineage: Ivan, whose name is the Russian version of John (the precursor of Christ), is by patronymic the son of Il'ia, or Elijah, the Old Testament precursor of the Messiah. The biblical resonance of the names in the story helps to generate an aura of seriousness and religious significance.

Thus the central issues the story deals with – the falseness of conventional life, the meaning of pain and death, the role of pity and compassion in authentic life – are suggested through Peter and his perception of Ivan's life and their society. This first chapter, which is both beginning and end, plays an important role in setting the context and establishing the values that are examined. The final chapter, however, is even more important; for here Tolstoy deals with the moral concerns of the dying man, not just the values of those who have come to his funeral. It is here, in the last chapter, that Tolstoy distinctively marks his moral purposes with his depiction of Ivan's vital transformation. The amazing variety of readings this chapter has stimulated gives testimony to its key position in the story as well as its mysterious richness.

Journey to the Light

Though we are told in the beginning of the story and in the last chapter that Ivan screams for his last three days, other events – mostly psychological – in the last chapter push our awareness of his pain into the background. His screaming, which begins when he recognizes that the end has come and presumably continues without abatement until the end, is much less noticeable than in previous chapters. And the sense we have that it is somehow less testifies to the shift in emphasis Tolstoy has directed as we make the transition to his presentation of the positive side of his truth.

In each of the previous chapters we watch minute changes in Ivan's perceptions and temperament, his physical and psychological condition; subsuming all is his suffering. Now the pain has begun to move into the background, yielding its place to Ivan's revelations, which are of such importance that they occupy the center of his consciousness. In fact, in his last hours Ivan seems unaware of his screaming; he is oblivious to his physical condition, undoubtedly because of his new view of life.

Ivan's mind-set in this last period of his life can be seen as a stage of dying, the end of his depression and the beginning of his acceptance of death.[15] Paradoxically, the proximity of death is linked to recurring thoughts of childhood and images of birth. Ivan loses his ability to speak, a development that intensifies for the reader the physical pain he feels, the inefficacy of all verbalization, the regressive quality of his experience. He tries to say something ("I don't want . . . [to die," presumably]) but instead merely howls with the sound of the final vowel of the word *want* (the long "u" sound of *khochu*). That Ivan's spiritual regeneration may lie in a return to the purity and innocence of childhood is suggested not only by the "babylike" sounds he makes as his defenses fall but also by recurring thoughts of his childhood. In chapter 10, for example, he recalls the flavor of plums he ate as a child, and the smell of his striped leather ball: more and more he realizes that life then had been full, fresh, innocent, and untainted.

Tolstoy accurately renders what many have observed about dying people: they are like children in their need for attention and their dependence on the care of others.[16] Screaming, of course, also fits the pattern of correspondences: that is how we come into the world and attract attention vital to our well-being. But also suggested is the inadequacy of language to convey the nature of Ivan's experience. Tolstoy, who used words so well, chose to make his moral statement in a different "language" here.[17] Tolstoy described the function of art as "laying the rails" for correct feelings. These rails are laid by paradox, metaphor, and Ivan's sudden insight.

We are told that during these three final days, time did not exist for Ivan, that he continued to struggle in a "black sack" or "black hole," forced into it by an invincible power.[18] But the source of his horror is ambiguous, both in his resistance and his yielding to the power forcing him deeper into the sack. The imagery suggests a high degree of disorientation, a life void of its customary points of reference:

> He struggled as one sentenced to death struggles in the hands of an executioner, knowing that he cannot save himself; and with each moment he felt that, despite all efforts in the struggle, he was getting closer and closer to what terrified him. He felt that his suffering came both from being shoved into that black hole and, still more, from not being able to crawl into it. What prevented him from crawling into it was his claim that his life had been good [*khoroshaia*]. That very justification of his life enchained him and did not allow him to pass forward, and tormented him more than anything. (26:112)

Trying to rationalize a bad life has kept Ivan from advancing to a higher state, though, paradoxically, this "advance" means "crawling" (*prolezt'*) deeper into the hole. The unconventional nature of Ivan's journey is captured in paradoxes, in the notion of advancing by crawling deeper. Recognition of what is really important in life is impossible with conventional perspectives. Seeing the truth through the abandonment of rationalization is difficult and demands radical reorientation.

Ivan is still at the level of "torment" (*muchen'e*), which will be contrasted with a later state yet to come. There is a new development, however: now his thoughts, not his physical condition, are causing him pain. All that is associated with his physical being recedes more and more into the background as he sheds old ways of looking at the world.

Ivan's new orientation is intimately connected with the recurring image of the black sack (alternatively, the black hole) from which he cannot escape. The image possibly originates in his visualization of his illness: he has earlier tried to make concrete what was causing him pain, vividly imagining the "blind intestine" or cecum, which some of his doctors had identified as the source of his ills. The black sack also suggests the womb, an identification that makes Ivan's pains analogous to labor pains. Labor pains can then be linked with his recollection of childhood, his nonverbal communication, and ultimately his "rebirth." Finally, the image of the black sack suggests the intestine again, and a particular situation: Ivan wishes to escape from a "constipated," restricted life. Tolstoy's linkage of scatology and eschatology is not without philosophical precedent.[19]

Within the "sack" Ivan is subjected to surrounding pressures; he wants to "crawl through," but something "did not allow him to pass forward" (*ne puskalo vpered*). The concept of "passing" from one plane to another is crucial. Shortly, in a slip of the tongue, Ivan will make a perhaps unconscious request to pass on to the next plane: "Let me pass" (*propusti*). This is one of a large number of verbs with the prefix *pro-*, which, though relatively common as a Russian prefix, appears in this section with uncommon frequency. Such a prefix, denoting actions and movements "through" something, as well as movements that are "complete," underscores Ivan's need to "pass through" to a different state. Multiple perspectives, all designed to intensify the event's meaning, come to bear on Ivan's "passage." First, while in pain, he feels a blow to the chest and side. The force impels him: "He fell through [*provalilsia*] into the hole, and there, at the end of the hole, something lit up." Now all that happens is beyond conscious control, and Ivan acts as if a force is working through him.

The narrator compares the experience of falling and then seeing a light to the sensations of a person in a train who is confused about which way the car is going: first confusion, then orientation, finally a realization of the car's true direction.[20] The train motif ironically closes what it began: it was on a train that Ivan first made the contact that led to his new job, a meeting that led to his move, his accident, his sufferings, his revelation, his death.

Ivan's spiritual turnabout is expressed in vivid terms of violence and disorientation. Coming to the truth is painful and involves radical reversals of former perspectives. Now Ivan understands that his past life was not right, and he explicitly says so:

> "Yes, everything was wrong [*ne to*]," he said to himself, "but that doesn't matter." "It's possible, it's possible to do it the 'right' way [*sdelat 'to'*]. But what is the 'right' way?" he asked himself, and then grew quiet. (26:112)

The moment of revelation comes at the end of the third day, only an hour before Ivan's death. This explicit reference to time, with its biblical suggestiveness, marks and sets up expectations for the approach of a redemptive moment, a "resurrection." The imagery, however, suggests a new birth, and thus a clean slate or state of originary purity rather than a resurrection or returning to life from the dead. Rebirth evokes the black sack with the light at the end, the pressures to remain in the sack but also to escape, and the final liberation from constraint and emergence into the light. Moreover, present at this rebirth is the archetypal family – father, mother, and son. The perspectives are skewed, however, for it is the father who is to be "born." The presence of other characters during Ivan's final moments expresses Tolstoy's belief that morality is a matter of compassionate actions and sincere feelings directed toward others. The relational, contextual, and interpersonal emphasis Tolstoy gives here to moral behavior is at odds with the customary representation of his ethics as bound by rule and logic.[21]

Ivan's son has crept (again a verb with a pro- prefix, *prokralsia*) into the room to join his mother and father. Ivan places his hand on his boy's head, with powerful effect on all: the boy grabs the hand and kisses it, tearfully expressing his compassion. This is a crucial scene, wordless, with a focus on spontaneous action, direct and unmediated human communication, not conscious and imitative behavior according to social dictate or moral rule. With biblical suggestiveness derived from the emphasis on compassion and Vasya's role (Christ urged people to become "as little children"), the scene makes vivid a significant feature of Tolstoy's religion.[22]

Disguised here is the general outline of Christ's crucifixion. The central figure is condemned to death, and next to him are two others, also condemned (as mortals); Ivan's wife and son stand here as tokens for the two thieves. The analogy is reinforced by Tolstoy's choice of verbs. Vasya "crept" or, literally, "stole" into the room: the association with theft exists in both Russian and English. What happens next underscores the analogy, making it clear that Vasya represents the unnamed thief who suffered alongside Christ, the one Christ consoled (Luke 23:42–43). In Tolstoy's extensively revised version of the Gospels, Christ says that the thief, by ignoring his physical well-being and asking Christ to remember him in his "kingdom," is already in "paradise." Paradise as something this side of death, as a state accessible to the living, is a notion with important implications for our understanding of Ivan's final experiences. Here Ivan's son, who already knows authentic compassion, is already in "paradise." Whether he will remain there or be seduced by the world of the pleasant and the proper is an open question at the end of the story.

Vasya's intuition and compassion give him an unerring sense of what could help his father. And this help is nonverbal, silent, simply tears and the pressure of a hand. Emphasizing the simultaneity of events, Tolstoy repeats what has happened to Ivan in these moments: he has fallen through, seen the light, realized that his life has not been what it should have been. But in addition – and this is the new element – he recognizes that it is still possible to correct matters. Falling silent, he listens for an answer to his question about the "right" way of life. And at this point he feels his hand being kissed. Tolstoy presents the same temporally limited series of mental and physical events from different perspectives, reinforcing Ivan's realization and its connection with the authentic emotional contact represented by his son's compassionate gestures.

Rebirth is appropriately connected with the parent-child model. But here the roles are unconventional, the perspective and orientation are different; for it is the father and son, not the mother and son, who are emphasized. Now Ivan looks at his son and pities him. Vasya is the only one in his world whom he has pitied: earlier, in chapter 8, the narrator said that Vasya "was always pitiable to him." What is more, "besides Gerasim, it seemed to Ivan Il'ich that Vasya alone understood and pitied him" (26:105). The glow of compassion is now extended to include Praskov'ia as well; for as she approaches him, he feels sorry for her, too. In practically all previous contacts with her in the story he has felt hatred for her. We know that earlier in their marriage he distanced himself from her emotionally because her querulousness and irritability during pregnancy were unpleasant to him, as they introduced into his well-ordered and rigidly controlled life an alien and threatening element. Immersing himself in his work and in his social games, he formalized the relationship with her so that Praskov'ia could not interfere with his "pleasant" life. But in the present, as his illness progressively worsens and as he comes closer to his "birth," she treats him as he has treated her, refusing to regard him as a suffering human being. He begins to hate her even more, as she represents to him his old way of life, the pleasure principle with all its hypocrisy; much of his anger, though displaced, is directed at her. Something has happened now, however, at the hour of his death; something in the situation has helped him to answer his question about the "right" way of life, and he no longer hates her but instead pities her.

This "something" is not the product of logical, rational thinking; rather, a new way of looking at the world has come to Ivan at a time when he is receptive to it, when he is ready to abandon rationalization for his past way of life. The model for realizing moral truth in Tolstoy's writing at this time is not one that depends on or utilizes conventional moral arguments. Tolstoy directs us to look at the world honestly, not through the elaborate defenses and rationalizations society has instructed us to build, and then to wait for the truth to be disclosed. The lies have heretofore distorted the one true perspective.

Ivan's new understanding of life is reflected in a new interest in others, an attention not to his own personal well-being but to the feelings of those around him. He recognizes that he is torturing his wife and son and that his death will make their life easier.

> "Yes, I am tormenting them," he thought. "They are sorry, but it will be better for them when I die." He wanted to say this but did not have the strength to speak. "But why speak? I have to do something," he thought. With a glance he indicated his son to his wife and said: "Take him away . . . sorry for him . . . and for you too . . . " He tried to say "Forgive," too, but said "Forward," and no longer having the strength to correct himself, waved his hand, knowing that whoever needed to understand would understand. (26:113)

The supreme moral attitude of compassion, the turn from the self to others, and the awareness of and concern for the suffering of others are emphasized repeatedly in the text, though English translations usually obscure this fact. The phrase "they are sorry" is too ambiguous in this context for "*im zhalko*"; better here is "they are sorry for him, they have pity for him." The expression exactly parallels Ivan's previous expressions of pity for his wife and son ("*Emu stalo zhalko ego*" and "*Emu zhalko stalo ee*"). The key word *zhalko* (an adverbial form for *pity* and *sorry for*) when used with noun or pronoun objects denoting people, suggests having pity for someone.

What is unusual now is that Ivan's wife, open-mouthed, with tears on her nose and cheeks and an expression of despair, is perceived by him as showing pity – and she may indeed be experiencing such a feeling. Compassion has united Ivan, his wife, and his son. Sympathy and feelings of pity are fundamental to Tolstoy's religion and to his ethics, and his attempts to spread his religion to others depend on the potential infectiousness of compassion. The scene illustrates this potential in exemplary fashion: authentic compassion is shown in all its glory. Its effects, however, are not lasting for Ivan's wife; for in the first chapter (depicting what happens after Ivan's death) she is shown to be, once again, in the world of the pleasant and the proper. The moment leaves its imprint only on Vasya, who has remained virtually untainted by society's evil influence.[23]

The didactic point of the story is transparent: examples of moral behavior have an infectious power, a power Tolstoy must rely on if his moral message is to be effective. The power can fade, however, once the example is gone and society's values have reestablished their dominance. The moral discussion focuses on behavior that is spontaneously and naturally moral: Ivan adjures talking, for he wants to do something. The need for action flows naturally from the feeling of compassion. Moreover, real compassion may itself be an action. The deed, not the words, is what is emphasized now. Action flowing spontaneously from the correct moral feeling has a much more important role than words and proper rituals.

The context makes it clear that Ivan has in mind not just action in general but completing an action already referred to (*sdelat'* is the verb); such an action could include dying, as well as showing compassion. But the verb has a mundane dimension as well. Ivan gives a concrete and specific indication to his wife that she should remove their son from the room ("*Uvedi,*" "lead him away"); but even in this case there is ambiguity, for the imperative could also suggest leading him away from the kind of life she and Ivan have lived, and from the values their society has supported. Ivan adds, again, that he feels sorry for her as well ("*zhalko* . . . / *tebia* . . ."). Feeling and expressing his compassion constitute Ivan's last actions.

Ivan's attempt to say "forgive me" has been subjected to various interpretations. His conscious intention to ask forgiveness has been embraced by those who have understood it as an appropriate response to his causing suffering in others; moreover, it would be the conventional thing for Christians to say, an expression of repentance. But there are other possibilities as well: the words point to Christ's, "Father, forgive them, for they know not what they do"; in this reading the attempt reinforces Ivan's Christlike role. And perhaps what he planned to say is no longer as important as what he actually said under the influence of his new perception of the world.

Ivan could not say "forgive" (*prosti*) but uttered instead a word with the same syllable (*pro-*): "Propusti," "Let me pass" (or possibly, "Let it pass"). The usual English translation, *forego*, and, to a lesser extent, the word used in translating it above (*forward*), obscures the possibilities inherent in Ivan's slip of the tongue: that he is asking to pass through into another state, to the light in the other realm, or, in effect, to death. On this reading, what is shown is Ivan's unconscious assimilation of what Tolstoy would view as real moral understanding rooted in authentic religious feeling, not conventional religious doctrine. Ivan wishes his spirit to pass out of his body into another state, to merge with God.[24]

Unable to correct what he said, Ivan nevertheless is confident that he has done what was required. Many English translations introduce a capitalized pronoun, suggesting that God is the one who would understand. The phrase in Russian is "*poimet tot, komu nado*," a very succinct "the one who needs to understand will understand." There are no capital letters in Soviet or pre-Soviet editions, although the possibility that God is the one who will understand is not excluded. In any case, there is no reason to think that the "one" referred to is a divinity. Praskov'ia, Vasya, and readers are privy to what Ivan says, and, if the message is compassion, then it has surely been understood.

Insights in these last moments come quickly:

And suddenly it became clear to him that that which had been wearing him down and which would not go away was suddenly and all at once going away, on two sides, on ten sides, on all sides. He felt pity for them, he had to do something so that it would not be painful for them. He had to release them and release himself from this suffering. (26:113)

Again pity and the need for active good are conjoined: releasing his wife and son from suffering flows naturally from his feelings of pity. The verb for "release himself" is *izbavit'sia*, with connotations of the biblical "deliverance from." Tolstoy's language aptly catches the exhilaration of freedom when everything that has been oppressing Ivan from all sides suddenly falls away. Deliverance here is concrete and of this world: it is action invoked and accomplished easily because it is derived from compassion. Freeing others from suffering, which is a variation of doing unto others as they would do unto you, is a notion shared by the conventional Christian ethos and Tolstoy's Christianity. But Ivan's behavior is not so much obedience to the rule as it is spontaneous action in accordance with it. And this spontaneity is an essential ingredient of Ivan's final experience.[25]

No longer subject to the power of the physical world, Ivan asks himself what happened to the pain. He even apostrophizes it: "How good, and how simple," he thought. "And the pain?" he asked himself. "Where was it? Well, where are you, pain?"

The pain has diminished and almost disappeared. It is totally under the dominion of Ivan's new consciousness of the "right" way, his new understanding of life. And when he senses it, he accepts it: "Yes, here it is. Well, what of it? Let the pain be" (26:113). The parallel question, "Where is death? Where is it?" leads to equally unexpected results:

He searched for his former habitual fear of death and did not find it. "Where is it? What death?" There was no fear because there was not death either. Instead of death there was light. "So that's it!" he suddenly pronounced aloud. "What joy!" (26:113)

In this simple experience Tolstoy expresses his alternative to the customary religious conception of "resurrection." It is a resurrection-rebirth that occurs before death, not after, and only after Ivan realizes how to live.

> For him all this happened in a single instant, and the meaning of this instant did not change anymore. For those present, his agony continued for another two hours. In his chest something rattled; his wasted body twitched. Then the rattle and the wheezing became less and less frequent. (26:113)

The sufferings (*muchen'ia*) have now turned into agony (*agoniia*), the "pre-death state of the organism." In this state there need be no mental or physical suffering, and, in Ivan's case, there is none; thus the English can be misleading, for our word *agony* usually has strong connotations of pain. Ivan is no longer suffering (or at least no longer conscious of his suffering), nor is he even in the realm of time and space, the physical and the changing ("the meaning of the moment remained unchanged").[26] The pain and mental torment that have preceded Ivan's death are replaced in his consciousness by light and life. There is just one more step:

> "It's all over!" said someone above him.
>
> He heard these words and repeated them in his soul. "Death is over," he said to himself. "It is no more."
>
> He drew in his breath, stopped in the middle of a sigh, stretched out and died. (26:113)

In Russian there is just a single word for "It is all over!": "*Koncheno!*" Having been uttered by someone "above," the word carries no little suggestiveness concerning divine origin. But because it provokes Ivan's response – his clarification that it is not life that is over but, paradoxically, death – it is doubtful that the word is God's. The meaning of Ivan's correction is clear: with his new knowledge of life, death no longer threatens him and no longer has any power over him. The solemnity and seriousness of the moment are enhanced by the religious connotations of the language and the context. It does not matter that the religious suggestiveness derives from a religion Tolstoy finds pernicious in its conventional forms. The feelings evoked by the scene are directed by Tolstoy.

The term *koncheno* is ripe with religious meaning. Ivan's final words, and the one uttered from above, parallel words spoken at Christ's death that suggested fulfillment of a divine plan ("It is accomplished!"). And of course this meaning is consistent with and finds its place in Tolstoy's ethics, which is also based on behavior according to a universal, "divine" plan. There is every reason to believe that Ivan's life is part of the same plan as Christ's: to Tolstoy, Christ was a man who died as men do. In his exegetical writings, Tolstoy denied any form of personal resurrection after physical death. When Ivan gives the completed action, "It's all over," a more specific referent, changing it to "Death is over; it is no more," he is giving expression to his pre-death "resurrection." Death is now a meaningless concept to him, for he had been born, in fact, into a new comprehension of life. Tolstoy has mapped out a new area for the application of the terms *life*, *death*, and *rebirth*. Ivan's banishment of death and his rebirth are derived from his newly discovered religion; in this new relationship (to Tolstoy, religion is one's relationship to the universe), he finds himself in harmony with the law of life, expressed as love and compassion for one's fellow human beings.

Death is a concept appropriate to the corporeal and the material sides of existence. It has no relevance to one who lives by the spirit. Tolstoy's new usage, translated into the old terminology, is that the rule of death over Ivan's life has been overthrown so that physical demands, including everything determined by or defined with concepts of space and time, no longer has any power. His "rebirth" inheres in his new view. Convincingly orchestrating this rebirth required the use of an array of sophisticated artistic devices.

The Strategy of the Final Chapter

Knowing well the powers of art, Tolstoy used them to make his new picture of life, rebirth, and death convincing. Within the story's complex structure, there is a fascinating interplay of verbal elements that belies the usual claims made about Tolstoy's stylistic transparency and directness.[27] We have already seen how he has manipulated conventional religious terminology to serve his purposes. If the music of Beethoven could lead to adultery and violence (*The Kreutzer Sonata*), then surely art's persuasive power could be utilized as a force for the good. His task was to put this power in the service of a higher moral purpose.

The devices he implemented in his moral strategy took a variety of forms. We have seen how he placed the end of the story in the first chapter, how he suggested some of the major themes in the story through the perceptions of Peter Ivanovich, how he manipulated imagery (of the black sack, for example) to expand the meaning of Ivan's rebirth. In addition, phrases with one meaning in Ivan's early life – he was described as the "phoenix" of the family, and he received a medallion inscribed "Respice finem" – took on a deeper, ironic meaning at the end of his life.

One of Tolstoy's most effective utilizations of language was his exploitation of the grammatical fact that the words for pain and death are both feminine and thus share the same pronoun (*ona*). Interweaving linguistic and psychological phenomena, he linked both words in Ivan's consciousness by their common pronoun (*it* in English) and used its indefinite referentiality to suggest the indefinite but paralyzing horror and fear Ivan experienced. Moreover, the interconnection of pain and death suggested an identical provenance, their common derivation from the same order or realm – the physical, the realm from which Ivan would eventually free himself. The preestablished connection of pain and death facilitated the natural turn from pain to death at the end of the story; both pain and death are by this time meaningless to Ivan, no longer oppressing him. And, ironically, the victory over pain and death is a victory for "life," also a feminine noun.

Other key words linked both thematically and linguistically are light and death. Thematically associated with the bottom of the black sack, *light* (*svet*) is also the word for world – a meaning that connects Ivan's seeing the light with his coming into the world (i.e., being born). The expression "that world" (*tot svet*) connotes, in Russian, a world beyond death, which in Tolstoy's philosophy means a life not in heaven but one lived on earth in accordance with God's plan. It is this life, which Ivan realizes is now living, that moves Ivan to exclaim "What joy!"

The narrative account of Ivan's life had opened (in chapter 2) with a statement from the narrator about Ivan's life being "most simple, ordinary, and horrible": "Proshedshaia istoriia zhizni Ivana Il'icha byla samaia prostaia i obyknovennaia i samaia uzhasnaia" (26:68). We discover in these simple, profound words that it was simple in the wrong way. His way of living was not right; for it was anchored in society's values, in the pleasant and the proper. And near death, he discovers that the right way to live is really very simple (though his reorientation was difficult). The right way entails pity, compassion, and living for others. Key words are again associated by sound texture, mostly by initial consonant clusters; their linguistic connection underlines their ironic relationship: *priiatno, prilichno* or *prilichie*, and *prostaia* (it is pleasant, it is proper or properness, simple) all lead, by the way of *provalilsia, prokralsia, prosti, propusti*, and finally *puskai* (fell, stole into, forgive, let pass, and allow) to Ivan's realization. Stylistic and structural devices all work harmoniously to present the moral message.

Tolstoy's use of the devices listed above can be approached from several perspectives. His linguistic play with prefix, pronoun, and metaphor is surely related to his plan of undercutting civilized, conventional life in society, with its ossified and complacent evasions, its card games and empty posturing designed to conceal authentic life. Tolstoy leads readers to look at this reality in new ways, to understand simple expressions like "it's a pity" in terms of real compassion – to distrust language, for it represents society's power to conceal authentic values. He dethrones language in its conventional forms through Ivan, who rejects it in favor of acting, or fails to say what he means, and who ultimately creates new meanings out of conventional terms. Compassion, pain, life, and death are revalued, uprooted from comfortable points of reference in the world of the pleasant and the proper.

Language is a sphere of power to Tolstoy; he will use it, turn it inside out, and create his own moral order and world (which he will call the real world). Tracing Christianity along its own fault lines with an iconoclastic severity, he will tear it from the hands of clerics and the grips of mystery and miracle, and embed it in an overarching philosophy more compatible with his own moral and metaphysical longings. His iconoclasm comes to a head in his reversal of customary distinctions and cherished dogmas: life, death, rebirth, resurrection. Challenging the conventional connections between signifier and signified, exposing the flimsy basis of his society's linguistic and perceptual frames, he offers a new philosophy of life which he thinks captures the way things really are. In his quest for what is primary he never doubted that it existed, that there was an origin brimming with moral purity. Tolstoy took what people considered primary and made it secondary, derivative, and morally suspect. He revised, rephrased, and reformulated Christian dogma, using its semiotic system but altering most of its signifieds on the basis of empirically grounded common sense. What resulted, beyond his own apostasy, was a religion focused on this world, on actions and behavior.

Despite Tolstoy's insistent claims that his philosophy was in conformity with the demands of reason, the source of the good remained something vaguely mystical, a God within to which one must yield, an originary principle of love carrying overtones of Schopenhauer, Eastern religions, and mystical Christianity.[28] This suprapersonal foundation (which Tolstoy did not find in conflict with reason) supported a practical moral edifice. Loving one another, having compassion, giving of oneself for others – all this is eminently moral, and all this is possible in our everyday world. Tolstoy's philosophy of life is testable, for the consequences of perceiving the world the way he wants us to are observable in our behavior and are authenticated in our personal experience.

Christian Readings

If we want a reading of the story that coheres with what we know of the author and with other works by the author, then it is obviously necessary to consider Tolstoy's religious views, as he expressed them in a wide variety of writings from the late 1870s until his death in 1910. Striving for this kind of coherence does not, of course, amount to denying the significance of other frames of reference on other levels; thus an account of the story that examines it from a hermeneutic Heideggerian perspective[29] can be fascinating and illuminating, even if such an approach carries with it concepts, assumptions, and terms quite unfamiliar to Tolstoy. Interpretations, of whatever cast, attain scope and power on the basis of what they do with whatever the text provides. Even moral-religious readings of a conventional sort can achieve a surface plausibility. But these sorts of readings, which run the usual risks associated with vague religious terminology and controversial theological conceptions, also come up against an even more formidable problem: it is hard to justify a reading based on notions we know the author inveighed against so persistently and vehemently for more than thirty years. One is then in the curious position of having to demonstrate that Tolstoy was an Orthodox Christian despite himself, and that, as V. V. Zenkovsky maintains, he actually believed in the divinity of Christ and the truth of the Church and its sacraments.[30]

But not all were willing to save Tolstoy for Christianity. The writer Vladimir Korolenko moved to the opposite position (which was equally unsatisfying), considering Tolstoy an atheist and Antichrist who concealed himself in religious rhetoric.[31] As George Kline observed, Tolstoy's radical reformation of religious conceptions was bound to provoke opposition; further, his habit of referring to his concordance and translation of the Gospels as "his" Gospels could only infuriate those steeped in the traditions of reverence for Holy Writ.[32] Also infuriating was the apparent simplicity of Tolstoy's religion (Ivan says, "How good and how simple!"): Lev

Shestov saw in this simplicity a potential compatibility with atheism, and Nikolai Berdiaev complained that there was no mystery, only rules. What is missing in the vast literature concerned with *The Death of Ivan Il'ich* is a satisfactory reading in Tolstoyan terms, a reading that relates the work to the philosophical and religious issues with which he was struggling in the years following his "conversion."[33]

Tolstoy's religious views rest on a distinction between carnal and spiritual life. Taking cues from the Bible, but always with a care to avoid its "mystification," he emphasizes the filial relation between God (the Father) and people. Those who fulfill God's basic teaching to love one another manifest the presence of God within them. "Life" is to be found in the proper understanding (he uses the term *comprehension*) of God's teaching and the filial relationship between God and people. A person who has comprehension lives spiritually, somehow beyond the limits and demands of physical existence. Life in this exalted spiritual sense cannot come to an end the way physical life does; for death, as well as our concepts of space and time, have no power over the spirit. Thus Christ, like Ivan, has no fear of death; both have the right notion of life. And Christ's teaching of love and sacrifice of one's life for another, which he expressed in the Sermon on the Mount, should be obeyed not as slaves blindly obey a master but as free people who understand the meaning of life.

Tolstoy underlines the primacy of love, which is the source of life.[34] It is God's plan that we love one another and act in behalf of the good. No one can know God, but people can nonetheless discover that love is the identifying mark of authentic life. People with the customary "comprehension" or understanding of life avoid pain and suffering and fear death as something alien, a violence from the outside. Death and suffering as they are customarily understood appear pointless and unfair, threatening, as they do, our very being and our right to exist. Ivan passes through the stage in which he deeply feels the injustice of his suffering, the unfairness of his dying when he has done nothing wrong. Only when he rejects this legalistic concept of life and death, with its notion of unfair and incommensurate suffering, does he conquer the power of this suffering and his fear of death.[35]

Tolstoy opposes to the customary view of life one that he ascribes to Christ. This view does not focus on justifying or accounting for death, endeavors that preoccupy conventional Christianity and all religions which promise that something better than present-day life will be given to people after they die. Tolstoy's focus instead is on the positive qualities of life, of which the most positive is the potential to love. This potential exists in everyone, but not all recognize it. If people would recognize love in themselves and yield to its power, "unite" with it, they would have no need to be concerned with death. Life is a gift, it is not "naturally" given, nor is it something to which people are in any way entitled; it is given for a purpose, associated with love and goodness, which Tolstoy believes he has discovered. Individuals do not and cannot have eternal life in any personal sense. Death and suffering are problems only to those who do not realize that life itself is an extraordinary gift of love.

Tolstoy's support for his view is borne, if not by logic and philosophical rigor, by the energy of his conviction and the comforting force of his terminology. His unconventional definitions of familiar terms map out a fairly familiar world: it is obvious that here in his religious writing, as in his story, he is building on the familiar only to mold it to a shape of his making, one he hopes will captivate readers. He argues that we should see our lives as something precious given to us by a higher power for a purpose we can discover by using our reason. If we adopt his picture of life, a gift that raised us out of nothingness, we will not complain of the cruelty and unfairness of death. Ivan's horrible suffering before he realized the "truth" should not be understood as punishment for having lived the wrong way; the reward-punishment model is not appropriate for assessing the way one lives. Ivan's initial pain and fear of death are merely indications that he has not had the "right" view, not punishment for having the "wrong" one.

Ivan's joy before his death is ultimately the product of a chain of realizations, all deriving from a newly found sense of compassion.

The transformation of grief into joy reflects an analogy Christ used in speaking to his disciples (in Tolstoy's version of the Gospels):

> When I am no longer in the carnal life, my spirit will be with you. But you are like all people and will not always feel the strength of this spirit i̇ ᷉ourselves. Sometimes you will weaken and lose this strength of spirit, and you will fall into temptation, and sometimes you will again awaken into true life. Hours of enslavement of the flesh will overcome you, but this will only be temporary; suffer and be born again in spirit, as a woman suffers in the pains of birth and then feels joy that she has brought a man into the world; you will experience the same when you, after enslavement of the flesh, rise up in spirit: you will feel then such bliss that there will be nothing left for you to desire. (24:753)

The metaphor of sorrow passing into a joyful birth is obviously relevant to Ivan's experience. After much inner struggle Ivan rejected the customary comprehension of life – he let go of it – and he no longer conceived of life as avoidance of the unpleasant. He was eventually given or led to the "right" direction by his son's gesture of pity and love. He felt the good as having a powerful source, love, and he "united" with this source. In giving himself up to it, he vanquished death's grip, together with all the power of the earthly and the physical. Just as the woman gave birth after labor, Ivan labored and was reborn.

The key to moral behavior is first attaining "comprehension" and then yielding to the force of love it discloses (24:737); when one yields totally, one's actions are good because they flow spontaneously from a divine source within and are not the products of abstract reflection and deliberation. The polarities Tolstoy established, which he elaborated in his later essay, "On Life" (1886–87), placed truth, life, and submission to a higher force at one end of the axis and the physical, animal, and personal life at the other (26:363–66). Again and again, until the end of his life, he would demand if not the "renunciation" of personality, its submission to a higher consciousness authenticated by reason (26:375–82).

Ivan's life and death are a vivid illustration of the lessons of love, self-sacrifice, and submission to "the God within" – lessons Tolstoy elaborated on in his exegetical writings and essays. Acting in accordance with God's plan means acting compassionately as the thief next to Christ did in Tolstoy's account of the crucifixion: "The thief had pity on Jesus, and this feeling pity was a manifestation of life, and Jesus said to him: you are alive" (24:781). Authentic life, pity, and love are all interwined. Right actions can be explained by reference to God's divine plan. God's plan stipulates our helping to realize divine goals, and helping in this way yields great joy.

The fundamental beliefs of other religions point to the same divine plan. To Tolstoy, the truths of other religions helped to prove that Christ's example was indeed a divine exemplification of the plan, not that Christ was a divinity. Using his empirical sensibility and his findings in the study of other religions, Tolstoy excised what he took to be irrelevancies and superstitions in Christian dogma. Above all, he appealed to common sense and reason, thereby undercutting the basic objection to moral theories based on revelation.

Though Tolstoy had no use for religion as an incentive for doing what is right – a system that is ultimately a form of egoism – he nonetheless utilized religion and religious example, as well as the concept of a divine plan, in establishing a foundation for his own moral theory. He found it necessary to have a divine, nonhuman basis for his theory of right and wrong; for Tolstoy, God and his plan were concepts consistent with reason.

Faintly perceptible in Ivan's final hours are features of a conventional Christian conversion.[36] Tolstoy follows the outlines of the traditional Christian final rite, but he gives it a new content based on his own religious and moral views. Ivan recognizes what has been wrong in his past life and chooses to act differently. Instead of a priest, it is his son who shows compassion. Instead of verbal refrains and incantations, there are compassionate actions. Instead of asking for forgiveness, Ivan asks to "pass through." And instead of being guided through a time of terror, Ivan touches his son, in a gesture of authentic compassion.

By now it is clear why it is misleading to say that Ivan, after his accident, becomes conscious of his sinful ways, becomes contrite, finds redemption through God's grace and the example of Jesus Christ, and ultimately finds salvation. This would be the interpretation of conventional Christianity which Tolstoy explicitly rejected in numerous places in his writings. The Christian framework can be imposed only with great difficulty, for there is no mention of Christ, sin, contrition, grace, and redemption; in fact, the role of the Christian Church (represented by the priest who comes to see Ivan) is hardly flattering: the Church's aid to Ivan is ineffective, and its role in the story remains insignificant.[37] Finally, it is doubtful whether any kind of conventional Christian interpretation can be made without ignoring or distorting not only Tolstoy's views, as expressed in his essays, but also, and more important, passages in the text.

The problem is that the story's religious suggestiveness – its numerological references, its biblical terminology, its references to a voice above Ivan, its use of names (Peter Ivanovich as well as Ivan Il'ich – John, son of Elijah), its parallels with the story of Christ (including peripheral parallels such as the "son" bringing the message of true life, the "son" as one of the "thieves," and the filial nature of compassion) – all this lends itself easily to "Christian" readings. But, as indicated above, Tolstoy uses the religious suggestiveness to enhance the seriousness of his statement and, at the same time, subtly to divert conventional views into new channels.

Although indirect allusions to Christ undeniably exist, they are deeply embedded, pointing to ironies that are far from obvious. Part of the subtext is readily apparent: both Christ and Ivan are condemned to death, both are in the hands of executioners, both suffer three days of torment (and wounds in their side), both experience a "resurrection," both exemplify their love by willingly yielding up their lives, and both conquer death.[38] Beyond the obvious is the parallel filial relationship: Ivan's early apostrophe to God (chapter 9): "Why do you torment me?" (which echoes Matthew 27:46: "My God, my God, why hast Thou forsaken me?"); Ivan's attempt to say "Forgive [me]"; and the expression from above, "It's all over!" ("*Koncheno!*" in both the story and Tolstoy's translation of the Gospels).

The surface similarities may be misleading, however. In his translation of the Gospels (24:781) Tolstoy renders the verses from Matthew as "My God, my God, in what has Thou left me?" (which he elucidated in a note as "in what, in what kind of exhausted body have you held my spirit?") and thus changes a complaint to a query suggestive of the spirit-flesh dualism he comprehends. Ivan, however, is made to echo traditional translations of Matthew in his words. But in what actually happened to him – his feelings of being in a black sack – it is Tolstoy's version of Christ's words that wins, in appropriateness, in the end. Finally, Ivan's slip of the tongue, with its emphasis on passing through rather than seeking forgiveness, indicates the presence of something more powerful beneath the surface, a more authentic kind of "religion," a force acting on the individual's psyche and carrying him away with it.

But the most striking deviation from conventional Christianity is the concept of rebirth or resurrection. To Tolstoy there is no personal life after death, and both Christ and Ivan prosaically illustrate this fact. Ivan may have said that death is finished, but the narrator had the last word: "He stretched out and died." Nothing could be more alien to Tolstoy's concept of morality than the notion that virtue will be rewarded in heaven with eternal life and vice punished in hell. Once again, Tolstoy disputes the picture of justice as fairness, as a strict balancing of actions with their appropriate rewards and punishments:

> Perhaps it is fairer to suppose that awaiting a person after this worldly life lived in the exercise of personal will is an eternal personal life in heaven with all kinds of joys; perhaps this is fairer, but to think that this is so, to try to believe that for good deeds I will be rewarded with eternal bliss, and for bad deeds, eternal torments – to think this way does not contribute to our understanding of the teaching of Christ; to think this way means, on the contrary, to deprive Christ's teaching of its main support. All

Christ's teaching promotes this goal: that his disciples, after understanding the illusoriness of personal life, will renounce it and convert it into the life of all humanity, the son of man ["*syna chelovecheskogo*"]. The doctrine of the immortality of the personal soul, however, does not urge us to renounce our own personal life but affirms personality forever.

According to the Jews, Chinese, Hindus, and all peoples of the world who do not believe in the dogma of the fall of man and his redemption, life is life as it is. People live, copulate, have children, raise them, grow old, and die. Children grow and continue the life of their parents which uninterruptedly leads from generation to generation exactly like everything in the existing world; stones, the earth, metals, plants, animals, stars, and everything in the world. Life is life, and we must use it as best as we can. (26:398–99)[39]

Immortality is impersonal, a spiritual potential dwelling in people, what Tolstoy sometimes referred to as "truth" or the "spirit of truth." Christ "saved" people only by illustrating with his life the power and truth of his message: there is no fear when one is in the power of the good, when God's plan is manifested through one's being. Thus the peasant servant, Gerasim, has no fear of death and no fear or discomfort in dealing with someone who is dying. In contrast to people around Ivan, he accepts pain and dirt as a matter of course. Healthy, strong, uncomplaining, and brimming with vitality, he casually accepts the most disagreeable functions in helping Ivan through his final days. Like a parent caring for a baby, he does not judge Ivan but only serves him, easing his final days. Gerasim is an illustration of the positive ideal – someone living totally, and unconsciously, the "right" way.

Conclusion

There is an extraordinary spirit of defiance – of the conventional, of traditional authority – in Tolstoy's moral elevation not only of a peasant but of an ordinary man like Ivan, whose banal, venal, and shallow life leads to a Christlike revelation and death. The conventional Christian perspective is not Tolstoy's, and it is hardly plausible in this story. Even though other kinds of readings are possible,[40] religious and moral interpretations have dominated critical discussion. And these interpretations, insofar as they adhere to conventional religious and moral categories, have been misleading, often relating only superficially to the text.

The tale makes concrete and personal what Tolstoy's moral and social commentaries exposit, expand on, and generalize. In their generalizing role, his essays elaborate on, and thereby enhance, the significance of Tolstoy's personal experiences; art also enhances this significance, and it does so by means of the feelings it generates. But feelings, too, can be interpreted and experienced in various ways. Tolstoy left the task of generalizing the personal to his readers, who read with their own frames of reference, through their own religious and philosophical glasses. Their feelings too were affected by their presuppositions; emotions generated and communicated are also part of a context that depends on interpretation, on what is brought to the text by the reader. Tolstoy relied on the power of the example he was giving to convey the appropriate moral truth, but, more important, to lay the rails for the proper emotional responses to questions about the meaning of life. However, these emotional responses have varied widely.

The very demands of fiction, and especially moral fiction (which must be alert to heavy-handedness and overly specific reliance on special doctrines), conditioned the open texture of the story. The danger of the open texture of the moral example is that it can yield multiple and diverse readings that may fail to do what Tolstoy intended. He may have underestimated people's ability to mold and distort what is alien and discomforting. On the positive side, the story's enduring value may very well reside in its broad suggestiveness, in its insights into pre-death experience – which Tolstoy characterized as including a rejection of materialism, a loss of the fear of death, and an absence of pain, a feeling that one is moving toward the light – whatever the specific nature of the philosophy of life projected through Ivan.[41]

Tolstoy believed that the artist's responsibility was to promote feelings that would bring people together and make them recognize that love and compassion are reasonable, that they function as the source of what is good in life. To convince people of the power of these emotions and the benefits of yielding to the tremendous impersonal source within that nurtures them, he presents a vivid example of how an ordinary man can emerge victorious in a confrontation with death. In a contest that mortals can never win, the only option is to yield to the very forces aligned with death; by reevaluating what has seemed negative as now positive, one can salvage a victory. Whether or not Tolstoy's efforts were mere wishful thinking or self-delusion, his attempt to change the rules of the game left its lasting imprint: *The Death of Ivan Il'ich* continues to be vital to generation after generation, its moral revelations from a man on the edge of death serving as a seemingly never-ending source of provocative readings.

Daniel Rancour-Laferierre (in an article included in this volume) raises an interesting issue in his contention that Ivan suffers from self-delusion until his death. Such a conclusion, of course, renders the story far more pessimistic than most interpretations (including my own) would have it. Of course, there is convincing evidence that Ivan's final dismissal of pain is bogus: we have the testimony of witnesses that he was groaning until the end, and we have his previous history of self-delusions. On the other hand, if we privilege Ivan's consciousness, which I believe Tolstoy wanted us to do (and, in fact, what the text pushes us to do by presenting everything through Ivan's consciousness), then what is important pragmatically is that Ivan believes he has vanquished pain; with this belief he is able to experience joy. And in his joy he finds victory over death.

All this is a matter of perspective: one could argue that it is irrelevant that Ivan's physical body is still undergoing pain. The more vulnerable issue is this: is Tolstoy not then guilty of promoting a religious view that denies reality in favor of some comforting vision, a vision, or philosophy, that allows one to defeat pain and death by simple and complete denial? How, then, is this philosophy better than that of any conventional religion that proposes any number of methods for coming to terms with death? Perhaps, again, the only reply is the pragmatic one: Ivan's method (and Tolstoy's) in fact works: he really does defeat pain and death, even if only in his own mind, when presumably others, with less powerful religious views, experience the pain until the end.

I see no inconsistency between these views – it is all a matter of emphasis. Having the right attitude banishes pain and death from consciousness. Pragmatically, it does not matter whether this attitude is self-delusion or based on a flawed view of the universe. Of course, the strength of attitude would give weighty support to the verity of Tolstoy's worldview here – the very effectiveness of it as a weapon against death and pain speaks well for its fundamental truth.

NOTES

1. John Gardner, who praised the moral energy and commitment of Tolstoy's art, was a notable exception ("Some Men Kill You with a Six-Gun, Some Men with a Pen," *Critical Inquiry* 3:4 [1977]: 741–71).

2. In recent years readings have appeared that are more or less consistent with Christianity in its conventional forms. James Olney, for example, emphasizes the power of Christ's example and the concepts of atonement, redemption, and grace ("Experience, Metaphor, and Meaning: *The Death of Ivan Ilych*," *Journal of Aesthetics and Art Criticism* 31 [1972]: 112). Olney's reading, complete with quotations from the Vulgate, molds the story into an acceptable Roman Catholic text. Robert Duncan adduces significant biblical allusions in the text to build a case for the centrality of repentance and faith in God as conventionally conceived ("Ivan Ilych's Death: Secular or Religious?" *University of Dayton Review* 15 [1981]: 99–106).

3. All textual citations to Tolstoy's writings, unless otherwise noted, refer to the ninety-volume Jubilee edition; translations are my own, except where otherwise noted.

The topic of Tolstoy's religious views in his later years deserves special study. As might be expected, his unorthodox thinking has generated considerable discussion and controversy. For a general account of how Russian philosophers have regarded Tolstoy's views, see George L. Kline, *Religious and Anti-Religious Thought in Russia* (Chicago: University of Chicago Press, 1968), 28–34; also see V. V. Zenkovsky, *A History of Russian Philosophy*, trans. George L. Kline, vol. 1 (New York: Columbia University Press, 1967), 392–96. George Steiner offers a fascinating discussion of the principal features of Tolstoy's religious philosophy; he focuses on Tolstoy's anti-Platonistic view of the kingdom of God, Tolstoy's attack on the theodicy of compensation, Tolstoy's chiliasm, his view of God as "enclosed" in man, and his concept of Christ as a man (*Tolstoy and Dostoevsky: An Essay in the Old Criticism* [New York: Vintage, 1961]), 249–68.

4. Edward Wasiolek, *Tolstoy's Major Fiction* (Chicago: University of Chicago Press, 1978), 109–12, 168–69, 199. Tolstoy has many characters in his fiction whose self-denial and self-sacrifice are not virtues but empty abstractions impoverishing their lives. Tolstoy's model is an "individualism" characterized by "at-one-ness with one's being and the sensuous flow about one" (78).

5. Edward Wasiolek (1967) explores the basic assumptions of Tolstoy's narrative style in efforts to exonerate Tolstoy from the charge of being overbearing ("Tolstoy's *The Death of Ivan Ilych* and Jamesian Fictional Imperatives," in *Tolstoy: A Collection of Critical Essays*, ed. Ralph E. Matlaw [Englewood Cliffs, N.J.: Prentice-Hall, 1967], 146–56).

6. "What Is Art?" elucidates the difference between persuading by logical demonstration and by artistic presentation: "And universal art, by uniting the most different people in one common feeling by destroying separation, will educate people to union and will show them, not by reason but by life itself, the joy of universal union reaching beyond the bounds set by life" (Lev Nikolaevich Tolstoi, *What Is Art? And Essays on Art*, trans. Aylmer Maude [New York: Oxford University Press, 1962], 288).

7. Gary Jahn, "The Role of the Ending in Lev Tolstoi's *The Death of Ivan Il'ich*," *Canadian Slavonic Papers* (September 1982): 231–33.

8. Mythic connections of the story with the stories of Job, Orestes and the Eumenides, and Satan are suggested by William V. Spanos ("Leo Tolstoy's *The Death of Ivan Ilych*: A Temporal Interpretation," in *De-Structing the Novel: Essays in Applied Postmodern Hermeneutics* [Troy, N.Y.: Whitston, 1982], 6ff).

9. See Gary Jahn, "*The Death of Ivan Il'ich* – Chapter One," in *Studies in Nineteenth and Twentieth Century Polish and Russian Literature in Honor of Xenia Gasiorowska* (Columbus, Ohio: Slavica, 1983), 37–43; Robert

Russell, "From Individual to Universal: Tolstoy's *Smert' Ivana Ilicha*," *Modern Language Review* 76 (1981): 630–32; and Wasiolek, *Tolstoy's Major Fiction*, 171.

10. See L. P. Grossman's remarks on the early drafts in Tolstoi, 26:679–91. The text of the story is in 26:61–113. For a history of the writing and a discussion of textual changes in successive editions, see L. D. Opul'skaia, *Lev Nikolaevich Tolstoi: Material k biografii s 1886 po 1892 god* (Moscow: Nauka, 1979), 7–16.

11. William B. Edgerton, "Tolstoy, Immortality, and Twentieth-Century Physics," *Canadian Slavonic Papers* 21 (1979): 293.

12. Mark Aldanov noted that Tolstoy first strove to "frighten the reader with death and then to reconcile him to it" (Mark Aldanov, *Zagadka Tolstogo* [Berlin 1923] [Providence, R.I.: Brown University Reprints, 1969], 60).

13. The importance of expressions referring to "pity" in the ideological fabric of the story is discussed by Russell ("From Individual to Universal," 631–32).

14. Thus I disagree with Spanos's pessimistic conclusion about the effects of Ivan's death on others: "What we discover – and are disturbed by – is that, despite the unspeakably terrible experience one of them has suffered, this 'community' has understood virtually nothing about it" (Spanos, "Leo Tolstoy's *The Death of Ivan Ilych*," 34). Conclusions about Ivan's redemption also seem questionable: "Ivan, that is, has redeemed his life, but he has died a terribly lonely, as well as painful, death. Unlike the Christ he imitates, his crucifixion has not redeemed the world" (34). I argue that Ivan's death is neither "lonely" nor "painful" and is, in Tolstoy's view, probably much like Christ's in its potential effectiveness.

15. Several efforts have been made to approach Ivan's death with a perspective derived from Elisabeth Kübler-Ross. It has been argued that Ivan's decline, for the most part, follows the pattern of denial, anger, depression, bargaining, and acceptance, with a final depersonalization and step-by-step withdrawal from the physical world ("decathexis"). According to Kübler-Ross, reaching this final stage marks a healthy and normal detachment – one achieved only by patients who have worked through their dying (Elisabeth Kübler-Ross, *On Death and Dying* [New York: Macmillan, 1969], 170). Ivan's final joy may mark a departure from the norm, however; usually the acceptance stage is totally devoid of feelings (113), though moments of emotion may precede it. For discussions using a thanatological perspective, see Y. J.

Dayananda, "The Death of Ivan Ilych: A Psychological Study on Death and Dying," *Literature and Psychology* 22 (1972): 191–98; Walter Smyrniw, "Tolstoy's Depiction of Death in the Context of Recent Studies of the Experience of Dying," *Canadian Slavonic Papers* 21 (1979): 367–79; and H. L. Cate, "On Death and Dying in Tolstoy's *The Death of Ivan Ilych*," *Hartford Studies in Literature* 7 (1975): 195–205.

16. Kübler-Ross comments on the relationship of dying to early childhood experiences (*On Death and Dying*, 112, 120). The complicated interconnections between deathbed regressions to childhood, feelings of rebirth, and immortality wish-formation recognized by psychoanalysis can easily be related to Ivan's story. For discussions from a psychoanalytic perspective of experiences associated with dying and the feeling of rebirth, see Richard S. Blacher, "Death, Resurrection, and Rebirth: Observations in Cardiac Surgery," *Psychoanalytic Quarterly* 52 (1983): 56–72; and G. H. Pollock, "On Mourning, Immortality, and Utopia," *Journal of the American Psychoanalytical Association* 23 (1975): 334–62; the connections of death and rebirth from a religious perspective are discussed by Duncan, "Ivan Ilych's Death," 103–4.

17. Spanos analyzes Ivan's replacement of one kind of language (his society's) by another, more authentic kind; language serves as a measure of the quality of Ivan's life: the more he rejects "public" language, the closer he comes to experiencing "the thing itself." Although some may not agree with Spanos's ontological presuppositions and concerns, it is difficult to disagree with his perceptive observations on the relationship of various "languages" in the text ("Leo Tolstoy's *The Death of Ivan Ilych*," 38–48).

18. As Kübler-Ross notes, "the harder they struggle to avoid the inevitable death, the more they try to deny it, the more difficult it will be for them to reach this final stage of acceptance with peace and dignity" (*On Death and Dying*, 114).

The powerful effect of Tolstoy's imagery is examined by C. J. G. Turner, "The Language of Fiction: Word Clusters in Tolstoy's *The Death of Ivan Ilych*," *Modern Language Review* 65 (1970): 116–21; Russell, "From Individual to Universal," 631.

19. Without denying the symbolic value of the black bag as womb or intestine, it is also possible to associate it with Ivan's ailment, as it was explained to him by doctors. Freud, in his *Introductory Lectures on Psychoanalysis* (New York: Norton, 1966), cites an 1861 study by K. A. Scherner that linked dreams with illness: "dreams seek above all to represent the organ

that sends out the stimulus by objects resembling it" (95, 479). Also see the discussion of the image of the black sack in Boris Sorokin, "Ivan Il'yich as Jonah: A Cruel Joke," *Canadian Slavic Studies* 5 (1971): 487–501, 503–4. W. R. Hirschberg ("Tolstoy's *The Death of Ivan Ilich*," *Explicator* 28, item 26 [1969]) gives a concise and convincing demonstration of how the image of the womb makes for a coherent and reasonable reading. The link with excretion is discussed by Sorokin, "Ivan Ilyich as Jonah," and Spanos, "Leo Tolstoy's *The Death of Ivan Il'ych*," 20–28, although the latter does not mention the black sack in this regard.

For Schopenhauer, with whose works Tolstoy was familiar, death is a natural part of the ongoing process of creation and destruction and does not differ in kind from excretion, which is also part of the process of creation and destruction within the body; something inessential is lost in both cases (Schopenhauer, *The World as Will and Idea*, trans. R. B. Haldane and J. Kemp [London: Routledge & Kegan Paul, 1883], 357). Tolstoy's affinities with Schopenhauer are well known; especially relevant are his philosophical impersonalism (the moral order is attained by giving up the personal self), his emphasis on compassion and on denying the will to live, and his unconventional concepts of death and immortality; see Sigrid McLaughlin, "Some Aspects of Tolstoi's Intellectual Development: Tolstoi and Schopenhauer," *California Slavonic Studies* 5 (1970): 187–245; and also Zenkovsky, *A History of Russian Philosophy*, 391–92.

20. Jahn, in "The Role of the Ending," points out how Tolstoy had used a similar metaphor of disorientation in describing his own conversion (in "What I Believe," cited on 232).

21. Tolstoy is promoting here an ethics of care, one that is "relational," emphasizing the universal need for compassion and care; see Carol Gilligan, *In a Different Voice: Psychological Theory and Women's Development* (Cambridge: Harvard University Press, 1982), 73, 98. This is the positive side of the socio-moral program suggested in the story – which Spanos's "ontological" perspective underplays ("Leo Tolstoy's *The Death of Ivan Il'ych*," 34).

22. Duncan, in "Ivan Il'ych's Death," 104, draws attention to the Christian parallel: Jesus said children and servants are ranked high in the kingdom of God (Matthew 18:3–4; Mark 10:14–16, 44–45). Ivan's final contact with Vasya, as well as his recollections of his own youth, underlines the theme of "innocent childhood" and suggests a biographical and subtextual dimension; see David Matual, *"The Confession* as a Subtext in *The Death of Ivan Il'ich*,"

International Fiction Studies 8 (1981): 124–28; Duncan, "Ivan Il'ych's Death"; and Jahn, "The Role of the Ending," for example, have conclusively demonstrated a biblical subtext, but how it relates to the story is still problematic.

23. Although it is true that Ivan's conversion does not have lasting results with respect to Praskov'ia, who continues to be caught up in the style of life of her class, for Vasya there is still hope: his father's conversion corresponds with the boy's incipient adolescence (the dark circles under his eyes are usually taken by critics to mean that he has begun to masturbate), and it was at approximately this age when his father first came under society's corrupting influence. The force of Ivan's example, together with the boy's yet untainted sincerity and compassion, offer the only protection from the coercive pressure and mendacity that invariably accompany life led according to the pleasure principle. His father's rebirth and death serve as a rite of initiation as the boy enters the adult world. Thus it is not so clear that Ivan's death was a total failure as far as its effects on others are concerned; it has had an effect on Vasya, as well as on Peter Ivanovich: it indicates the "right" way, and now it is up to them to act on what they have learned.

24. Here critics part ways, depending on the significance they give to the power of the unconscious. Most give prominence to Ivan's intention, not what he said, since it is a traditional request for forgiveness and suggests repentance (contrition) of a conventional sort. Hirschberg, in "Tolstoy's *The Death of Ivan Ilich*," and I find a deeper meaning in Ivan's slip of the tongue: he is falling under the control of positive inner forces that will eventually direct him into the light. The expression "*propusti*" suggests that death will be a "transition" (see Edgerton, "Tolstoy, Immortality, and Twentieth-Century Physics," 298).

25. In his theological writing, Tolstoy emphasized not Christ as savior but as a man who lived and died in exemplary fashion. It is evil to strive for personal gain and pleasure, and the meaning of life will never be discovered by those who do. Living for others is the key to fulfillment and immortality. By showing compassion and by loving others one adds "something to the life and the salvation of others," and this loving spirit lives on in others long after one's own physical death. Tolstoy accumulates numerous examples of how organized Christianity has perverted Christ's simple and eminently practical message of love for one's neighbors and salvation through this love; salvation is not eternal and personal salvation (in a heavenly paradise) but liberation from lies and deceptions. It is also joy now on earth. Christ was not teaching

salvation by faith or asceticism (which Tolstoy respectively labels "salvation by deceit of the imagination" and "by voluntary tortures in this life"); rather, he taught a way of life that would give people less suffering and more joy by saving them from the pain of a personal life ("*V chem moia vera*," 23:401–2).

26. True life is beyond concerns of the flesh, beyond the limits of space and time; see "O zhizni," 26:401–9.

27. The structural properties of the story, including its temporal development, have been examined in great detail by Jahn, "The Role of the Ending"; Gunter Schaarschmidt, "Theme and Discourse Structure in *The Death of Ivan Il'ich*," *Canadian Slavonic Papers* 21 (1979): 356–66; Irving Halperin, "The Structural Integrity of *The Death of Ivan Il'ych*," *Slavic and East European Journal* 5 (1961): 334–40; and Spanos, "Leo Tolstoy's *The Death of Ivan Il'ych*."

28. See Edgerton, "Tolstoy, Immortality, and Twentieth-Century Physics"; McLaughlin, "Tolstoi and Schopenhauer"; and Zenkovsky, *A History of Russian Philosophy*.

29. See Spanos, "Leo Tolstoy's *The Death of Ivan Ilych.*"

30. Zenkovsky, *A History of Russian Philosophy*, 394.

31. Cited in Edgerton, "Tolstoy, Immortality, and Twentieth-Century Physics," 293.

32. George Kline, *Religious and Anti-Religious Thought in Russia*, 28–29, 33.

33. Although they were expressed in different ways in his essays, letters, and fiction, Tolstoy's ideas about the "right way of life" remained much the same from the 1880s on. His work in this period, in particular his translation and exegesis of the Gospels, clearly presents his religious views. Especially rewarding for our purposes is his discussion and translation of chapters of John (14–16) that relate Christ's final discourse (24:734–37) and his commentary on Christ's final hours and the meaning of his death (24:790–98).

34. Temira Pachmuss, "The Theme of Love and Death in Tolstoy's *The Death of Ivan Ilych*," *American Slavic and East European Review* 20 (1961): 72–83.

35. Part of what makes Ivan's suffering seem so incommensurate with his sins is the assumption that the world is basically just and that life is fair. Tolstoy rejected this notion, replacing it with another: suffering does not vary with the quality of one's life; it is always there, sometimes very intense and sometimes less so. It can be minimized only by adopting the right

attitude toward life (Tolstoy's comprehension). Adopting an alternative picture not dependent on our sense of balance and fairness is a tactic adopted by twentieth-century thinkers as well; for examples, see D. Z. Phillips, *Death and Immortality* (London: Macmillan, 1970), 52–55.

36. The issue of whether the story is secular or religious usually arises at this point. Duncan, for example, adduces the numerous New Testament parallels and allusions, together with Ivan's final "revelation," to prove that Tolstoy's vision is religious in the broad sense, and Christian besides. R. F. Christian, however, rejects the Christian conclusion (of Mirsky and others) that Ivan does not see at the bottom of the sack "God's love or immortality, but only a release from suffering" (R. F. Christian, *Tolstoy: A Critical Introduction* [Cambridge: Cambridge University Press, 1969], 237). Tolstoy thus, according to Christian, avoids a "facile 'religious' solution." While it is clear that Tolstoy avoids the "facile" solution, it seems equally clear that there is much more than "release" at the bottom of the sack: for Ivan, besides the absence of pain, there are the feelings of having vanquished death and of intense joy.

37. Duncan reads this differently; it is not a failure of conventional religion, represented by the priest and the rite of confession, but of Ivan, who is still clinging to his sinful ways and not yet ready to receive confession ("Ivan Il'ych's Death," 102). This explanation will seem unsatisfactory, I suspect, to anyone who has read Tolstoy's vitriolic response to his excommunication, particularly his discussion of Church sacraments (34:245).

38. See Duncan, "Ivan Il'ych's Death," 103–4, for the biblical significance of "three," and the connections between death and baptism, rebirth (the black sack as a "womb"), and Ivan's "change of mind," which to Duncan represents "repentance."

39. Tolstoy devoted considerable discussion to the matter of Christ's resurrection and "life after death" in the conclusion to his harmonization and translation of the Gospels (24:790–98); as might be expected, he was highly critical of conventional, and theologically official, understandings of this important part of Christian dogma.

40. Wasiolek suggests Marxist and psychoanalytic possibilities (*Tolstoy's Major Fiction*, 169–70); also see Edward Wasiolek, "Wanted: A New Contextualism," *Critical Inquiry* 1 (1975): 623–39. For a Marxist analysis of the story, see B. Tarasov, "Analiz burzhuaznogo soznaniia v povesti L. N. Tolstogo, *Smert' Ivana Il'icha*," *Voprosy literatury* 3 (1982): 156–76. This

approach seems particularly suitable for analyzing what was wrong with Ivan's life, namely, the constant flight from the facts of existence, such as birth, death, and love (171–72).

41. See, for example, Kenneth Ring, *Life at Death: A Scientific Investigation of the Near-Death Experience* (New York: Coward, McCann, and Geoghegan, 1980).

Signs on the Road of Life:
The Death of Ivan Il'ich

RIMGAILA SALYS

Ia kak budto zhil-zhil, shel, shel i prishel k propasti.
   —Ispoved'

[*It's as if I kept on living, kept on walking, and came at last to an abyss.*
   —A Confession]

     The narrator of *The Death of Ivan Il'ich* tells his hero's story with relentless and devastating assurance. He relates the steps leading to Ivan's death – his pleasant and decorous life, his illness, spiritual crisis, and conversion – with the absolute certainty of one who fully knows the nature and consequences of such a life: "most simple and ordinary and most terrible."[1] It is not immediately evident, however, that the narrative's imagery and metaphorical language also tell and foretell Ivan's physical decline and spiritual renewal. The peripeteias of Ivan's progress are conveyed through a complex pattern of motion: as he traverses the road of life, his misdirection is suggested in the impedimenta of physical objects that clutter his path and by half-understood warnings in foreign languages, signs that point ironically toward his true destination. Critics have noted that Ivan gradually erects a series of screens to protect himself against all that is unpleasant in life.[2] His work, faith in doctors, wonder-working icons, even the last rites, all provide a temporary protection that death inevitably penetrates. Among these screens against the fact of mortality are Ivan's beloved objects, the stock expressions in foreign languages, and his belief in the conventional road of life or career path. As these screens fall it becomes clear that objects are also mortal; the stock phrases all have a second, telling meaning; and, ultimately, that Ivan has been traveling in the wrong direction.

"Things" abound in *The Death of Ivan Il'ich* because of the acquisitiveness of the story's upper-class characters. Like their owners, they are born, live, and die. Ivan's marriage is accompanied by new furniture, new dishes, and new linens. To those in the midst of life, fresh, new things blunt or screen the awareness of mortality. Paradoxically, Ivan's death is announced by a "newborn" newspaper, fresh and still smelling of printer's ink. The living, however, see no paradox: to them Praskov'ia Fedorovna's announcement is "news" rather than a reminder of death. Ivan's death triggers only surprise and thoughts of their immediate, professional future, not of the day when their names will be announced in black borders. At the funeral service (*panikhida*), they fail to heed the dead man's warning and hastily return to the card game of life, reassured by four fresh candles (we recall the usual symbolism when Ivan drops his candle in chapter 5) and the pleasure of opening and snapping a brand new deck of cards.

Other objects relate to their owners in a more complex, metonymical fashion. At Ivan's funeral, the rebellious pouffe – no longer new but not yet on its last legs – resembles the middle-aged Petr Ivanovich. Giving voice to its decrepitude in an audible snap of its misaligned springs (*shchelknul*), the pouffe conveys perfectly the agitating consciousness of death that he struggles to subdue during his conversation with Praskov'ia Fedorovna ("*puf stal volnovat'sia*" [65]).[3] The lengthening ash on Petr Ivanovich's cigarette – another *memento mori* – likewise upsets the decorum of their conversation, when Praskov'ia Fedorovna is obliged to pass him an ashtray to protect Ivan's "new" antique table. Just as the cigarette threatens the table, the table endangers Praskov'ia Fedorovna's black lace mantilla when she snags it on the carving – a rebellion analogous to the pouffe's assault on Petr Ivanovich. The snagging of the black mantilla, an obvious symbol of mourning, is emblematic of the ways in which objects or material concerns impede or screen even the formal expression of grief in the widow's conversation with Petr Ivanovich.

The ominous (if comical) interplay of table, pouffe, cigarette, and mantilla in Ivan's knickknack-cluttered living room prefigures his growing awareness of the mortality of objects during the time between his fall and the first unmistakable signs of illness. Every spot on the tablecloth or upholstery, every broken curtain cord begins to irritate him. Later, as Ivan is forced to face his own mortality, he wanders into his beloved living room and notices a scratch on the lacquered table. Ivan finds that "the expensive album which he had lovingly arranged" (151) – like his living room and his life – has damaged the table. The torn and topsy-turvy photos upset him because they are a record of his life (the formally posed Victorian album chronicling, among other things, his career progress, e.g., the group photo taken when he leaves his first job), and they are particularly important during his mortal illness as an attempt to freeze time. Like the family snapshots, his life has been turned upside down, and he is trying to right it. He fails, just as he fails to stop the progress of his illness. Ivan's growing, subconscious recognition of his impending death is reflected in his decision to shift the albums to another corner by the flowers, the very same flowers from which a moment later death peeps out at him (151). At the funeral service Praskov'ia Fedorovna, while justifying her unimpaired practical abilities to Petr Ivanovich, casually moves the albums to one side, as if to sweep aside the life Ivan had so carefully constructed. The dying man had called the table and albums "this whole *établissement*" (151); the foreign phrase (as we will see later) underscores the narrator's ironic view of Ivan's life.

In the same way, throughout the story the narrator takes a skeptical view of the euphemistic aspect of language, consistently removing its figurative screens to expose literal meanings, all of which convey a truth about Ivan. The French and Latin maxims and phrases in chapter 2 all have a second, "telling" meaning. Ivan Il'ich supposes that his wife is disrupting their pleasant and proper life purely on a whim (*de gaité de cœur*), when in fact she is hurt by his neglect and lack of sympathy for the complications of childbearing and takes her revenge on purpose – out of "*tristesse*" rather than "*gaité*." The other foreign phrases all pertain to Ivan Il'ich, and just as death eventually penetrates all the screens in his existence, the reader notices that with Ivan's illness, all foreign expressions revert to their literal meanings. Ivan is *le phénix de la famille*, the well-adjusted middle child, who has revived the family's fortunes; yet the phrase ultimately points to his death and spiritual rebirth rather than his material success.[4] The *respice finem* medal he wears attached, appropriately, to his watch is a lawyer's affectation, but also conveys a warning to "look to the end."[5] Ivan's youthful sins are excused with a tolerant shrug – *il faut que jeunesse se passe* (the chic of a French phrase screens his ugly behavior all the better), yet the reader is warned that youth is passing, too. In society Ivan is considered a good fellow (*bon enfant*). Years later, as he reviews the past, he sees that his morally good childhood was the only patch of light in a life that led inexorably into the black sack: "There's one bright spot there at the back, at the beginning of life, and afterwards all becomes blacker and blacker" (163). Ivan and his entire life are very much *comme il faut*, yet during his illness the affirmation of decorum re-verses to doubt: "Maybe I didn't live as I ought to have done?" (161) (*ne tak kak dolzhno?*), and in death his face again reveals the literal meaning of the phrase: "The expression on the face said that what was necessary (*chto nuzhno bylo sdelat'*), had been accomplished, and accomplished rightly" (125).[6]

Although objects and language both point the way to Ivan's desti-nation, the central metaphor for his physical decline and spiritual renewal is the road of life and related directional body movement. The archetypal familiarity of the "road of life" must have attracted Tolstoy because of its accessibility to all readers – a major aim of his postconversion writings.[7] Waking, stepping, and other related meta-phors consistently record Ivan's moral progress along the road of life and later, when he can no longer walk, mirror his shifting state of mind at different stages of his illness.

Ivan Il'ich is already dead as the story begins. Because his life's journey has been completed, his spatial immobility is emphasized: "The dead man lay, as dead men always lie, in a specially heavy way"

(125). Chapter 1 is, in fact, concerned with the living, the other characters, who either ignore Ivan's silent warning or are annoyed and discomfited by this indecorous reminder of their own mortality. Petr Ivanovich, another Ivan still en route to his destination, looks at his feet during the funeral service and then ignores the dead man's warning. Two other characters reflect Ivan's own evasions at different stages of his life. Entering Ivan's house, Petr Ivanovich sees the dapper Shvarts, whom Ivan had earlier recognized as his double (145), at the head of the stairs. Having reached the pinnacle of worldly success, Shvarts is in his prime, and therefore stands at the top of the staircase of life. Ivan's son, Vasya, just beginning his climb, materializes from under the lower part of the staircase. Each double recalls a different though already corrupt stage of the dead man's existence – Ivan as sex-obsessed but still sensitive adolescent and later as callous and complacent man of the world.

The rest of the story (chapters 2–12) chronicles Ivan's life, illness, and death. Commentators have pointed out that the content ironically reverses the meaning of the title. Ivan's existence turns out to have been a living death, while his death is a rebirth into a new spiritual life.[8] In keeping with this reversal, Ivan sets out on the path of (or rather *to*) life not in childhood or adolescence but only when he falls ill and begins to question the ideas on which his existence is predicated. In spite of all his activity on the conventional road of life in chapter 2 (schooling, love affairs, marriage, children, and career peripeteias), the stepping/walking imagery that appears later in the story is missing at this point because Ivan, before his illness, has been on the wrong road.[9]

The first stage of his progress is marked by a step, albeit a false one. While showing the upholsterer how to hang curtains, the hero misses a rung and falls, banging his side against the knob of the window frame. Ivan is injured by the naked reality of life – essentially indecorous, unbeautiful, and Darwinian – as seen through the bare window which he has just been trying to cover up with one of the many screens against reality he sets up in the course of his life. In his preoccupation with decorating the new apartment, which supersedes even his interest in the coveted appointment, Ivan reaches new heights of trivial and frivolous materialism (a judge concerning himself with pink cretonne and knickknacks), and it is just at this point, at the pinnacle of material success, recalling the staircase of chapter 1, that he stumbles and falls off the ladder. Ivan later boasts to his family about his lucky escape ("Another man might have been killed" [138]), yet he is already morally dead.

The consequences of Ivan's fall, the first step toward a spiritual life, are at first suppressed; all is well for a time, or so Ivan wants to think. He seems healthy: "I feel fifteen years younger" (138) (*Chuvstvuiu, chto s menia soskochilo let 15* [79]), but in its literal meaning, the phrase in fact hints at the fifteen years of life he has lost through his fall. The narrator's simple but devastating summary conveys Ivan's complacent sense of invulnerability and tranquil motion. "So they lived, and all went [*shlo*] well, without change, and life flowed pleasantly" (141). Ivan realizes he is dying only after his brother-in-law's visit, when the progress of his illness, as well as his own increasing superfluity to the world, are expressed in terms of walking, approaching ever closer to an unavoidable abyss: "I kept coming [*vse shel*] closer and closer" (148); "it came about step by step" (151). Ivan tries twice to light a symbolic candle of life in the dark room, but fumbles and drops it, cannot find the matches, and finally throws himself back onto the bed in despair. As his wife brings him another candle, he lies panting, very much like one who is no longer walking the path of life, but is now running a race against time and death: "He lay there breathing heavily and quickly, like a man who had run a thousand yards" (149). As Ivan's disease progresses, physical movement becomes more difficult. Rising from the commode, he is horrified by the sight of his emaciated, weak thighs (152). When physical mobility (with its implied link to the outside world) is restricted, Ivan sets out on the mental journey that will lead first to awareness of the hypocrisy of his past life and eventually to his conversion.[10]

At the stage of his illness when he is no longer able to move about freely, Ivan requires the assistance of Gerasim, who serves as a model

of Christian behavior. Unlike his physically and spiritually debili-
tated master, the kind-hearted and cheerful peasant walks with a
distinctively light step, an obvious metaphor for the way he goes
through life – with the simplicity, ease, and acceptance of God's will
born of religious faith. Gerasim half carries, half helps Ivan walk
across the room from commode to bed and then spends hours holding Ivan's legs aloft on his shoulders. This is viewed as a sick man's
eccentricity by those around Ivan; in reality Gerasim is helping (as if
bearing) his master along the path to a new spiritual life. The narrator stresses metaphorical "carrying" in his explanation of Gerasim's
motives: "He is not oppressed by his work precisely because he bears
it [*neset ego*] for a dying man and hopes that when his time comes
someone will also do the same [*poneset tot zhe trud*] for him" (154).
Gerasim's act is foreshadowed in the earlier reference to Princess
Trufonova, the sister of the founder of the society "Unesi ty moe
gore" (Carry Away My Sorrow). The parodistic name of the charita-
ble organization, derived from a colloquial expression of disapproval,
like all the foreign phrases pertaining to Ivan's earlier life, undergoes
an ironic "unscreening" or literalizing in the context of his illness. It
is the peasant Gerasim, close to the tradition of the folk song "Unesi
ty moe gore, bystra rechenka, s soboi" ("Carry my sorrow away with
you, swift stream"), and not the society ladies, who will bear the
burden of Ivan's sorrow or misfortune.

Before Ivan Il'ich can be saved, he must recognize the moral
wrongness of his entire adult life, a truth he resists and the last screen
he maintains, up to the very moment of his death. The first step in
the process is his gradually developing awareness of "the lie," the
hypocrisy governing all levels of human contact which torments him
even more than his physical pain (153). Chapter 8 distills and con-
centrates the various social screens (feigned conjugal love and society's refusal to acknowledge, i.e., speak about, death) which Ivan's
heightened consciousness now penetrates.

Realizing the hypocrisy around him leads Ivan to doubt for the
first time the direction of his past life, and once again his thought is
expressed in terms of concrete physical motion: "It is as if I had been

going [*shel*] steadily downhill while imagining that I was going uphill. . . . I was going uphill in public opinion, but to the same extent life was ebbing away from me" (161) (*rovno nastol'ko iz-pod menia ukhodila zhizn'*, 107).[11] The mountain of worldly success here again recalls Shvarts's complacent pose at the top of the staircase in chapter 1.

As Ivan's illness progresses, his living space contracts – from the world to his apartment, to his study, and finally to the sofa on which he dies.[12] In the absence of external events, Tolstoy now turns to the movement of Ivan's mind to maintain the momentum of the story. Because Ivan can no longer walk, his movements on the sofa take on particular significance, although most of the motion of the story, the train of thought leading to his conversion, now takes place in his head. Beginning with Ivan's realization in chapter 5 that he is dying, that life is escaping him (148) (*Da, zhizn' byla i vot ukhodit, ukhodit* [Yes, there was a life and now it's going, going; 91]), the figurative phrases of mental motion ("train of thought or memory," "current of feeling") enter the text: "*On pytalsia vozvratit'sia k prezhnim khodam mysli'* [He tried to return to his previous train of thought]" (93); "*vmeste s etim khodom vospominaniia* . . . [together with this chain of memories]" (108).[13]

As Ivan's spiritual life intensifies in his steadily constricting physical space, mental motion increases (his struggles to get into and out of the black sack in his first dream). Simultaneously, his actual physical motion wanes: he awakens and lies looking at his emaciated legs (160). Ivan's shifting positions on the sofa also seem to relate to specific aspects of his mental perambulations. When he first begins to think about the reasons for his illness, he turns onto his side, weeps in self-pity, and seeks from God an explanation of his torment. As the internal dialectic – really court briefs for and against the correctness of Ivan's life – intensifies, he turns over to his other side, toward the wall, and begins to think. Refusing to believe his life could have been wrong, he reaches an impasse in his search for justification of his pain; literally and metaphorically he faces the wall: "But however much he pondered, he found no answer" (162).

For the entire next chapter, Ivan continues in the same position, his physical isolation now corresponding to his total estrangement from those around him. When he is completely confined to the sofa, his mental activity increases even more, as if the spatial compression engendered a previously unknown density of memories. Ivan now journeys in time (*khod vospominanii*) from the present to childhood and then back. The movement of Ivan's thoughts through time provides him with a perspective from which he can weigh the contrasting values of his childhood and maturity, and come to see the direction of his entire life. A button on the sofa and wrinkles in the leather (an even narrower spatial focus) impel him on another journey from the materialistic present ("Morocco is expensive, but it doesn't wear well: there had been a quarrel because of it" [163]) to his childhood and unselfish mother-love ("It was a different kind of quarrel and a different kind of morocco that time when we tore Father's briefcase and were punished, and mamma brought us tarts" [163]).

This *Recherche du temps perdu* leads to yet another train of thought about the progress of his illness: "Then together with that chain of memories another series passed through his mind – of how his illness had progressed and grown worse" (163) ("*vmeste s etim khodom vospominaniia, u nego v dushe shel drugoi khod vospominanii – o tom, kak usilivalas' i rosla ego bolezn'*" [108]). Ivan identifies the course of his life – morally all downhill – with the course of his disease ("Just as the torments get [*idut*] worse and worse, so all of life grew [*shla*] worse and worse" (163), thereby progressing toward an acknowledgment of spiritual death in life, the reversal implied by the story's title.[14] Mental motion accelerates even more as Ivan compares his life to a stone gathering speed in its fall – another image of concrete spatial movement (163). The inevitable progress of Ivan's life, its temporal and spatial movement toward death, has assumed the incontrovertible authority of physical law. Yet, in spite of his mental peregrinations, as the chapter concludes, Ivan is again at a dead end, facing the back of the sofa, because he still refuses to follow the line of thought and memory to its logical conclusion – the incorrectness of his life.

Two weeks later, on the crest of another worldly success (Petrish-chev's long-awaited proposal to Liza), the sick man takes a turn for the worse (i.e., the better) and for the first time not only thinks but also speaks the unscreened truth to his family and doctor: "For Christ's sake, let me die in peace" (164); "you know you can do nothing for me, so leave me alone" (164). Both before and after this scene the narrator stresses that Ivan is now lying in a different position: "He lay down on his back and began to review his whole life in a completely new way" (164). In its spatial openness, Ivan's body position (the same as in his dignified coffin repose) clearly parallels his acknowledgment of the incorrectness of his life, and contrasts to his earlier doubts about its value and the rejection of these doubts while lying on his side, facing the wall.[15]

Ivan's acceptance of his wasted life in chapter 11 is short-lived. Soon he is again assailed by doubts, abandons the open position, and begins to toss about on the sofa, as if in mental and physical uncertainty. The screen of religion soothes him temporarily, but the sight of Praskov'ia Fedorovna and his false answer to her query about his health ("You feel better, don't you?" [165]) place the lie squarely before him once again. By agreeing that he is better, Ivan actively participates in the deception, and consequently his spatial reaction is all the more extreme: "Having said 'yes,' looking her straight in the face, he turned face down with a rapidity extraordinary in his weak state" (165). In complete negation of the earlier open position, he turns over on his belly, just as he has once again turned away from an admission of guilt: "At the moment he answered his wife he realized that he was lost . . . that the end had come . . . and his doubts were still unsolved" (165–66).

During the last three days of his life Ivan's space narrows to the tunnel of the black sack, but mental motion continues with even augmented intensity in the decreasing area: "he struggled," "thrashed about," "can't squeeze through."[16] Two related images of spatial motion express the final train of thought that leads to his change of heart. In the first, Ivan himself is trapped and finds release; he struggles inside the black sack and eventually falls out through a hole. At the same time, within Ivan there is a blockage that is eventually expelled: "What had been oppressing him and would not come out" suddenly was coming out all at once, from all sides (167). The images narrow in spatial sequence: Ivan is inside the sack struggling to escape; yet at the same time something is inside him and wants to come out.

The two parallel struggles represent Ivan's isolation in sickness and in health. All his life Ivan has set up screens between himself and others, practiced voluntary isolation, in effect a negative self-enclosure. With the onset of his illness, however, isolation is forcibly imposed from without: his space contracts from the total openness of life in the world to the progressively more constricted area of apartment and sofa. Confined to the sofa, turned to the wall, his forcible isolation (the opposite of his lifelong self-imposed isolation) leads to productive reflection on the past and present.

Ivan's bad life has steadily darkened into the black sack of pain and doubt, the epitome of the isolation forced on him by his illness; the blockage he labors to expel is the moral defect within himself – his self-absorption and subsequent lack of compassion for others that caused him to set up screens against them – which he has refused to recognize up to this moment. Ivan breaks out of the sack at the same time that he admits the badness of his life and makes human contact, when his hand falls on his son's head. His internal blockage dissipates when he stops thinking only of himself, asks forgiveness for his indifference toward his wife and son ("He tried to add, 'forgive me,' but said, 'Let me through'" [166] – another way out of the sack), and acts to express compassion. The direction of both actions is from confinement (also implying darkness) to openness and light. When Ivan is able to pity someone other than himself, he breaks through the external barrier of the sack and at the same time breaks down the barrier within.

The moment of illumination in Ivan's journey, when he finally admits that he has lived badly, is expressed in a modern equivalent of the road of life metaphor: "What happened to him was what he used to experience in a railway car when you think you are going forward, but you are going backward, and suddenly you become aware of the real direction" (166).[17] Tolstoy had employed the same metaphor in *Anna Karenina:* returning to Petersburg after her first meeting with Vronskii, Anna thinks about him and gradually loses her moral bearings. Her confusion is reflected in her perception of the train's direction: "She continually had moments of doubt; was the car going forward or backward, or not moving at all?"[18] When Ivan Il'ich recognizes the right direction, his journey comes to an end: "He drew in a breath, stopped in the midst of a sigh, stretched out, and died" (167). The climactic motion of Ivan's journey fulfills the logic of reversal that governs the story's structure. Having arrived at its destination, his body stretches out and relaxes, assuming the ease and natural dignity it lacked in a life constricted by the moral rigor mortis Ivan escapes only in the moment of death.

NOTES

1. *The Death of Ivan Il'ich*, in Leo Tolstoi, *Tolstoy's Short Fiction*, ed. and trans. Michael R. Katz (rev. trans.) (New York: Norton, 1991), 129. In several instances the Maude-Katz translation obscures the specificity of Tolstoy's spatial-directional language. For these I have supplied a more literal rendering. The source for Russian references is L. N. Tolstoi, *Smert' Ivana Il'icha, Polnoe sobranie sochinenii*, 90 vols. (Moscow: Gosudarstvennoe Izdatel'stvo Khudozhestvennoi Literatury, 1928–58), vol. 26; hereafter, *PSS*. All further references to this work appear in the text.

2. Most recently Gary R. Jahn, *"The Death of Ivan Il'ich* – Chapter One," in *Studies in Nineteenth and Twentieth Century Polish and Russian Literature in Honor of Xenia Gasiorowska*, ed. Lauren G. Leighton (Columbus, Ohio: Slavica, 1983), 41–42.

3. This nuance is completely obscured by the translation in which the pouffe simply *rises* when relieved of Petr Ivanovich's weight (127).

4. Boris Sorokin, "Ivan Il'ich as Jonah: A Cruel Joke," *Canadian Slavic Studies* 5, no. 4 (1971): 502.

5. M. Eremin, "Podrobnosti i smysl tselogo. Iz nabliudenii nad tekstom povesti *Smert' Ivana Il'icha*," in *V mire Tolstogo*, ed. S. Mashinskii (Moscow: Sovetskii pisatel', 1978), 246.

6. Also "I've not lived as I ought to" (163); "he had not spent his life as he should have done" (164).

7. When advising others how to proceed with their lives, Tolstoy employs the metaphor in his correspondence: "You can come to nothing but despair along the path you walk; that means the road is not the right one and you must turn back" (letter to N. N. Strakhov [*Neotpravlennoe*], 19 . . . 22 November 1879, Letter 535, *PSS*, vol. 62, 502). See also letter to M. A. Engel'-gart, 20[?] December 1882–20[?] January 1883, Letter 140, *PSS*, vol. 63, 123.

8. Gary R. Jahn, "The Role of Ending in Lev Tolstoi's *The Death of Ivan Il'ich*," *Canadian Slavonic Papers* 24, no. 3 (1982): 229.

9. In an earlier version of chapter 2 Ivan's disappointment in his wife is described as the first pothole in the road of life: "Okazalos', chto zhena byla revniva, skupa, beztolkova i chto v domashnei zhizni nichego ne vykhodilo, krome tiazhesti i skuki. Pridat' zhizni s nei veselyi, priiatnyi i prilichnyi kharakter ne bylo nikakoi vozmozhnosti. Eto byl pervyi ukhab, v kotoryi zaekhala kativshaiasia tak rovno do tekh por zhizn' Ivana Il'icha [It turned out that his wife was jealous, stingy, muddle-headed, and that nothing came of their home life except difficulty and boredom. There was no possibility whatsoever of imparting a cheerful, pleasant, and proper character to life with her. This was the first pothole in Ivan Il'ich's life which had, until then, rolled along so smoothly]" (variant 4, *PSS*, vol. 26, 521). A crossed-out section of variant 56 treats Ivan's first job failure in the same way: "Sluchilsia drugoi ukhab. Buduchi eshche tovarishchem prokurora, i luchshim, i pravia vsegda dolzhnost' pro-kurora, Ivan Il'ich zhdal, chto ne oboidut pri pervom naznachenii v prokurory. Okazalos', chto Goppe, tovarishch prokurora, zabezhal kak-to vpered v Peter-burg, i ego, mladshego, naznachili, a Ivan Il'ich ostalsia [Another pothole came along. As assistant public prosecutor, and the best one, and as the one who always managed the duties of public prosecutor, Ivan Il'ich expected that he would not be passed over when the next public prosecutor's appointment came up. It turned out that Goppe, an assistant public prosecutor, somehow ran ahead to Petersburg and he, the younger man, was appointed, while Ivan Il'ich remained where he was]" (521). "Goppe," from "gop," jumps ahead of Ivan Il'ich in the career race. In the coming months, as Ivan begins his zigzagging spiritual odyssey, the doctors will diagnose a "wandering kidney" (*bluzhdaiushchaia pochka*) and the dead end of a diseased "blind gut" (*slepaia kishka*).

10. In "Master and Man," a conversion story written some ten years after *The Death of Ivan Il'ich*, the hero sets out on a business trip which in spatial terms

parallels his life's journey. The tale unfolds in two parts, each characterized by a distinct pattern of motion. In the first, Brekhunov is linked to the world by a comfortable sleigh journey, during which he has social contacts with others. At midpoint in the story the sleigh and Brekhunov's life are forced to an abrupt halt and his spiritual journey commences. Physical motion continues but is now painfully cramped in the isolation of ever-narrowing space. Forced to lie still in the sleigh, Brekhunov beings to think. His reflections on his wealth, his attempts to put up screens against the fear of death (tobacco, the coming dawn, wonder-working icons) are as fruitlessly circular as his three escape attempts, two of which bring him back to the wormwood and the third to the sleigh and Nikita. As Brekhunov approaches death, the space in which he moves becomes more restricted, as does Ivan's in the course of his illness. Toward the end Brekhunov lies freezing, and physical movement ceases completely. At this point he embarks on the spiritual journey that leads to his conversion. Like Ivan before his death, Brekhunov feels the need to do something and realizes he must save Nikita. In Brekhunov's dreams of the world, physical motion gradually ceases; only when he is completely confined to his bed does he become spiritually "mobile," rejecting the world and going to meet Christ: "'I'm coming! [*Idu!*],' he cried joyfully" (268).

11. Cf. Tolstoy's letter of 30 November 1875 to Strakhov about climbing the mysterious mountain of life (*PSS*, vol. 62, 226–27).

12. Jahn, "The Role of the Ending," 231. "How Much Land Does a Man Need?" was written in 1886, the same year Tolstoy completed *The Death of Ivan Il'ich*. Clearly, Pakhom's walk in chapters 8–9 symbolizes his life's journey. Greed drives him in a circular path, as it does Brekhunov in "Master and Man," and his living space contracts from the world (no matter how much land he acquires, he always feels cramped) to the three *arshiny* (approx. 7 ft.) in which he is buried.

13. Also "*khody chuvstva* [course of feeling]" (93), "*khod myslei* [train of thought]" (106). "*Khod*" expressions also occur in *A Confession*, as Tolstoy recounts the steps by which he arrived at religious belief: "I ia stal proveriat' khod rassuzhdenii moego razumnogo znaniia [And I began to check the line of reasoning of my rational knowledge]" (33), "Khod razmyshleniia pravilen [The line of reasoning is correct]" (34); also pages 36, 43, 57 in *PSS*, vol. 23. The Maude translation of *The Death of Ivan Il'ich* dilutes with synonyms Tolstoy's emphatic repetition of the construction.

14. The analogy between the development of a terminal illness and the stages of a spiritual crisis has its source in *A Confession*. See David Matual, "*The*

Confession as Subtext in *The Death of Ivan Il'ich*," *International Fiction Review* 8, no. 2 (1981): 126.

15. In earlier sections of the story, before Ivan is confined to a particular place, the correlation of physical position and mental activity is less firmly established. In chapter 5, after talking to Petr Ivanovich's doctor, Ivan lies on his back and thinks about the salutory effects of the medicine he has just taken. However, reality intrudes when he turns onto his side; the pain begins again, and for the first time he is forced to admit the seriousness of his illness: "It's not a question of my appendix or my kidney, but of life and . . . death" (148). At this point the later consistent relationship of patterned movement to thought begins to operate. Just as in chapters 9–10 when Ivan, while lying on his side, begins to question the value of his life and ends by repressing his doubts, here Ivan (also on his side) begins to think about impending death, but then suppresses the idea. He fumbles twice with the candle, flings himself back on the bed, and, staring ahead in this open position, ends by acknowledging the approach of death: "Breathless and in despair he fell on his back, expecting death to come immediately" (148).

16. In *O zhizni* (*About Life*), written soon after *The Death of Ivan Il'ich*, Tolstoy compares the course of life to a cone, the narrowest part of which represents the beginning of consciousness and the widest the higher relation to life which he has now achieved: "Reason places man on that unique path of life which, like a cone-shaped widening tunnel, amidst the walls surrounding him from all sides, opens up to him in the distance the indubitable infinity of life and its blessings" (*PSS*, vol. 26, 419, 423). Thus, if Ivan's bad life narrows into the black sack, a life lived rightly moves toward the ever-widening base of the cone of *O zhizni*. More on Tolstoy's spatial, almost geometrical way of thinking: the sine curve of nineteenth-century Russian literature (letter to N. N. Strakhov, 3 March 1872, Letter 362, *PSS*, vol. 61, 275); the geometry of religion (letter to V. Frei, 1–31 March 1886, Letter 490, *PSS*, vol. 63, 339); and the diagram of the progress of marriage partners on the road of life (letter to I. L. Tolstoi, October 1887, Letter 151, *PSS*, vol. 64, opp. 116 and 117).

17. This crucial passage is rendered incorrectly in the Maude-Katz translation.

18. L. N. Tolstoi, *Anna Karenina*, *PSS*, vol. 18, 107. In "Master and Man," when Brekhunov causes Mukhortyi to go off the road after pausing in Grishkino and just before the horse stops on the edge of the ravine, he experiences a loss of directional sense analogous to his spiritual confusion: "At times the sleigh seemed to stand still and the field seemed to run backwards" (252).

Narcissism, Masochism, and Denial in *The Death of Ivan Il'ich*

DANIEL RANCOUR-LAFERRIERE

Death is life's greatest insult. Psychoanalytically speaking, death is the greatest possible narcissistic injury. Nothing forces one to think so much about one's very self as the imminence of death – not just anyone's death, but *my death*.

Freud believed death to be such a blow to the ego as to be virtually incomprehensible. In his psychoanalytic classic *Mourning and Melancholia* (1915), and again in the same year in *Thoughts for the Times on War and Death*, Freud attempted to characterize the enormity of death:

> So immense is the ego's self-love, which we have come to recognize as the primal state from which instinctual life proceeds, and so vast is the amount of narcissistic libido which we see liberated in the fear that emerges at a threat to life, that we cannot conceive how that ego can consent to its own destruction.
>
> It is indeed impossible to imagine our own death; and whenever we attempt to do so we can perceive that we are in fact still present as spectators. Hence the psycho-analytic school could venture on the assertion that at bottom no one believes in his own death, or, to put the same thing in another way, that in the unconscious everyone is convinced of his own immortality.[1]

Denial of death is thus to be expected, even when death is certainly approaching, as in terminal cancer.[2]

Tolstoy's Ivan Il'ich illustrates Freud's point: he cannot conceive of his own destruction; he is never truly reconciled with what is about to happen to him. For most of the duration of *The Death of*

Ivan Il'ich Tolstoy's hero is busy fending off thoughts of death. For example, Ivan Il'ich cannot accept Kiesewetter's simple logic:

> In the depth of his heart he knew he was dying, but not only was he unaccustomed to the thought, he simply did not and could not grasp it.
>
> The syllogism he had learnt from Kiesewetter's Logic: "Caius is a man, men are mortal, therefore Caius is mortal," had all his life seemed to him correct only as applied to Caius, but not at all to himself. That Caius – man in the abstract – was mortal, was perfectly correct, but he was not Caius, not an abstract man, but a creature quite separate from all others. He had been little Vanya, with a mamma and a papa, with Mitya and Volodya, with toys, a coachman and a nanny, afterwards with Katenka and with all the joys, griefs, and delights of childhood, boyhood, and youth. What did Caius know of the smell of that striped leather ball Vanya had been so fond of? Had Caius kissed his mother's hand like that, and did the silk of her dress rustle for Caius? Had he rioted like that at school when the pastry was bad? Had Caius been in love like that? Could Caius preside at a session as he did? "Caius really was mortal, and it was right for him to die; but as for me, little Vanya, Ivan Ilych, with all my thoughts and emotions, it's altogether a different matter. It cannot be that I ought to die. That would be too terrible." (149–50; 26:92–93)[3]

I have quoted Tolstoy at length here in order to indicate the psychological depth ("*v glubine dushi*") of Ivan Il'ich's denial of death. The denial occurs not only in successive moments of the ongoing narration, but has always been there in the past ("all his life").[4] It will also be there in the future, right until the very end, as I will demonstrate. Ivan Il'ich does realize what is happening to him on some intellectual level, and he is especially gratified when his servant Gerasim, unlike most other people around him, does not pretend that the illness will pass. But this does not mean that Ivan Il'ich actually accepts his coming death. He intensely dislikes the falsehood of those doctors and family members who deny he is dying. But that is because they remind him of himself and of his own denial.

Of course, toward the very end, Ivan Il'ich does weaken and appears to be reconciled with his coming death. There is a passage in *The Ego and the Id* (1923) where Freud says that when the ego understands that death is actually drawing near, "it sees itself deserted by all protecting forces and lets itself die."[5] I think Freud's phraseology here (i.e., after he had developed his theory of the "death instinct"[6] and stopped insisting that the ego is categorically opposed to its own destruction) may be applied to Tolstoy's hero at the end of the novella. Ivan Il'ich does "let himself die," at least in some respects. He ceases to fear death. He experiences joy. He feels sorry for his previously hated wife and at least attempts to say "Forgive me" to her before he dies – the proper Russian thing to do, at least among the folk.[7] One could even argue that Ivan Il'ich's acceptance of death constitutes a religious conversion or spiritual rebirth.

Yet there is also something incomplete or unconvincing about Ivan Il'ich's acceptance of death. Edward Wasiolek says: "It is hard to make artistic sense of Ivan Ilych's conversion."[8] The conversion is there, but denial of death seems to lurk close by in the background as well. Part of Ivan Il'ich has changed, but another part has not. What happens to Ivan Il'ich could be read as more an accommodation to dire circumstances than acceptance, as David Shepherd has recently argued. At one level, says Shepherd, "Ivan Il'ich has not changed one bit."

> He may come to renounce much of what he formerly believed in and lived for, but this is because it is no longer available to him, available to reinforce his *sense of his self and its worth*. The moment when he sees the light is not a moment of epiphanic access to some truth previously hidden from him, but a moment of discovery of a new way to conceptualize *his own relationship* to his (temporally and spatially reduced) circumstances. His apparent embracing of the ethics of empathic pity is not the sublimation of his

ego in a Karataevan sense of himself as a part of the whole, but the *apotheosis of an ego* whose driving imperative is to order the world around it in such a way as to ensure its continuing security.[9]

I have italicized certain items in this quotation to indicate Shepherd's implicit attention to Ivan Il'ich's narcissism, that is, concern with the self. The thought of one's own death is an inconceivable blow to the ego, an unacceptable narcissistic injury, as stated earlier.

In my opinion Ivan Il'ich's "conversion" is a mental maneuver designed to avoid confrontation with the narcissistically wounding fact of death. Death is denied until the very end:

> "And death . . . where is it?"
>
> He looked for his former accustomed fear of death and did not find it. "Where is it? What death?" *There was no fear because there was no death* [*smerti ne bylo*].
>
> In place of death there was light.
>
> "So that's what it is!" he suddenly exclaimed aloud. "What joy!"
>
> To him all this happened in a single instant, and the meaning of that instant did not change. For those present his agony continued for another two hours. Something rattled in his throat, his emaciated body twitched, then the gasping and rattle became less and less frequent.
>
> "It is finished!" said someone near him.
>
> He heard these words and repeated them in his soul.
>
> "*Death is finished* [*Konchena smert'*]," he said to himself. "*It is no more* [*Ee net bol'she*]!"
>
> He drew in a breath, stopped in the midst of a sigh, stretched out, and died. (167; 26:113; emphasis added)

The negations could not be plainer, and the denial is apparent. If in the first instance Ivan Il'ich is denying death within the structure of the omniscient narrator's report, in the second he denies death directly: "*Ee net bol'she.*" He means of course that his own death does not exist anymore.

Not that it had existed *before*, however. He had been denying it all along. This belated denial only adds a further layer of defense. Note also that the narrator does *not* say that the process of dying is over – that would have been "*Koncheno umiranie*," rather than "*Konchena smert'*." Nor does he *only* say that the fear of death is now gone (although he does say that). Ivan Il'ich is clearly happy and fearless in his final moments. But his belief that death does not exist is simply false, it is a delusion.[10] The narrator, after all, steps in and contradicts him with the last word of the novella: "*umer*." The reader is left to choose between believing Ivan Il'ich or believing the narrator – and certainly an Ivan Il'ich *in extremis* is not as credible as an omniscient narrator.[11]

Yet Ivan Il'ich does accept something in his final moments, even if he remains in a state of frozen denial regarding his own death. What this something is may be defined as pain and suffering. Indeed, pain and suffering are not only accepted, they are welcomed:

> "And the pain?" he asked himself. "What has become of it? Where are you, pain?"
>
> He turned his attention to it.
>
> "Yes, here it is. Well, what of it? Let it be [*Nu chto zh, puskai bol'*]." (167; 26:113)

In a draft the pain is welcomed even more:

> "And the pain?" he asked himself. "What has become of it? How to deal with it? Where are you, pain?" He turned his attention to it. "Yes, here it is. The same as ever. Well, carry on in good shape! More! Do your thing! The more, the quicker. That's the way!"[12]

In the psychoanalytic literature this welcoming attitude to pain is part of what is meant by (moral) masochism.[13] Ivan Il'ich ceases to struggle against the pain, and instead turns masochistic – even as he is still denying death ("*smerti ne bylo*"). Pain is acceptable; death is not. Masochism is permissible, but narcissism will not permit a death blow.

True, the pain does seem less noticeable or prominent in the final chapter than in previous chapters, where Ivan Il'ich was resisting it.[14] But this is as much because Ivan Il'ich is coming to accept the pain in masochistic fashion as because new psychological processes are coming into the foreground.

The pain continues for some time after death has been denied: "For those present his *agony* continued for another two hours" (167; 26:113; emphasis added).[15] At the same time denial of death also persists: "the meaning of that instant did not change." The masochistic acceptance of pain and the narcissistic denial of death now go hand-in-hand until death actually occurs at the very end of the novella (*"umer"*).[16]

Previous readings of the novella have tended not only to miss the masochism and the narcissism but also to conflate their immediate objective correlatives, that is, pain and death. Thus Wasiolek speaks of the "pain-death" that takes over the end of Ivan Il'ich's life[17] – as if the two items were interchangeable because they are both feminine nouns in Russian (*"bol'"* and *"smert'"*). Even the psychological reading offered by Y. J. Dayananda does not bother to distinguish the two processes. Dayananda says that Ivan Il'ich reaches the "final stage of acceptance" and that he "shows a new understanding and acceptance."[18] But acceptance of what? Not death (*"smerti ne bylo"*) but pain is what Ivan Il'ich accepts (*"puskai bol'"*). Curiously, Dayananda misquotes the final passage of the novella, deleting Ivan Il'ich's acceptance of pain.[19] The misquotation is repeated without comment in the Katz edition of Tolstoy.[20] Understandably, masochism is something one would rather forget.

But what motivates Ivan Il'ich's last-minute shift to a masochistic attitude? Before this moment, after all, Tolstoy's hero, being an ordinary, normal person, resists the pain and suffering: "'If I could only understand what it's all for!'" Ivan Il'ich can make no sense of what is happening to him. But he suspects something is wrong (*"ne to"*) about the way he has lived his life, and this suspicion offers an opportunity for him eventually to make sense of what he has been enduring: "'An explanation would be possible if it could be said that

I've not lived as I ought to. But it's impossible to say that,' and he remembered all the legality, correctitude, and propriety of his life" (163; 26:109). The moral breakthrough to masochism cannot occur until this opinion is reversed, that is, until, a few pages later, the narrator reports: "At that very moment Ivan Ilych fell through and caught sight of the light, and it was revealed to him that though his life had not been what it should have been, it could still be rectified" (166; 26:112).

But how to "rectify" ("*popravit'*") the situation? There is so little time left – less than a page of the *siuzhet* (plot), a little more than two hours of the *fabula* (story). Yet, surprisingly, time is not an issue.[21] After all, Ivan Il'ich has already been screaming in continual pain for the previous three days, and he was in pain for months before he started screaming. He has already "rectified" the situation in large measure simply by suffering. What remains is to reinterpret the suffering once and for all, that is, understand that he has indeed lived badly, admit his guilt, and give all that previous pain a meaning. Ivan Il'ich has been suffering all along, but only now does he begin to think his suffering is deserved (this reversal of his attitude toward his suffering fits in well with the overall pattern of semantic reversals that Gary Jahn has discerned in the novella).[22] Ivan Il'ich admits he (so he thinks) has lived badly, and he even tries to say "Forgive me" to his hated and hateful wife – which is to say he recognizes he has sinned against her. As Richard Gustafson says, Ivan Il'ich "suffers from his sins."[23]

But are the sins commensurate with the suffering? Without mentioning the masochism, Edward Wasiolek makes an important point: "The life is not that bad, and the pain and terror are too much. The life is too trivial for the pain to be so great."[24] It does not seem right that Ivan Il'ich should be "bludgeoned" by pain, as Wasiolek puts it. Many of Tolstoy's contemporaries felt that same way, for example, the critic D. N. Ovsianiko-Kulikovskii, who felt there were "insufficient grounds" for Tolstoy to treat Ivan Il'ich so harshly: "Tolstoy demands too much."[25] One gets the impression that Tolstoy was treating the inconsequential Ivan Il'ich as he would have treated himself – great man that he was, and great sinner that he imagined himself to be. As Gustafson has demonstrated, Tolstoy not only suffered from chronic guilt feelings but believed that others should so suffer.[26]

There are other Tolstoy characters who, like Ivan Il'ich, accept guilt as a necessary condition for making a breakthrough to love. One thinks of the wounded Prince Andrei, who has to realize how badly he had treated Natasha before he can love her; or Dmitrii Nekhliudov, who decides to give up everything for Katia Maslova when he takes responsibility for having made a prostitute of her and blames himself for her prison sentence. Then of course there is Lev Tolstoy himself who, in an 1889 letter to his friend Vladimir Chertkov, explained how important it was to him to be able to feel the weight of his own guilt:

> In order to stop being angry at a person, in order to make peace, to forgive – if there is something to forgive – even to feel sorry for or to start loving the person, what should one do? The best thing is to recall your own sin against this person, the same as his. This is a special kind of happiness, followed by an instant healing.

"If you do this sincerely," Tolstoy continues to Chertkov, "if you seriously and vividly recall your own vileness, you will forgive, you will make peace and, God willing, you will feel sorry and start to love [*pozhaleesh' i poliubish'*]." In order to accomplish this, however, you must not have forgiven yourself for your previous sins: "Do not forgive yourself, then you will forgive others" (86:262).

In other words, your own burden of guilt is precious. You must hold on to it, for otherwise you will not be able to love (forgive) others.[27] You need the guilt not only because your sufferings would otherwise be senseless but also because they facilitate a loving union with others who, like you after all, are also suffering and burdened with guilt. Those others out there constitute a convenient and necessary reflection of your own torments.

Thus the suffering Ivan Il'ich, in his last moments, perceives and appreciates how much those around him are also suffering:

> He felt that someone was kissing his hand. He opened his eyes, looked at his son, and felt sorry for him. His wife came up to him and he glanced at her. She was gazing at him open-mouthed, with undried tears on her nose and cheek and a despairing look on her face. He felt sorry for her too.
>
> "Yes, I am making them all wretched," he thought. "They're sorry, but it'll be better for them when I die." He wished to stay this, but didn't have the strength to utter it. "Besides, why speak? I must act," he thought. With a look at his wife he indicated his son and said:
>
> "Take him away . . . sorry for [*zhalko*] him . . . and for you too . . ." He tried to add "Forgive me" [*prosti*], but said "Let me through" [*propusti*] and waved his hand, knowing that He whose understanding mattered would understand. (166–67; 26:112–13)

Now Ivan Il'ich believes that by feeling sorry for his wife and son, he can alleviate both his sufferings and theirs: "He was sorry for them, he must act so as not to hurt them: release *them* and free *himself* from these sufferings. 'How good and how simple!' he thought" (167; 26:113; emphasis added).

Good indeed, but not so simple. How is it possible for an immobile, nearly dead human being to "act"? How can he "release" his family from suffering? Certainly he cannot "release" them by commiting suicide. He has neither the wish nor the means to kill himself. On the contrary, he cannot even accept death and denies it until the end, as we have seen. But Ivan Il'ich can "act" in the performative sense, that is, he can express his compassion for those around him, and he can (at least attempt to) ask their forgiveness. This is an important psychological move for him to be able to make, even if it has no visible impact on those around him (in his narcissistic isolation Ivan Il'ich does not even notice whether his words have any psychological effect on his wife and son, nor does the narrator).

The act Ivan Il'ich accomplishes may be characterized as an out-
burst of compassion, even love. If in the definitive version of the
novella the Russian word is "zhalko," in an earlier draft quoted by
Vladimir Zhdanov the phrasing is: "*I vdrug on* poliubil *ikh*" (And
suddenly he *started loving* them).[28] For Tolstoy, of course, compassion is the highest form of love.[29] Compassion is indeed God's own
way of loving humanity, for it was divine compassion that led Christ
to redeem the sins of humankind by suffering and dying on the cross
(Tolstoy's well-known rejection of the church doctrine of redemption did not affect his awareness of Christ's compassionate nature).
Christ's compassion, moreover, was tied to his innocence and perfec-
tion. Christ certainly did not suffer for his own sins. His sufferings
constituted the most important and exemplary act of moral masochism in the history of humanity, for Christ was God and therefore
without sin, without guilt. The pain and suffering he welcomed were
utterly undeserved.

That Ivan Il'ich accepts much more pain and suffering than he
really deserves indicates how truly masochistic is his final psychological move. Yet there is something about the masochism that is not
an exaggeration, provided we consider the narration as a whole and
recall the negative impression produced by the self-centered, hypocritical characters Tolstoy introduces at the beginning of his novella.
Most of the novella is, after all, an extended flashback to Ivan Il'ich's
life and dying before the funeral service takes place in the opening
chapter, that is, before Ivan Il'ich's scheming associates, "so-called
friends," and unsavory family members make their initial impression
on us. Ivan Il'ich's widow sins in the reader's eyes by appearing to be
more interested in obtaining money from the government than in
mourning her husband. So, too, does Petr Ivanovich, who manages
to fit in a game of cards right after contemplating his friend Ivan
Il'ich's corpse. These people leave such a bad aftertaste that the
dying Ivan Il'ich seems noble by comparison. The extremity of *his*
suffering seems to cancel *their* evil. We all too readily forget that,
right after Ivan Il'ich completes his sufferings and sees the light,
these characters will start their disgusting behavior of the first chap-

ter. I think Tolstoy wanted it that way. He wanted that uplifting, masochistic sense of forgiveness of the final chapter to stay with the reader, but it would have been erased by any subsequent depiction of sinning. How many readers, after all, remember that Aleksei Karenin at one point actually forgave Anna her adultery?

Like the exemplary masochist Jesus Christ, then, Ivan Il'ich seems to be suffering for sins other than his own; that is, his sufferings have a virtual redemptive power – they help erase our awareness of the sinfulness of the sinners around him. This parallel with Christ fits in well with the other parallels that Gary Jahn has already detected.[30] If Christ on the cross calls out "My God, My God, why hast Thou forsaken me?" (Matthew 27:46), Ivan Il'ich, lamenting the cruelty and absence of God, calls out to God: "Why, why dost Thou torment me so terribly?" (160; 26:105). Whereas Christ is wounded in the side with a lance, Ivan Il'ich suffers a blow to the side when he falls from a ladder. The deaths of both Christ in Tolstoy's *Harmonization and Translation of the Four Gospels* and Ivan Il'ich in the novella are depicted by the phrase "It is finished" ("*Koncheno*"). There is also a hint of Christ's resurrection from the dead in the characterization of Ivan Il'ich as "*phenix de la famille*," as Jahn observes.[31] This hint is corroborated by Vladimir Zhdanov's detailed examination of drafts and variants of the novella. Zhdanov quotes a passage in which Ivan Il'ich believes he is resurrected from the dead: "*On pochuvstvoval, chto on voskres*" (He felt that he had risen from the dead). This passage did not make it into the final version. In addition, the word *resurrection* (*voskresenie*) appears near the ending in several manuscript variants.[32] Certainly Tolstoy intended Ivan Il'ich to be a Christ figure, and it is difficult for the educated reader to miss this intention. What psychoanalysis adds to our understanding of the intention is at least a partial motive for it: in the masochistic Jesus Christ, Tolstoy found a handy model or justification for Ivan Il'ich's terminal masochism.

Although Ivan Il'ich shows Christian compassion for those around him just before he dies, he does so for his own personal reasons, and he remains narcissistically isolated.[33] Here Ivan Il'ich is very different from Christ. The "release" is purely internal or mental. Those around Ivan Il'ich in his last moments are merely reflections of his internal self, and he does not – nor does the narrator – register any feedback to his act of compassion, as I mentioned earlier. When someone above Ivan's head says "It is finished," Ivan hears these words and responds *to himself:* "Death is finished." Apart from the need to deny death, there is no effort whatsoever to communicate. No contact is made with those around Ivan Il'ich who are witnessing the approach of objective death. Subjective Ivan Il'ich has retreated entirely into himself. Narcissus is closed off from the world.

Or rather, Narcissus enters another world. It is as though Ivan Il'ich has passed through a mirror (*propusti*) and entered a new and joyful noumenal existence. The key phrase here again seems very Christian: "In place of death there was light." What does this new light signify?[34] In what sense does light constitute a convincing replacement for the death which – to the analytic mind at least – is unconvincingly denied?

One of the main representations of Jesus Christ's earthly presence in the New Testament is *light.*

A light for revelation to the Gentiles. (Luke 2:32)

In him was life, and the life was the light of men. The light shines in the darkness, and the darkness has not overcome it. (John 1:4–5)

The true light that enlightens every man was coming into the world. (John 1:9)
"I am the light of the world." (John 8:12)

Examples could be multiplied. Tolstoy was particularly impressed by the first passage from John's gospel (1:4–5) quoted here, for he made use of it in *War and Peace* (in one of Pierre Bezukhov's dreams)[35] as well as in the title of his unfinished autobiographical play *The Light Shines in the Darkness (I svet vo t'me svetit).*

For Ivan Il'ich, light replaces death. Even as he is dying Tolstoy's hero denies death and affirms light, experiences it, *becomes* it even in his intense joy. For just as light replaces death, joy also replaces death: the rhetorical question *"Kakaia smert'?"* [What death?] becomes the exclamation *"Kakaia radost'!"* [What joy!]. Suffused with joy, Ivan Il'ich is virtually identified with the light (cf. also the topos *"svet*laia radost'"). But if the light is Christ, then Ivan Il'ich is identified with Christ.

Whereas earlier in the narration death was a personified or animate "it" stalking Ivan Il'ich,[36] now the stalker has been vanquished by divine light, that is, light personified. Instead of becoming dead, Ivan Il'ich becomes Christ. Ivan Il'ich does not merely imitate Christ by suffering on a metaphorical cross and loving those around him in a Christlike fashion just before he dies; he actually becomes Christ, that is, he becomes God the Son instead of dying.

On the one hand, this transformation is appropriate because, in the same passage from John's gospel, God is both light and *life:* "The life was the light of men." Not only is there "no death," there is what is normally considered to be its opposite, that is, there is life. Death is thus doubly denied: first directly ("There was no death"), then indirectly ("In place of death there was light," i.e., in place of death there was the equivalent of life).

On the other hand, the life Ivan Il'ich attains by his mental maneuver is no ordinary life, it is divine life. The grandiosity is breathtaking. Ivan Il'ich is not merely not dead, he is God. Ivan Il'ich's death illustrates the general Tolstoyan tendency to characterize death as "discovery of the *divine* self."[37] Ivan Il'ich's internal transformation is truly incredible. It is as if a man walking in a dark forest were approached by robbers who threatened to kill him, but then bowed down to worship him instead. Or, to resort to the anal-fecal imagery that pervades earlier portions of the narrative,[38] it is as if a "blocked" Ivan Il'ich finally emerges from an intestinal "black sack," and is immediately transformed from a sinful piece of shit into pure, bright gold.

Such is Tolstoy's covert religious message. One becomes God upon dying, or rather, one becomes God instead of dying. Instead of the end of the self, there is what Kohutian analysts would term the grandiose self.[39] Instead of dying (*"vmesto smerti"*), the self of Ivan

Il'ich expands infinitely to become God. Instead of images of confinement – the black frame of the obituary, the edge of the coffin, the black sack – [40] there is an image of omnidirectional release from confinement: "What had been oppressing him and would not leave him was all dropping away at once from two sides, from ten sides, from all sides" (167; 26:113). Light shines in darkness, that is, it radiates from a point in all directions. Anything, even imminent death, can be denied in deference to an expanding, luminous, and grandiose self. Such a self is omnipotent; it brooks no peers.

The Death of Ivan Il'ich is a great and deceptive fiction. When Ivan Il'ich thinks "Death is finished," he is terribly mistaken. Death is in fact about to occur. It is not finished, and Ivan Il'ich is jumping the gun. *It* is not over until it is over. But since, when it is over, there is no reporting that it is over, we have to settle for Tolstoy's marvelous depiction of what it might be like to be over.

NOTES

I wish to thank Barbara Milman for her constructive comments on an earlier draft of this essay.

1. Sigmund Freud, *Standard Edition of the Complete Psychological Works of Sigmund Freud* (hereafter, *SE*), trans. under direction of J. Strachey, 24 vols. (London: Hogarth, 1953–65), 14:252, 289.

2. Even suicide is no exception, according to Freud, for the person who commits suicide is not so much killing the self as covertly killing another against whom sadistic feelings cannot be openly acknowledged: "the ego can kill itself only if, owing to the return of the object-cathexis, it can treat itself as an object – if it is able to direct against itself the hostility which relates to an object and which represents the ego's original reaction to objects in the external world" (*SE*, 14:252; cf. 18:162–63).

3. All annotations to *The Death of Ivan Il'ich* are from Lev Nikolaevich Tolstoi, *Polnoe sobranie sochinenii*, ed. V. G. Chertkov et al., 90 vols. (Moscow: Gosudarstvennoe Izdatel'stvo Khudozhestvennoi Literatury, 1928–64). References to the English text are from Leo Tolstoi, *Tolstoy's Short Fiction*, ed. and trans. Michael R. Katz (rev. trans.) (New York: Norton, 1991). Page

numbers from the English text are given first and then those of the Russian text.

4. I have had to correct the Katz translation slightly to make this diachronic depth visible.

5. *SE*, 19:58.

6. It was in *Beyond the Pleasure Principle* (1920; *SE*, 18:7–64) that Freud introduced the "death instinct." According to this new idea the seeds of self-destruction are inherent in all life: "*The aim of all life is death*" (18:38). The ego manages not to destroy itself only because it redirects aggressive impulses outward toward the external world. Sexual impulses are merely a temporary stage. Thanatos eventually conquers Eros.

Even psychoanalysts were appalled by Freud's new theory, rejecting it for the most part (the Kleinians being the notable exception: see Otto Fenichel, *The Psychoanalytic Theory of Neurosis* [New York: Norton, 1945], 58–61). For my own part, I was able to write an entire book on self-destructive behavior of Russians (including, for example, mass suicides of Old Believers) without ever having to resort to the death instinct as an explanatory tool (Daniel Rancour-Laferriere, *The Slave Soul of Russia: Moral Masochism and the Cult of Suffering* [New York: New York University Press, 1995]).

7. Compare, for example, the dying Petr who begs Nikita's forgiveness in *The Power of Darkness*, or the Nikita who thinks he is dying and begs Brekhunov's forgiveness in *Master and Man*. Even the aristocratic Anna begs Karenin's forgiveness when she thinks she is dying. On the enormous importance of forgiveness in *Anna Karenina*, see Dragan Kujundžić, "Pardoning Woman in *Anna Karenina*," *Tolstoi Studies Journal* 6 (1993): 65–85.

8. Edward Wasiolek, *Tolstoy's Major Fiction* (Chicago: University of Chicago Press, 1978), 175.

9. David Shepherd, "Conversion, Reversion, and Subversion in Tolstoi's *The Death of Ivan Il'ich*," *Slavonic and East European Review* 71 (1993): 403, 410; emphasis added.

10. Cf. Shepherd, "Conversion, Reversion, and Subversion," 409, who suggests that because of the morphine that Ivan Il'ich takes, "perhaps the key moments of his conversion are, at least in part, hallucination." Shepherd does not pursue this line of thinking, however.

11. On Tolstoy's personal rejection of the possibility of life after death, cf. George J. Gutsche, *Moral Apostasy in Russian Literature* (De Kalb: Northern Illinois University Press, 1986), 96.

12. Quoted by Vladimir Aleksandrovich Zhdanov, *Ot "Anny Kareninoi" k "Voskreseniiu"* (Moscow: Kniga, 1967), 121.

13. For a review of the current psychoanalytic literature on masochism, see Rancour-Laferriere, *The Slave Soul of Russia*, chap. 5.

14. See Gutsche, *Moral Apostasy*, 80–81.

15. The Russian word *agoniia* suggests immense pain and suffering, according to the *Academy Dictionary:* "*poslednii, samyi muchitel'nyi period umiraniia; predsmertnye muki.*" See ANSSSR, *Slovar' sovremennogo russkogo literaturnogo iazyka*, 17 vols. (Moscow: Nauka, 1950–65), 1:46.

16. This pairing is also visible elsewhere in postconversion Tolstoy. For example, the "madman" at the end of *Notes of a Madman* (1884) believes that death no longer exists and welcomes his sufferings.

17. Wasiolek, *Tolstoy's Major Fiction*, 176.

18. Y. J. Dayananda, "*The Death of Ivan Il'ich:* A Psychological Study on Death and Dying," *Literature and Psychology* 22 (1972): 197–98.

19. Ibid., 198.

20. Leo Tolstoi, *Tolstoy's Short Fiction*, ed. and trans. Michael R. Katz (rev. trans.) (New York: Norton, 1991), 433.

21. Cf. Boris Sorokin, "Ivan Il'ich as Jonah: A Cruel Joke," *Canadian Slavic Studies* 5 (1971): 501.

22. Gary R. Jahn, *The Death of Ivan Il'ich: An Interpretation* (New York: Twayne, 1993), 30, 63, 77–82, 97. Cf. Rimgaila Salys, "Signs on the Road of Life: *The Death of Ivan Il'ich*," *Slavic and East European Journal* 30 (1986): 25–26.

23. Richard F. Gustafson, *Leo Tolstoy: Resident and Stranger* (Princeton, N.J.: Princeton University Press, 1986), 158.

24. Wasiolek, *Tolstoy's Major Fiction*, 175.

25. D. N. Ovsianiko-Kulikovskii, *L. N. Tolstoi kak khudozhnik*, 2d ed. (St. Petersburg: Orion, 1905), 264.

26. Gustafson, *Resident and Stranger*, 143–55.

27. It is difficult to imagine a worse kind of psychotherapy (one of the aims of most forms of psychotherapy in the West today is self-forgiveness). But holding on to guilt apparently worked for the aging Tolstoy who, like the dying Ivan Il'ich, was filled with hatred for his wife and family.

28. Zhdanov, *Ot "Anny Kareninoi" k "Voskreseniiu,"* 112; emphasis added.

29. See Gustafson, *Resident and Stranger*, 186–90.

30. Jahn, *The Death of Ivan Il'ich*, 70, 73–75; cf. also Gutsche, *Moral Apostasy*, 83–89, 95–96.

31. Cf. Sorokin, "Ivan Il'ich as Jonah," 502.

32. Zhdanov, *Ot "Anny Kareninoi" k "Voskreseniiu,"* 121.

33. On Ivan Il'ich's isolation from others, cf. Kathleen Parthé, "The Metamorphosis of Death in Tolstoy," *Language and Style* 18 (1985): 205–14.

34. Here I am searching for the light's significance apart from its intrinsic meaning within the novella's pattern of light and dark imagery (see David S. Danaher, "Tolstoi's Use of Light and Dark Imagery in *The Death of Ivan Il'ich*," *Slavic and East European Journal* 39 [1995]: 227–40). It is interesting in this connection that a vision of light or radiance often accompanies the so-called near-death experience or deathbed vision (see Rosemary Ellen Guiley, *Harper's Encyclopedia of Mystical and Paranormal Experience* [Edison, N.J.: Castle Books, 1991], 141–43, 399–400). Tolstoy seems to have been ahead of his time in accurately characterizing the subjective experience of dying in his fiction (see, especially, Walter Smyrniw, "Tolstoy's Depiction of Death in the Context of Recent Studies of the Experience of Dying," *Canadian Slavonic Papers* 21 [1979]: 367–79).

35. See Daniel Rancour-Laferriere, *Tolstoi's Pierre Bezukhov: A Psychoanalytic Study* (London: Bristol Classical Press, 1993), 149–50.

36. See Parthé, "The Metamorphosis of Death," 207.

37. Gustafson, *Resident and Stranger,* 154; emphasis added.

38. Sorokin, "Ivan Il'ich as Jonah," 503–4.

39. On the occurrence of grandiosity in the clinical context, see Heinz Kohut, *The Analysis of the Self* (Madison, Conn.: International Universities Press, 1971), 25–34, 114–15, 168–75. For a Kohutian analysis of Prince Andrei's grandiosity and otherwise disturbed narcissism, see Ruthellen Josselson, "Tolstoy, Narcissism, and the Psychology of the Self: A Self-Psychology Approach to Prince Andrei in *War and Peace*," *Psychoanalytic Review* 73 (1986): 77–95.

40. See Jahn, *The Death of Ivan Il'ich*, 37–39.

Scrooge on the Neva: Dickens and Tolstoy's *Death of Ivan Il'ich*

PHILIP ROGERS

Writing to Dickens in 1849, Irinarkh Vvedenskii, his first Russian translator, informed him that he was "read with great zeal from the banks of the Neva to the remotest limits of Siberia."[1] Among his zealous Russian readers of that time was the twenty-three-year-old Tolstoy, who first encountered Dickens – a Russian translation of *David Copperfield* – in 1851, while serving in the Caucasus campaign.[2] "How delightful *David Copperfield* is!" he noted in his diary (*PSS*, 46:140), and soon thereafter requested that his brother send him a copy of the novel in English along with his English dictionary (*PSS*, 59:251). Dickens was, he later concluded, "incomparably better in English."[3] More than fifty years later, in spite of the religious conversion that led him to speak of *Anna Karenina* as "excrement," the special pleasure Tolstoy found in Dickens was undiminished. Rereading the complete works in 1905, probably for the third time,[4] he noted with satisfaction: "I read them all. Now I am reading *David Copperfield* for the *n*th time, I'm sucking it like a caramel."[5] His final estimate of Dickens was succinct and unambiguous: "I consider him the greatest novelist of the nineteenth century" (*PSS*, 75:24). Dickens's portrait was prominently displayed at Iasnaia Poliana,[6] and as Nikolai Apostolov notes, "everyone, from Tolstoy's relations down to his old servant, Il'ia Vasil'ich, looked on it as the picture of 'the favorite author.'"[7]

Tolstoy appears to have read almost everything Dickens wrote, including the lesser known nonfiction such as *Pictures from Italy*, *A Child's History of England*, and *American Notes*.[8] While in London in 1861 he enriched his reading of the novels by witnessing Dickens's dramatic interpretation of his own characters in a public reading of *A Christmas Carol*,[9] a performance that moved Tolstoy to tears.[10] Many years later he recalled Dickens's "wonderful dramatic power" and the "lean strength" of his physical presence.[11] Apostolov relates that in his storytelling Tolstoy dramatized each role, as Dickens did in his public readings, thus adopting the storyteller's manner along with his stories.[12]

Just two years before his death Tolstoy remarked that if he had time he would like to write something about Dickens because "he gave me great pleasure and influenced me."[13] The essay on Dickens was never written and, consequently, the "influence" Tolstoy attributed to Dickens can only be inferred from random comments in his letters and conversations, his markings in his personal copies of Dickens's works,[14] and, of course, from the complex evidence of Tolstoy's writings themselves. Scholars have generally limited their study of the Dickens influence to the identification of resemblances – analogous characters and scenes – primarily in the early works; they assume as well that Tolstoy's interest in Dickens originates in his fondness for Dickens's characters (on which some of his own in *Childhood* are obviously based) and his approval of Dickens's Christian morality, as he explained in *What Is Art?* While these assessments are not incorrect, they are far from complete: the influence of Dickens extends to Tolstoy's postconversion works and, in all periods, consists of both formal and thematic features.[15] Further, it must be stressed that Tolstoy made Dickens his own – appropriated, possessed, and re-created him – sucked the Dickens caramel until it was absorbed into his own fictional system. Tolstoy entertained children at Iasnaia Poliana not with readings from Dickens but with retellings of Dickens in Tolstoyan adaptations.[16] Tolstoy's impulse to *re*tell Dickens, re-creating his works to suit the knowledge and interests of a Russian audience according to the prompting of his own aesthetic sensibility and moral ideas, became formalized in later years in Tolstoy's publication of adaptations of Dickens in *Posrednik*. Editing and rewriting A. A. Rytsen's translation of *A Christmas Carol*, he produced his own Tolstoyan Scrooge.[17]

For Tolstoy, sucking the caramel also involved the appropriation of Dickens's typology of characters to describe himself and others. In conversation and correspondence he footnoted his analyses of persons and relationships with references to Dickens. His brother's letters, he observed, resembled Mr. Micawber's (*PSS*, 59:120); his sister-in-law (Tat'iana Bers) had the personality of Bella Wilfer of *Our Mutual Friend* (*PSS*, 48:65).[18] More important, Tolstoy, in a serious frame of mind, saw himself in the light of analogous Dickens characters. As the high-minded young writer wooing a frivolous beauty (Valeriia Arsen'eva), Tolstoy recognized that he was repeating David Copperfield's error with Dora Spenlow, and told Arsen'eva so (*PSS*, 47:88).[19] Angered by Archduke Nikolai Romanov's patronizing attitude toward his impractical "idealism," he compared himself at length to Daniel Doyce (of *Little Dorrit*), the inventor who is treated as if he were an ineffectual child by the bourgeois banker, Mr. Meagles.[20] This Tolstoyan self-analysis through Dickens continues almost directly in his fiction; the analogous condescension of untalented mediocrity to creative genius finds its literary expression in the Vronskii-Mikhailov relationship in *Anna Karenina*. Vronskii's aristocratic scorn for the true artist, as F. R. Leavis has shown, also appears to have been influenced by *Little Dorrit*, in the character of the aristocratic painter Henry Gowon; the latter's defensive rationalization of his mediocrity (all art is really "mere humbug") – seen by Dickens as a debasement and insult to art itself – anticipates Vronskii's reduction of Mikhailov's inspiration to mere training and technique.[21] Dickens and Tolstoy both felt obliged to defend true art and artists – ultimately their sense of self and vocation – from the self-justifying opinions of triflers and dilettanti. Tolstoy's recurrent appropriation of *Little Dorrit*'s vein of commentary on the predicament of genius in a stifling bourgeois world exemplifies, I think, at least one aspect of what he meant by Dickens's "influence."

Analogues of moral and psychological circumstance similar to the Gowon-Vronskii parallel occur throughout Tolstoy's works and are especially numerous in *Childhood*. Although much remains to be said regarding the extent and nature of Dickens's influence on the major novels,[22] I want to focus here on Tolstoy's use of Dickens in *The Death of Ivan Il'ich*, a co-authoring evident both in the work's central themes – death, judgment, and brotherhood – and in the formal properties of its narration, genre, and rhetoric.

The Death of Ivan Il'ich is of particular importance for the study of the Dickens-Tolstoy relationship because Tolstoy's writing of it, his first major creative achievement after his conversion, coincided with a rekindling of his interest in Dickens and a reappraisal of his works: "Just recently I reread Dickens's novels *Little Dorrit* and *Bleak House*. I think Dickens is still not fully appreciated. We don't know Dickens, but what a force he is. Formerly these novels seemed heavy and boring to me, but now – no. What a force!"[23] The occasion of Tolstoy's rereading Dickens appears to have been the need, beginning in 1884, to select suitable material for *Posrednik*. On 8 May 1885 (when he was literally in the middle of writing *Ivan Il'ich*), he wrote to Chertkov recommending all of Dickens for *Posrednik*: "They're all wonderful – the short stories and novels" (*PSS*, 85:188).[24] In October 1885, while working on the final version of *Ivan Il'ich*, Tolstoy wrote to his daughter that he was simultaneously reading *Bleak House* "in snatches and thinking about *Oliver Twist*." "Just imagine if you had read them at school," he characteristically notes (*PSS*, 63:293). The reading of *Bleak House* appears to have continued throughout the period of his writing the final version of *Ivan Il'ich*, a time when, according to Gusev's chronology, he was reading nothing else. Toward the end of November he advised Chertkov to "try translating all of Dickens's *Bleak House* or *Little Dorrit* in its entirety . . . it's worth trying, and particularly with Dickens, to convey all the subtlety of irony and feeling – to teach [them] to understand subtleties. For this there is no one better than Dickens" (*PSS*, 85:286–87). In February 1886, just a month after completing the final version of *Ivan Il'ich*, Tolstoy's enthusiasm was still waxing: "Dickens interests me more and more," he wrote to Chertkov, recommending that *Posrednik* publish versions of *A Tale of Two Cities*, *Little Dorrit*, and *Our Mutual Friend*, and wishing he had the time to do *Our Mutual Friend* himself (*PSS*, 85:324). The final phase of Tolstoy's preoccupation with Dickens during this period was his rewriting of *A Christmas Carol* for *Posrednik* in March 1886 – two months after completing *Ivan Il'ich* – a project that had probably originated the previous March when Tolstoy was suggesting Dickens titles to Chertkov.

That Tolstoy's reading of Dickens may have stimulated the creative impulse that produced *Ivan Il'ich* is suggested by a diary entry of his wife, Sof'ia Andreevna, concerning his inability to write. On 23 October 1878, she noted: "Leva said today that he had read so much historical material that he would like a rest and read Dickens's *Martin Chuzzlewit* for a change. I know that when Leva begins to read English novels he is sure to start writing again himself" (1:99–100). Two weeks later, she recorded that Tolstoy, still unable to write, had found a germ of inspiration in Dickens: "It worries him not to be able to write. In the evening he was reading Dickens's *Dombey and Son* and suddenly said to me: 'I've got an idea!'" (1:103)[25]

The nature of Tolstoy's renewed interest in Dickens is partly explained by comments he made in late November 1885, probably about *Bleak House:*

> He has ten characters on stage and as you read you don't forget a one; each of them hits you in the eye. In his works all of their English institutions appear in an ironic light, everything is clothed with such irony. . . . His heroes . . . are not lords and the like, but ragamuffins with faces blemished by smallpox – the people – they are the real heroes.[26]

What Tolstoy admired in Dickens in 1885 was at least partly a rediscovery of qualities he had valued from the time of his earliest reading and continued to praise in his old age. As he explained in *What Is Art?*, Dickens's works exemplify the highest form of Christian art; they "illustrate and promote the love of man and God" (*PSS*, 30:160–61). Long before his conversion Tolstoy had appreciated the morally edifying aspect of Dickens. Almost thirty years earlier, reading *Bleak House* for the first time, he had vowed to adopt Esther Summerson's resolutions as his own:

> Esther (in *Bleak House*) says that her childish prayer consisted of promises she had made to God:
> 1. Always to be industrious
> 2. To be sincere
> 3. To be contented, and
> 4. To try to win the love of all around her.
> How simple, how sweet, how easy to accomplish, and how great are those four rules. (*PSS*, 47:11–12).

In 1885, however, Tolstoy stresses qualities different from those he admired in Esther's sweet and simple rules. The first of these is the power of Dickens's art, especially his subtle irony and memorable characterizations; the other, an aspect of Dickens's thinking congenial to the views of Tolstoy, the convert – his democratic sympathy for the common man. Both of these newly discovered interests are reflected in *The Death of Ivan Il'ich*.

Although *A Tale of Two Cities*, *The Chimes*, and *A Christmas Carol* exemplified for Tolstoy "the highest form of Christian art" (*PSS*, 30:160–61), his remarks on Dickens's style suggest that Dickens's influence on him was by no means limited to the realm of moral ideas. In his study of style in *War and Peace*, R. F. Christian points out that "the most characteristic single feature of Tolstoy's style" is repetition. One of his most obvious uses of repetition is "the constant reiteration of some detail designed to characterize an individual . . . No one can fail to notice how the essence of a Tolstoyan character is distilled into a mannerism, a gesture, a physical feature, an outward and visible sign which recurs continually and is the permanent property of that character."[27] As examples, Christian notes from *War and Peace* Napoleon's small white hands, Hélène's bare white shoulders, and Princess Mar'ia's radiant eyes.[28] This mode of characterization is, of course, quintessentially Dickensian – perhaps the most conspicuous single feature of his style. Uriah Heep writhes in false humility, Peggoty pops her buttons, Lady Dedlock is bored to death. Mrs. Merdle displays her husband's jewels on her metonymical show-window bosom, Mr. Dorrit ha-hums, and, in perhaps the best-known example of the Dickens verbal tag, Scrooge bah-humbugs.

As Christian notes, another common form of repetition in Tolstoy is that of single words. As examples he cites the seven uses of *plakat'* at the death of Prince Andrei, the five references to *priemnaia* as Andrei waits in the drawing room of Count Arakcheev, and the use of *kruglyi* five times in a single sentence describing Platon Kara-taev.[29] Examples of single-word repetition are equally numerous (and even more unabashedly reiterative) in the works of Dickens. The first chapter of *Bleak House* repeats *fog* twelve times in a single paragraph; describing the nouveau-riche Veneerings in *Our Mutual Friend*, Dickens repeats *new* fourteen times (2:6);[30] *stare, stared*, and *staring* are employed seventeen times in the first two pages or so of *Little Dorrit*; Steerforth's servant, Littimer, in *David Copperfield* is described as "respectable" more than twenty times in two pages (21:299–300).

Tolstoy's conscious awareness of Dickens's stylistic mannerisms, especially his rhetoric of repetition, is revealed in his recollection of a disagreement with Turgenev concerning Dickens's style. The dispute arose from Turgenev's criticism of Dickens's description of grape harvesting in Switzerland, the passage that introduces part 2 of *Little Dorrit*:

> It was vintage time in the great valleys on the Swiss side of the Pass of the Great Saint Bernard, and along the banks of the Lake of Geneva. The air there was charged with the scent of gathered grapes. Baskets, troughs, and tubs of grapes stood in the dim village doorways, stopped the steep and narrow village streets, and had been carried all day along the roads and lanes. Grapes, split and crushed under foot, lay about everywhere. The child carried in a sling by the laden peasant woman toiling home was quieted with picked-up grapes; the idiot sunning his big goiter under the eaves of the wooden chalet by the way to the waterfall

sat munching grapes; the breath of the cows and goats was redo-
lent of leaves and stalks of grapes; the company in every little
cabaret were eating, drinking, talking grapes. A pity that no ripe
touch of this generous abundance could be given to the thin, hard,
stony wine, which after all was made from the grapes! (2:1:431)

To Turgenev, this passage was merely an example of Dickens's "artificial, mannered" descriptions. Never loath to disagree with Turgenev, Tolstoy found the vineyard description "excellent" and concluded that although Turgenev was a perceptive critic, he sometimes
missed the mark.[31] In comparison with Dickens, Tolstoy remarked
on another occasion, Turgenev was "a mouse in front of a mountain."[32] When Tolstoy related this anecdote to Makovitskii and Sergeenko almost fifty years later, he omitted (or had perhaps forgotten)
its epilogue: his final defense of the disputed vineyard description –
Tolstoy's way, one suspects, of having an incontrovertible last word
in the argument – was an imitation of both its form and content in
his own description of the grape harvesting in *The Cossacks*:[33]

It was the month of August . . . The vineyards, thickly over-
grown with twining tendrils of green, lay in cool, deep shade.
Everywhere ripe heavy clusters showed black from behind the
broad transparent leaves. Creaking ox carts heaped with black
grapes moved slowly along the dusty road leading to the vineyard.
Clusters crushed by the wheels lay about on the dusty road. Boys
and girls in smocks stained with grape juice ran after their
mothers with clusters in their hands and mouths. Everywhere
along the road one met Nogai labourers in tattered clothes carrying baskets of grapes on their splendid shoulders. Cossack girls,
their kerchiefs pulled down to their eyes, led bullocks harnessed
to carts heaped high with grapes. Soldiers who passed a cart
would ask the Cossack girls for grapes and the Cossack girls,
climbing up on the moving carts, would take an armful of grapes
and drop them into the outstretched coats of the soldiers. They
were already pressing grapes in some of the yards and the smell of
juice filled the air . . . Grunting pigs gobbled up the pressed skins

and wallowed in them. The flat roofs on the huts were completely covered with black and amber clusters which were withering in the sun. (*PSS*, 6:109–10)[34]

In these descriptions, the repetition of the word *grapes* is only the most obvious feature of a more complex rhetorical design. In both, grapes are the recurring central detail in a social panorama stressing relationships: man and woman, parent and child, human and animal come together in the harvesting, eating, giving, and receiving of grapes. In both passages as well the pervasive odor of grapes and the omnipresence of gathered grapes in baskets and crushed grapes along the road evoke the sense of burgeoning harvest, a cornucopia abundant almost to repletion. As prefigurations of significant actions to follow, the two descriptions also serve analogous functions. In *Little Dorrit*, the vineyard scene introduces "Riches," part 2 of the novel; the harvest represents the Dorrits' newly acquired wealth, which, like the Swiss grapes, ironically yields only a hard and stony life. In spite of its obvious source in *Little Dorrit*, however, Tolstoy's description in *The Cossacks* is altogether subdued to his own thematic purposes. Here the fecund abundance of the harvest, reinforced by the physical splendor of the workers and the hint of flirtation between the soldiers and the Cossack girls, provides a suggestive background for Olenin's ripening passion for Marianka. This, along with his emphasis on the heavy grape clusters warmed by the sun, gives Tolstoy's description a sensuality altogether lacking in Dickens's.

Examples of analogous uses of repetition in Dickens and Tolstoy are so numerous that my analysis will be limited to passages that serve to illustrate a thematic affinity and that bear directly on the main ideas of *The Death of Ivan Il'ich*. The Tolstoyan reiteration associated with *Ivan Il'ich* is "pleasant and decorous" (131, 133, passim),[35] a tag more memorable in the formulaic, alliterating Russian original, "*priiatno i prilichno*." In Dickens, the analogous province of the pleasant and decorous is chiefly that of Mrs. General, whose role in *Little Dorrit* is to help the Dorrit children to "form a surface" suitable to their level in society. The formula conveying the essence of her teaching is "prunes and prism," continually repeated and alliteratively expanded. "Prunes and prism," she tells them, are "very good words for the lips" and "serviceable in the formation of a demeanor; if you sometimes say to yourself in company – or entering a room for instance – Papa, potatoes, poultry, prunes and prism, prunes and prism" (2:5:476). The tranquility of Mrs. General's existence, like Ivan's, requires the suppression of the disagreeable. Where Ivan "erects screens" against unpleasant realities, Mrs. General is said to "varnish" them: "Mrs. General was not to be told of anything shocking. Accidents, miseries, and offenses were never to be mentioned before her. Passion was to go to sleep in the presence of Mrs. General, and blood was to change to milk and water. The little that was left in the world when all these deductions were made, it was Mrs. General's province to varnish . . . The more cracked it was, the more Mrs. General varnished it" (2:2:450–51). Mrs. General's "deductions" of unmentionables – sexuality, contingency, poverty, death – "life itself" (*Ivan Ilych*, 165), as Ivan comes to realize are, of course, also Ivan's. Rebuking Amy Dorrit for having taken notice of the vagrants in Venice, Mrs. General elaborates the prunes and prism principle: "nothing disagreeable should ever be looked at . . . A truly refined ["comme il faut"] mind will seem to be ignorant of anything that is not perfectly proper, placid and pleasant" (2:5:447) – that is, "*priiatno i prílichno.*" The pervasiveness of prunes and prism in English society is suggested in Dickens's further extension of the alliterating "*pr-*" series to include "precedent and precipitate," repeated invocations of which (the former to extol tradition, the latter to deplore reform) epitomize the Barnacle family strategy in Parliament. Considering Tolstoy's use of Daniel Doyce, Henry Gowon, and the grape harvesting from *Little Dorrit*, it is not perhaps far-fetched to think of *Ivan Il'ich's* "*priiatno i prilichno,*" echoes of "prunes and prism" both in sound and sense, as Tolstoyan addenda to Dickens's alliterating list.

The use of repetition to convey the monotony of middle-class social and professional routines is characteristic of both Dickens and Tolstoy. Ivan "got up at nine, drank his coffee, read the paper, and then put on his undress uniform and went to the law courts" (139). At work his chief aim is "to exclude everything [that] disturbs the regular course of official business," especially the "fresh and vital" (139) – the quite literal vitality of life itself as Tolstoy suggests when Ivan escapes into "official business" to avoid confronting his wife's pregnancy (134). The mechanism by means of which subversive vitality is suppressed is the official: in his "official capacity," Ivan admits "only official relations with people, and then only on official grounds"; does business on "officially stamped paper," always separating "his real life from the official side of affairs" (139). In the evening Ivan reads official papers or a book everyone else is also reading at the time. Podsnap, Dickens's analogous arch-bourgeois (*Our Mutual Friend*) is also wholly defined by routines and restraints: he "got up at eight, shaved close at a quarter past, breakfasted at nine, went to the City at ten, came home at half-past five, and dined at seven" (11:128). Of special significance to Tolstoy's concern for the fate of the arts and artists in bourgeois society is the way in which Podsnap's routines define his taste.

> Mr. Podsnap's notions of the Arts in their integrity might have been stated thus. Literature; large print, respectively descriptive of getting up at eight, shaving close at a quarter-past, breakfasting at nine, going to the City at ten, coming home at half-past five, and dining at seven. Painting and Sculpture; models and portraits representing Professors of getting up at eight [etc.]. Music; a respectable performance (without variations) on stringed and wind instruments, sedately expressive of getting up at eight [etc.]. (11:128–29)

Only in his suppressions is Podsnap passionate; the arts must adhere to Podsnap's formula, especially in the avoidance of sexuality, against which manifestation of life screens like Ivan's must be imposed: "Nothing else to be permitted to those same vagrants the Arts, on pain of excommunication. Nothing else To Be – anywhere!" (11:129). The Podsnap formula requires "everything in the universe to be filed down and fitted to it" (11:129). Like Ivan, Podsnap maintains his self-satisfaction by suppressing the disagreeable:

> He felt conscious that he set a brilliant social example in being particularly well satisfied with most things, and, above all other things with himself . . . Thus happily acquainted with his own merit and importance, Mr. Podsnap settled that whatever he put behind him he put out of existence. There was a dignified conclusiveness – not to add a grand convenience – in this way of getting rid of disagreeables, which had done much towards establishing Mr. Podsnap in his lofty place in Mr. Podsnap's satisfaction. (11:128).

The monotonous social rituals where one hears only "the sort of conversation that is always repeated and always the same" (*Ivan Ilych*, 159) are typically evoked by Dickens and Tolstoy in the rhetoric of iteration. The chief social activity of Ivan's life is giving little dinner parties. In his pleasures, too, Ivan's life reiterates all other middle-class lives: "Just as his drawing room resembled all other drawing rooms so did his enjoyable little parties resemble all other such parties" (140). In an elaborately extended metaphor expressive of weary familiarity, Dickens in *Little Dorrit* compares the guests seated opposite one another at the dinner table to dull houses facing one another on opposite sides of the street. Just as the sameness of Ivan's parties mirrors the sameness of his drawing room, the guests at Mr. Merdle's fashionable dinner party are merely objects, as predictable as, and no lovelier than, their houses:

> Indeed, the mansions and their inhabitants were so much alike . . . that the people were often to be found drawn up on opposite sides of dinner tables . . . staring at the other side of the way with the dullness of the houses. Everybody knows how like the street the two dinner rows of people who take this stand by the street will be. The expressionless uniform twenty houses, all to be knocked at and rung at in the same form, all approachable by the same dull steps, all fended off by the same pattern of railing, all

with the same impracticable fire escapes, the same inconvenient fixtures in their heads . . . who has not dined with these? (1:21:246)

Dickens elaborates the metaphor to describe a variety of people-houses, punctuating his catalogue with repeated questions: "Who was not dined with these? . . . who does not know her? . . . who is unacquainted with that haunted habitation?"

Tolstoy uses an analogous extended (and markedly Dickensian) metaphor expressing the mechanical aspect of social ritual in the famous opening scene of *War and Peace*, in which Anna Pavlovna is compared to the foreman in a spinning mill; to keep the conversation machine in constant motion she must attend to each spindle in turn, "approaching now a silent, now a too-noisy group, and by a word or slight rearrangement" keep the machine in "steady, proper, and regular motion" (1:10). In his introduction of the guests at Anna Pavlovna's, as Christian points out,[36] Tolstoy employs one of his most characteristic kinds of repetition, that of introductory verbs. Here, the repetition of "there arrived" suggests monotonous formality: "There arrived the highest Petersburg society . . . ; there arrived the daughter of Prince Vasilii . . . There arrived Prince Ippolit . . . ; there arrived too the Abbé Morio and many others." This sentence structure, in which the initial verb is repeated in successive sentences or clauses, is often used by Dickens for the identical purpose – the mechanical introduction of dinner party guests at mechanical dinner parties. In the episode of the Veneering's dinner party in *Our Mutual Friend*:

> The great looking glass above the sideboard reflects the table and the company. Reflects the new Veneering crest . . . Reflects Mrs. Veneering; fair aquiline-nosed and fingered . . . Reflects Podsnap; prosperously feeding . . . Reflects Mrs. Podsnap . . . [and six more "reflects"]. (2:10)[36]

In describing the arrival of Lord Decimus at Mr. Merdle's dinner party in *Little Dorrit* Dickens employs a similar device: "Lord Decimus was . . . glad to see the Member. He was also glad to see Mr. Merdle, glad to see Bishop, glad to see Barnacle, glad to see Physician, glad to see Tite Barnacle, glad to see Ferdinand his private secretary" (2:12:561).[37]

In addition to their analogous use of repetitions to mirror the sameness of lives restricted by social decorums, both Dickens and Tolstoy employ repetitions to evoke emotional intensity. Thus in *Ivan Il'ich* repetition depicts not only Ivan's decorous screens against unpleasantness but also the process by which those screens are ultimately penetrated, the irresistible incursions of what Ivan calls *It* (150–51), his impending death. Ivan struggles to suppress, control, and finally to discover a meaning in *It*; repeatedly he reaches the inevitable conclusion that he is dying, only to retreat. Each retreat, however, leads directly back to the inescapable truth.[38] Tolstoy's repetitions convey Ivan's stubborn belief that the mortality of Caius (the Everyman of Kiesewetter's *Logic*) has nothing to do with him, because, unlike Caius, he is a real man. He vacillates from pole to pole of a dead-end contradiction: although he isn't mortal, like man in the abstract, he is nonetheless dying:

> Could Caius really know the smell of that striped leather ball Vanya had been so fond of? Could Caius really kiss his mother's hand like that and could the silk of her dress really rustle so for Caius? Could Caius really riot like that at school when the pastry was bad? Could Caius really be in love like that? Could Caius really preside at a session as he did? Caius really was mortal and it was right for him to die, but for me, little Vania, Ivan Il'ich . . . it's altogether a different matter . . . It can't be. It can't be, but it is . . . It can't be! Can't be, but is. (149–50)[39]

In *A Christmas Carol* Dickens dramatizes the dynamics of Scrooge's conversion in a similar rhetoric of repetitions. Like Ivan, Scrooge struggles to believe that he has led a good and proper life. At first he denies the reality of Marley's accusing ghost:

> Every time he resolved within himself, after mature inquiry, that it was all a dream, his mind flew back again, like a strong spring

released, to its first position, and presented the same problem to be worked all through, "Was it a dream or not?" Scrooge went to bed again, and thought, and thought, and thought it over and over, and could make nothing of it. The more he thought, the more perplexed he was; and the more he endeavored not to think, the more he thought. (2:23–24)

For Scrooge, too, it can't be, but is. Rationalizing the propriety of his obsession with profit, Scrooge protests that Marley made good use of his life and has no reason to feel remorse: "But you were always a good man of business, Jacob." Repeating the word *business*, Marley attacks Scrooge's complacent sense of a life well spent: "Business! . . . Mankind was my business. The common welfare was my business; charity, mercy, forbearance, and benevolence were all my business. The dealings of my trade were but a drop of water in the comprehensive ocean of my business!" (1:20). In an analogous exchange, Ivan's "inner voice" (his Marley) challenges his self-estimate by throwing his words back at him:

> "What is it you want?" [his voice asks him.] "What do you want? What do you want?" he repeated to himself. "What do I want? To live and not to suffer," he answered . . . "To live? How?" asked his inner voice. "Why, to live as I used to – well and pleasantly." "As you lived before, well and pleasantly?" the voice repeated . . . "Then what do you want now? To live? Live how?" (160–61)

Their sufferings, too, are expressed in similar forms: "'Spirit,' said Scrooge, 'show me no more! . . . Why do you delight to torture me?' 'One shadow more!' exclaimed the Ghost. 'No more!' cried Scrooge – 'no more. I don't wish to see it. Show me no more!'" (2:35). Ivan addresses his protest to God: "'Why hast Thou done all this? Why hast Thou brought me here? Why, why dost Thou torment me so terribly? . . . Go on! Strike me! But what is it for? What have I done to Thee? What is it for?'" (160). In the latter questions Ivan voices doubts that carry him far beyond the more narrowly defined limits of Scrooge's moral concerns. Scrooge recoils from the consequences of his actions; Ivan's fears arise from thoughts on being and nonbeing, the realm of Tolstoy's prevision of death in the dark night of Arzamas: "I was here and now I'm going there! Where? . . . I won't be, so what will be? Nothing will be. And where will I be when I won't be? . . . Can this be dying? No, I don't want to!" (148).

Tolstoy's most insistent repetition in *Ivan Il'ich* emphasizes the irresistible onset of *It*, the death he cannot screen out. The repetition (fifteen times in the last two pages of chapter 6) is further stressed by italics:

> *It* would come and stand before him and look at him . . . And what was worst of all was that *It* drew his attention to itself not in order to make him take some action but only that he should look at *It* . . . And to save himself from this condition Ivan Il'ich looked for consolations – new screens – and new screens were found and for a while seemed to save him, but then they immediately fell to pieces or rather became transparent, as if *It* penetrated them and nothing could veil *It* . . . He would go to his study, lie down, and again be alone with *It*: face to face with *It*. And nothing could be done with *It* except to look at it and shudder. (150–51)

In a strikingly similar passage from *Dombey and Son*, the idea of death projected as "it" (lacking, however, italics) is repeated by Dickens sixteen times in one page. Devoting his entire life to the family firm, Dombey (another Ivan Il'ich prototype) has deliberately cut himself off from the love of his wife and daughter. When the firm fails, Dombey, like Ivan, realizes that his life has been wrong; the culmination of his remorseful despair is the discovery of "it," the haggard mirror image of himself, which contemplates the killing of Dombey – an internal conflict analogous to the schisms of Scrooge and Marley, Ivan and his "inner voice." Dombey sees in the glass:

> A spectral, haggard, wasted likeness of himself . . . Now it lifted up its head, examining the lines and hollows in its face; now hung it down again and brooded afresh. Now it rose and walked about; now passed into the next room, and came back with something from the dressing-table in its breast. Now, it was looking at the

bottom of the door and thinking . . . It was thinking that if blood were to trickle that way . . . it must be a long time going so far . . . Now it was thinking again! What was it thinking? [etc.] (59:795)

But the influence of Dickens's style on Tolstoy consists of far more than the example of his penchant for repetition. In structure and genre, no less than in theme, *A Christmas Carol* provides obvious models for *The Death of Ivan Il'ich*. The example of Dickens is clearly relevant: in the hope of reaching a large audience, he abandons the lavish profusion of detail characteristic of his novels in order to create in the Christmas stories sharply focused, broadly popular didactic short fiction. Of the various Dickens works Tolstoy had been considering for publication in *Posrednik*, the self-contained brevity of *A Christmas Carol* made it the easiest to adapt, the obvious first choice for *Posrednik*, just as, for similar reasons, it had always been Dickens's favorite work for public reading.[40]

Stripped of whimsy and sentiment, *A Christmas Carol* closely resembles *The Death of Ivan Il'ich* in its gross anatomy. The narrative begins in present time, flashes back to Scrooge's earliest past, and returns to present time in a series of episodes tracing his ascent to worldly success and simultaneous decline into selfish withdrawal from human love and obligation. The movement of his mind through time as he confronts his past, present, and future leads him to realize that he has lived wrongly.[41] Returned to present time, the story ends with Scrooge's joyful rebirth as he emerges from his self-absorption determined to act so as to help others while there is yet time. As the type of utilitarian philosophy's economic man, Scrooge, like Ivan, represents an entire society gone wrong.[42] His life, too, is most simple and most ordinary and therefore most dreadful.

In spite of their superficially different tones, the narrators of the two works speak from the same vantage point. Both are more than merely omniscient: they have in a sense passed through the grave and address the reader with the confidence of immortals who possess transcendent knowledge of life's purpose. What Ivan discovers only with his last breath ("So that's what it is. What joy!") (167), the narrator knows all along. Scrooge learns from Marley's ghost the impotent frustration of the dead as they walk invisibly among the living, who repeat their errors. Dickens's narrator hints that he himself is the story's fourth spirit, standing invisibly at the reader's side (2:24). The converted Tolstoy, raised from the "death" of his unregenerate life, has seen the light and rattles Marley chains of admonition to awaken his readers. "The warning and reproach to the living" (125) that Ivan's corpse conveys to Petr Ivanovich is exactly analogous to Marley's admonition to Scrooge to change his ways while there is yet time; both warnings, moreover, function as thresholds to the main narratives, introducing the stories of Ivan and Scrooge, respectively, the lives whose direction and form elaborate and justify the warnings.

A second quality common to Dickens and Tolstoy's narrators is their irony, the aspect of Dickens's writing that Tolstoy singled out for special praise in the fall of 1885,[43] and that dominates the first three chapters of *Ivan Il'ich*. From the time of his earliest reading of Dickens, Tolstoy took special note of Dickens's ironical treatment of the hypocrisy of funerals and feigned bereavement. In *Childhood* Nikolenka's sense that his insincere display of sorrow has cheapened his genuine grief at his mother's funeral obviously recalls David Copperfield's self-conscious affectation of dignified melancholy at the death of his mother.[44] In his personal copy of *Oliver Twist*, Tolstoy marked with his characteristic double fold the page (36) on which Mrs. Sowerberry, the undertaker's wife, decides that Oliver would make an ideal professional mourner for children's funerals: "a mute in proportion, it would have a superb effect" (5:33). The episode of Anthony Chuzzlewit's funeral in *Martin Chuzzlewit* (1:351) is also marked with Tolstoy's double folding. Here the hypocritical behavior of Anthony's family and friends is markedly similar to that of the mourners at Ivan's funeral. Mr. Mould, the undertaker, struggles to conceal pleasure at his profit from the lavish ceremony; Mr. Tacker winks at Mrs. Gamp (recalling Svart's reassuring wink to Petr Ivanovich); the doctor pretends not to know the undertaker, while the real grief of Anthony's servant, Chuffy, is scorned by all as indecorous. In the chapter of *Bleak House* ironically titled "Our Dear

Brother," Dickens invokes night and darkness to hide Captain Hawdon's burial in a festering, shallow pauper's grave (11:151). The paragraph was marked in pencil by Tolstoy 1:157.[45] Like Anthony Chuzzlewit, Hawdon is mourned by only one poor friend, Jo, the illiterate crossing sweeper, who, like Chuffy in *Martin Chuzzlewit*, is scorned by all for his ignorance and refused as a witness at Hawdon's inquest (11:148), a passage also noted by Tolstoy with a marginal pencil mark (1:153). At Ivan's funeral, the sole true mourner, whose genuine emotion is revealed in his "tear-stained eyes," is his son. The scene in which Scrooge's merchant colleagues in the city learn of his death also resembles the opening scene of *Ivan Il'ich* in the law courts. "What was the matter with him?" they ask, and "what has he done with his money?" (4:59). Ivan's colleagues are no more moved than Scrooge's, wondering "but what was really the matter with him?" and "did he have any property?" (*Ivan Ilych*, 124).

What *was* the matter with them? The apparent difference in their behavior – Ivan the "bon enfant" and Scrooge the misanthrope – is merely superficial. Ivan and Scrooge in fact arrive at the crises of their respective lives by following quite similar paths. Doing the "proper" thing – Ivan's downfall – is also Scrooge's. Mere stinginess (the popular understanding of Scrooge) is not the basis of his misanthropy. Scrooge's rejected fiancée provides the most revealing analysis: "You fear the world too much," she tells him. "All your other hopes have merged into the hope of being beyond the chance of its sordid reproach" (2:43). Not wealth but the respectability of wealth is Scrooge's raison d'être. Scrooge's faith in prisons, workhouses, and the Poor Laws – the socially approved utilitarian solutions to Bob Cratchit's problem – is also what was "considered the right thing by the most highly placed of his associates" (*Ivan Ilych*, 130). Like Ivan, Scrooge is "strict in the fulfillment of what he considered to be his duty" (*Ivan Ilych*, 130), as duty is understood in utilitarian economics. In both *A Christmas Carol* and *Ivan Il'ich* "respectability" – the values guiding the lives of the "best people" – is the ultimate source of evil.

The conversions of Ivan and Scrooge are also similar; for both, the recognition that they have lived badly entails a review of their entire lives from a vantage point affording both distance and intimacy – the memory of childhood. This bright beginning, from which they descended (in Rousseau's paradigm) to the darkness of respectability, is crucial: childhood for both is the source of the healing emotions and sensations that foster an emerging sympathy for others. Scrooge evinces no sympathetic feeling until he is shown the world of his boyhood, when his eyes fill with tears. Like Ivan's most intimate recollections of childhood – the smell of the striped leather ball, the touch of his mother's silk dress, the sensation of plum stones in the mouth (10:150) – Scrooge's feelings are triggered by sensory memory – "a thousand odours floating in the air, each one connected with a thousand thoughts" (2:26). Paradoxically, his first sympathy for another is self-pity for his former self as a lonely boy: "Poor boy!" he feels, but immediately retrieves the newly recovered emotion for present-time altruistic purposes when he regrets not having given something to a "poor boy" who came to his door singing Christmas carols (2:28). For Ivan, too, it is pity for his past self, for "Little Vania with a mama and papa and toys" (149) that leads to his desire to be pitied like a child, to weep like a child, emotions which at the story's end become redirected outward into concern for others – for his son (a little Ivan, the image of his past self) and even his wife. In both, the alienated and self-justifying adult ego dissolves in a flood of tears, liberating the genuine self that had been repressed by conformity to the stifling values of respectability. Ivan's emergence from death-in-life into renewed life-in-death is, of course, a birth out of the black sack into a new world of joy and light; Scrooge celebrates restoration to the bright world of Christmas morning with the discovery that his youth has been restored to him. "I'm a baby," he exclaims, "I'd rather be a baby" (5:723). Both works can be read as glosses of Matthew 18:3: "Except ye . . . become as little children, ye shall not enter into the kingdom of heaven."

As Edward Wasiolek explains, Ivan is saved by the rediscovery of his individuality, "his own forgotten, personal, and individualized life."[46] Scrooge's salvation obviously arises from the same recovery of long-abandoned individuality. The Spirits of Christmas do not tell Scrooge how to live; they merely show him what he was and what he has become. The impulse to change emanates entirely from within. Tolstoy's rewriting of *A Christmas Carol* in the *Posrednik* version makes this aspect of Scrooge's psychology even more explicit: when Tolstoy's Scrooge asks Marley how he should have lived, Marley replies, "I cannot tell you . . . Every living being decides that for himself."[47]

Tolstoy's use in *Ivan Il'ich* of *Bleak House*, whose ironical view of "all the English institutions" he had singled out for praise while writing *Ivan Il'ich* in November 1885,[48] is primarily evident in the theme of justice. Both writers juxtapose the inflexible, legalistic justice of the state – of lawyers and judges – with the divine judgment of God and the divinely inspired self-judgment of individuals. "I expect a judgment," says (repeatedly) the mad Chancery suitor, Miss Flite, "shortly. On the Day of Judgment. I have discovered that the sixth seal mentioned in the Revelation is the Great Seal [of England]" (3:33). The same double meaning is suggested in the account of the death of Gridley, another perennial suitor in the Court of Chancery, in the chapter ironically titled "An Appeal Case." Gridley's "appeal" is heard only at what he terms "the great eternal bar" (15:215). Ivan's dying similarly entails both meanings of judgment. As *it* penetrates the screens of officialdom, the judge, too, must submit to judgment, first to that of the hypocritical doctors, who know the verdict but conceal it lest decorums be upset by the acknowledgment of death, and finally to his own self-judgment. As his illness progresses, his ability to judge, to administer the forms of state justice, fails him. Significantly, *it* first confronts him while he presides in court; he becomes confused and makes procedural errors. On his deathbed he remembers the call that formerly proclaimed his arrival in court, "'The judge is coming! The judge is coming, the judge!'" (*Ivan Ilych*, 161), now ironically anticipating his own last self-judgment. The idea of a hierarchy of judicial powers in which the judgment of any judge may be invalidated or reversed owing to uncertainties of jurisdiction and the possibility of appeal subtly pervades *Ivan Il'ich*, arising first in the opening scene, when jurisdiction (rather than the merits) of the Krasovskii case is being debated (*Ivan Ilych*, 123); then in Ivan's discussions with Shebek concerning decisions in the Court of Cassation (*Ivan Ilych*, 154) – the highest court of appeals; and even more subtly in the game of *vint*, when Ivan is unable to muster his hierarchy of diamonds for a grand slam and is overtrumped (metaphorically reversed) once again by It (*Ivan Ilych*, 145). Dickens's Court of Chancery in *Bleak House* is, of course, a court of equity to which suitors appeal, in vain, for justice, receiving ultimately only their last judgment.

As in *A Christmas Carol*, the world's blindness to the evil in *Bleak House* derives from the unimpeachable respectability of its perpetrators; the direst human suffering results from the most respectable of sources. Dickens's most sinister and malevolent lawyer, the "very respectable" (Dickens repeats the word seven times in one paragraph [39:547–48]) Mr. Vholes, is more obviously a cause of evil than the official villain of *Bleak House*, the murderess Hortense. Vholes rationalizes his parasitism by repeatedly invoking his domestic responsibility – his three daughters and dependent father – and in turn serves the legal community at large as a justification for not remedying its worst abuses and reforming the court: How can the System be changed without injuring Vholes, his father, and three daughters? (39:551–53). How can my life have been wrong, asks Ivan, when I have done nothing but right things? Vholes breaks no laws; he represents his indifference to others as a laudable objectivity: "professional duty" and his "good name" require that he be "cool and methodical," like Ivan, "completely excluding his personal opinion of the matter, while above all observing every prescribed formality" (*Ivan Ilych*, 132). Perhaps the most telling irony in *Bleak House* is Dickens's depiction of the Lord High Chancellor himself – the one individual most clearly responsible for the abuses of the Court of Chancery: he is described by Esther Summerson as "pleasant," "affable," "polite," "courtly," "kind," and "courteous" (3:30–32), a witty, unpretentious, and perceptive man – one, in sum, who could not be seen as anything other than – as Tolstoy describes Ivan – "an intelligent, polished, lively, and agreeable man" (*Ivan Ilych*, 130) – the model English gentleman. In *Bleak House*, however, the Devil has assumed the mask of respectability: "For, howsoever bad the devil can be in fustian or smock frock (and he can be very bad in both) he is a more designing, callous, and intolerable devil when he sticks a pin in his shirt front" and "calls himself a gentleman" (26:363), a passage Tolstoy seconded with a double underlining in his copy of the novel.[49]

The corollary of viewing the established classes and their values as the source of evil is to locate virtue among the humble and, as noted above, in children, childhood, and the childlike. Thus the peasant Gerasim's simple acceptance of Ivan's death, as well as his nursing of Ivan, form an important stage in Ivan's conversion. Likewise, as Tolstoy noted in November 1885, Dickens's real heroes often are not gentry but the ordinary people, "ragamuffins with pock-marked faces."[50] Dickens's pock-marked ragamuffin is, of course, Jo, the crossing-sweeper of *Bleak House*, the blankness of whose ignorance appears to have fascinated Tolstoy: "a wild boy in the middle of London," he wrote of him, marveling that he and many others could be completely deprived of the heritage of civilization that comprises "our spiritual, moral humane essence" (*PSS*, 30:465). In his copy of *Bleak House* Tolstoy underlined the passage in which Jo is questioned at Hawdon's inquest:[51]

> Name, Jo. Nothing else that he knows on. Don't know that everybody has two names. Never heerd of such a think. Don't know that Jo is short for a longer name. Thinks it's long enough for *him*. *He* don't find no fault with it. Spell it? No. *He* can't spell it. No father, no mother, no friends. Never been to school. What's home? Knows a broom's a broom, and knows it's wicked to tell a lie. (11:148)

In spite of his almost total ignorance, however, Jo expresses the essence of brotherhood for Dickens. He knows Hawdon "wos very good" to him and, wanting to do him good in return, he sweeps the steps leading to Hawdon's grave. He further proves his common humanity by infecting Esther Summerson with smallpox, symbolically uniting Chesney Wold and Tom-all-Alone's, the summit and nadir of British society, in the fact of their common mortality.

Gerasim's counterpart in *Bleak House* is not Jo, however, but Trooper George Rouncewell, the simple soldier who shelters both Jo and Gridley, the chancery victim, in their final illnesses and later nurses Sir Leicester Dedlock after his stroke. George Rouncewell, especially in his kindness to Phil Squod (another ragamuffin), appears to have piqued Tolstoy's special interest. The section of the chapter "Sharpshooters," in which Phil recalls George's rescue of him, the history of his misfortunes, and his devotion to George, are all underlined in Tolstoy's copy of the novel.[52]

But it is in the episode in which George, a former servant at Dedlock Hall, sits through the night at Sir Leicester's sickbed that the similarity of George and Tolstoy's Gerasim is most evident. The analogy has two related aspects: first, like Ivan, Sir Leicester derives comfort from the strong shoulders of the vigorously healthy younger man and seeks to prolong it.

> Sir Leicester . . . tries to raise himself among his pillows a little more. George, observant of the action, takes him in his arms again and places him as he desires to be . . . He has put Sir Leicester's sounder arm over his shoulder in lifting him up, and Sir Leicester is slow in drawing it away again . . . Overpowered by his exertions, he lays his head back on his pillows, and closes his eyes . . . in the rendering of those little services, and in the manner of their acceptance, the trooper has become installed as necessary to him. (58:793–95)

Second, the almost womanly gentleness of both George and Gerasim revives in Sir Leicester and Ivan the needs and emotions of childhood: "The trooper takes him in his arms like a child, lightly raises him . . . 'Thank you. You have your mother's gentleness,' returns Sir Leicester, 'and your own strength.' He looks at the trooper until tears come into his eyes" (58:792). Gerasim similarly satisfies Ivan's need for "someone to pity him as a sick child is pitied.

He longed to be petted and comforted. . . . In Gerasim's attitude towards him there was something akin to what he wished for, and so that attitude comforted him. Ivan Il'ich wanted to weep, wanted to be petted and cried over" (154). Ivan's weeping "like a child" after a night attended by Gerasim immediately precedes the recollection of his childhood noted above. In both works, the contrast of the vigorous and cheerful servants with their emaciated masters suggests that power, authority, and wealth are inversely related to vitality and joy. The fate of Ivan, the judge, and Sir Leicester, the baronet, is paralysis.[53] For both, their illness constitutes a symbolic retribution in the mode of Dante: assuming in their persons the rigidity of the social institutions and values they represent, they become immobile, fixed forms. At the same time, however, the coming together of master and servant in the familial intimacy of the sickroom, like the bond of contagion that links Jo and Esther, implicitly acknowledges the brotherhood of mankind in the face of common mortality, a unity Tolstoy underscores in Gerasim's simple acceptance of Ivan's death: "It's God's will. We shall all come to it some day" (129).

Dickens's presence in *The Death of Ivan Il'ich* is clearest in the story's central concern: the discovery of meaning in death. In *The Old Curiosity Shop* – of all Dickens's novels the one most preoccupied with death – he preaches (at the graveside of Little Nell) that the consciousness of death is morally edifying:

> It is hard to take to heart the lesson that such deaths will teach, but let no man reject it, for it is one that all must learn, and is a mighty, universal Truth. When Death strikes down the innocent and young . . . a hundred virtues rise, in shapes of mercy, charity and love to walk the earth and bless it. Of every tear that sorrowing mortals shed . . . some good is born, some gentler nature comes. In the Destroyer's steps there spring up bright creations that defy his power, and his dark path becomes a way of light to Heaven. (72:544)

Tolstoy underlined this paragraph, almost his only marking in the novel.[54] Dickens's "universal Truth" has several aspects, all of which relate to Tolstoy's ideas about death. First, and most obvious, the sorrowful tears of death are themselves a source of goodness and of the changed outlook on life implied in "gentler nature." The good born from tears is clearly exemplified in the consequences of Ivan's weeping like a child, as noted above. The goodness arising from the consciousness of mortality is also more than merely understanding right and wrong: it manifests itself in moral acts of "mercy, charity and love," "creations" of the living that "walk the earth."[55] Similarly, the culmination of Ivan's dying is not simply the realization that he has lived wrongly but rather the subsequent awareness that he must act. Having learned "the right thing," he feels sorry for his wife and son, but realizes that telling them he is sorry for them is not important: "'Besides, why speak? I must act,' he thought" (166). Learning "the right thing" must be confirmed in action. Thus Ivan's dying is depicted as an accomplishment, as Tolstoy emphasizes in describing the expression of his corpse: "what was necessary had been accomplished and accomplished rightly" (125).

A further aspect of Dickens's view of death is revealed when the narrator of *The Old Curiosity Shop* discovers in the clock of St. Paul's Cathedral (the "Heart of London," he calls it) a symbol of human brotherhood, a unity arising from mankind's shared fate as victims of death.[56] The clock measures time with a sledge-hammer beat, "as if its business were to crush the seconds as they came trooping on, and remorselessly to clear a path before the Day of Judgment" (6:107). From his sense of time as Destroyer he derives a moral: in its every stroke he hears a voice which bids him to "have some thought for the meanest wretch that passes, and, being a man, to turn away . . . from none that bear the human shape" (6:109).

The idea that the inevitable mortality of all men, their shared fate, is the ultimate basis of human brotherhood is also at the heart of Tolstoy's moral psychology in *The Death of Ivan Il'ich*. As Wasiolek explains, "Death, for Tolstoy, as the supremely shared experience, is the model of all solidarity, and only the profound consciousness of its significance can bring one to the communion of true brotherhood . . . The consciousness of death, Tolstoy is convinced, is the cement of true brotherhood."⁵⁷ This view of death and brotherhood is also the main theme of *A Christmas Carol*. Scrooge's nephew, clearly speaking for Dickens, explains that the consciousness of shared mortality is the heart of the Christmas spirit. He tells Scrooge that Christmas is "the only time . . . in the long calendar of the year, when men and women seem by one consent to open their shut-up hearts freely, and to think of people below them as if they really were fellow passengers to the grave, and not another race of creatures bound on other journeys" (1:10).⁵⁸ For Scrooge, the culminating experience leading to his spiritual rebirth is the revelation by the Ghost of Christmas Yet to Come of his own corpse, deathbed, and gravestone. The resulting consciousness of his inevitable, impending death gives urgency to his reform and impels him, like Ivan, to act while there is yet time. "I am not the man I was," Scrooge protests after seeing his grave, "I will not be the man I must have been" (4:70). "Best and happiest of all," the narrator assures us, "the Time before him was his own, to make amends in!" (5:71). The lavish celebration of Scrooge's amends (Christmas morning, prize Turkey, "God bless Us, Every One!") undergoes in *Ivan Il'ich* a painful contraction: Ivan mumbles his incomprehensible request for forgiveness; the darkness of his life is replaced by light, he briefly experiences the joy of knowing "what it is," and dies. The ratio of suffering to solace in the two works is not to be compared, either as to duration or profundity. However seriously we may take *A Christmas Carol*, we are not apt to liken Scrooge to Job, a comparison that Ivan's agonized questioning of God clearly evokes.

Tolstoy's editing of *A Christmas Carol* was a curiously appropriate epilogue to the writing of *The Death of Ivan Il'ich*. Having rewritten Scrooge as Ivan, he proceeded to rewrite the original as well, to make it conform more closely to his own, more austere version. Tolstoy took the same kind of liberty with Dickens as he had in producing his own version of the New Testament: just as he had purged the Bible of Christ's miracles and the resurrection, he banished the Ghosts of Christmas Past, Present, and Yet-to-Come from *A Christmas Carol*. Tolstoy's Marley – the only remnant of Dickens's fantasy – exists only in Scrooge's dream. Dickensian whimsy and sentimentality held little appeal for Tolstoy;[59] one of his very few criticisms of his favorite writer was his observation that the Christmas stories in general were flawed by sentimentality.[60] For Tolstoy, the interest of Dickens's tale lay not in the supernatural machinery or the (un-vegetarian) Christmas turkey but rather in its exploration of the central question Ivan repeatedly asks himself, the quintessentially Tolstoyan question he makes Scrooge ask Marley in the *Posrednik* version: "How then is one to live?"[61]

NOTES

1. I. Katarskii, *Dikkens v Rossii* (Moscow: Nauka, 1966), 1.

2. L. N. Tolstoi, *Polnoe sobranie sochinenii L. N. Tolstogo*, 90 vols. (Moscow: Gosudarstvennoe Izdatel'stvo Khudozhesvrennoi Literatury [GIKhL], 1907–60), 59:120. Henceforth cited in text as *PSS*.

3. S. I. Elpat'evskii, "L. N. Tolstoi," in *L. N. Tolstoi v vospominaniiakh sovremennikov*, 2 vols. (Moscow: GIKhL, 1960), 2:177.

4. A. Sakhaltuev, "Lev Tolstoi chitaet Charl'za Dikkensa," *Innostrannaia literatura* 6 (1970): 224–26. Sakhaltuev's claim is impossible to prove on the basis of Tolstoy's diary and letters or Gusev's chronology. Clearly, however, Tolstoy read almost all of them on three different occasions: first in the 1850s and 1860s, many of them, for example, *Little Dorrit* and *Our Mutual Friend*, as they were issued serially by Tauchnitz; second during the 1880s when he was considering them for Chertkov's *Posrednik* (*The Intermediary*), a publication devoted to producing inexpensive translations and adaptations of Western literature for Russian readers; and finally in 1905. Sakhaltuev also provides a partial account of Tolstoy's marking in his copies of Dickens.

5. D. P. Makovitskii, *U Tolstogo: "Iasnopolianskie Zapiski" D. P. Makovitskogo*, 5 vols. (Moscow: Nauka, 1979), 1:442.

6. G. A. Rusanov, "Poezdka v Iasnuiu Polianu," in *L. N. Tolstoi v vospominaniiakh sovremennikov*, 2 vols. (Moscow: GIKhL, 1960), 1:308–26.

7. Nikolai Apostolov, "Tolstoy and Dickens," in *Family Views of Tolstoi*, ed. Aylmer Maude (London: Allen and Unwin, 1926), 72.

8. Two novels are mentioned neither in Gusev's *Letopis'* nor in Tolstoy's diary or letters: *Barnaby Rudge* and, more surprisingly, *Great Expectations;* however, since an adaptation of *Great Expectations* ("The Convict's Daughter,

or from the Forge to Riches") was published in *Posrednik*, Tolstoy must have read it. "The Convict's Daughter" was read to Tolstoy's youngest child, Vanichka, shortly before he died in 1895 (S. A. Tolstaia, *Dnevniki*, 2 vols. [Moscow: GIKhL, 1978], 1:512). Both novels are in his collection.

9. Several major sources (Gusev, Christian, Simmons) erroneously claim that Tolstoy heard Dickens lecturing on "education," but Sergeenko makes it clear that Tolstoy attended a literary reading (P. A. Sergeenko, "Zapisi," *Literaturnoe nasledstvo 37–38* [Moscow: Izdatel'stvo akademii nauk, 1939], 557). See also A. V. Knowles's account of Tolstoy in London in "Some Aspects of L. N. Tolstoy's Visit to London in 1861: An Examination of the Evidence," *Slavonic and East European Review* 56 (1978): 106–14.

10. S. L. Tolstoi, *Tolstoi Remembered by His Son Sergei Tolstoi* (New York: Atheneum, 1962), 67.

11. Sergeenko, "Zapisi," 557.

12. See Apostolov, "Tolstoy and Dickens," 73; see also Elpat'evskii's amusing account of Tolstoy's acting the part of Tony Weller ("L. N. Tolstoi," 177). A remark made by Tolstoy to A. F. Koni suggests that Tolstoy saw a connection between Dickens's manner in the public readings and his representation of characters in writing: "The genuine teacher of literary language is Dickens. He always knew how to put himself in the place of the character being described and clearly imagined to himself what kind of language each of them had to speak" (A. F. Koni, "Lev Nikolaevich Tolstoi," *L. N. Tolstoi v vospominaniiakh sovremennikov*, 2 vols. [Moscow: GIKhL, 1978], 2:173).

13. Makovitskii, *U Tolstogo*, 3:325; Tolstoy also spoke of wanting to write about Dickens in 1905 (1:466).

14. Tolstoy marked his books in several ways: with black pencil (underlining and occasionally bracketing individual words and sentences; with marginal lines, check marks, and X's), fingernail impressions, and turned back, double-folded page corners. Tolstoy's personal copies of Dickens's works are kept at the Estate-Museum, Iasnaia Poliana. My comments on Tolstoy's markings are based on my examination of the books at Iasnaia Poliana. Although almost all of Dickens's works are represented in Tolstoy's collection, some of his original copies of favorite novels are unfortunately missing, for example, the Russian translation of *David Copperfield*, volumes 2 and 3 of *Dombey and Son*, and his first copies of *Little Dorrit* and *Our Mutual Friend* (the archive copy of *Little Dorrit* is a later edition; neither of the two copies of *Our Mutual Friend* is fully cut). N. N. Ivanov tells of Tolstoy's giving him

his own copy of *Our Mutual Friend* ("U L. N. Tolstogo v Moskve v 1886 gody," in *L. N. Tolstoi v vospominaniiakh sovremennikov*, 2 vols. [Moscow: GIKhL, 1960], 1:346). I am indebted to the Estate-Museum, Iasnaia Poliana, for permission to use its archive and also to the Tolstoi Museum, Moscow, for the use of its library.

15. P. Waddington's view is typical: "Tolstoy's later development as a novelist appeared to leave no room for Dickens" (*Turgenev and England* [New York: New York University Press, 1981], 76). Discussions of the influence of *David Copperfield* on *Childhood* include those of Apostolov, "Tolstoy and Dickens," 79–84; R. F. Christian, *Tolstoy: A Critical Introduction* (Cambridge: Cambridge University Press, 1969), 27–29; Boris Eikhenbaum, *The Young Tolstoi* (Ann Arbor, Mich.: Ardis, 1972), 58–59; and Philip Rogers, "A Tolstoian Reading of *David Copperfield*," *Comparative Literature* 30 (1990): 1– 28. Eikhenbaum sees only a limited influence of Dickens on Tolstoy: "It is characteristic that [Tolstoy] assimilates Dickens only in that area which assimilates him with Sterne, i.e., in the elaboration of details, the consistent miniaturism of description" (*The Young Tolstoi*, 51); "In Dickens . . . Tolstoi feels the tradition of the English "domestic" (*semeinyi*) novel and evidently assimilates this, and not other elements of Dickens' creation" (29–30). See also Popova's comparison of the role of memory in the two writers (P. Popova, "Stil' rannikh povestei Tolstogo," in *Literaturnoe nasledstvo 35–36* [Moscow: Izdatel'stvo akademii nauk, 1939], 85–87). Useful general accounts of Dickens's influence on all stages of Tolstoy's development are those of Michael H. Futrell, "Dickens and Three Russian Novelists: Gogol', Dostoyevsky, Tolstoy," unpub. Ph.D. dissertation, University of London, 1955, and T. K. Naumenko, "Charl'z Dikkens v vospriiatii L. N. Tolstogo," *Nauchnye trudy novosibirskogo gos. ped. instituta* 65 (1971): 232–50.

16. I. M. Ivakin, "Zapiski," in *Literaturnoe nasledstvo* (Moscow: Izdatel'stvo akademii nauk, 1939), 2:76.

17. L. N. Tolstoi, "Ch. Dikkens rozhdestvenskaia skazka," in *Tolstoi redaktor*, ed. I. A. Pokrovskii (Moscow: Kniga, 1965).

18. Waddington notes that Turgenev often made similar allusions: "The extent to which Dickens crept beneath his skin is shown by his use of the term 'Micawber' to describe emotionally – or financially – unstable colleagues, or by the fact that in advising one young writer on the choice of heroes' names as titles the first example to enter his head was that of Oliver Twist" (*Turgenev and England*, 76).

19. Tolstoy's Irish setter was named after Dora (David's pet). Another of the family dogs was named for Boffin of *Our Mutual Friend* (S. L. Tolstoi, *Tolstoi Remembered*, 73).

20. L. N. Tolstoi, "Perepiska Tolstogo s N. M. Romanovym," *Literaturnoe nasledstro 37–38* (Moscow: Izdatel'stvo akademii nauk, 1939), 305–6. Tolstoy incorrectly remembered Doyce as a character from *Hard Times*. Doyce's earnest commitment to creative striving appears to have impressed Tolstoy, who assumes (probably correctly) that Doyce speaks for Dickens: "Dickens said a very clever thing," he remarked to Gor'kii: "'Life is given to us on the definite understanding that we boldly defend it to the last'" (A. M. Gor'kii, "Lev Tolstoi," in *L. N. Tolstoi v vospominaniiakh sovremennikov*, 2 vols. [Moscow: GIKhL, 1978], 2:477). Doyce's words were these: "You hold your life on the condition that to the last you shall struggle hard for it" (16:176).

21. F. R. Leavis, *D. H. Lawrence, Novelist* (New York: Simon and Schuster, 1955), 297–98.

22. The most useful discussions of Dickens's influence on the major novels are those of F. R. Leavis, *D. H. Lawrence, Novelist* (New York: Simon and Schuster, 1955); Q. D. Leavis, "Dickens and Tolstoy: The Case for a Serious View of *David Copperfield*," in *Dickens the Novelist* (London: Chatto and Windus, 1970); and Futrell, "Dickens and Three Russian Novelists." See also Tom Cain, "Tolstoy's Use of *David Copperfield*," *Critical Quarterly* 15 (1973): 237–46.

23. Ivakin, "Zapiski," 76.

24. Tolstoy's admiration of Dickens, despite his recommending all the novels for publication in *Posrednik*, was not uncritical. In addition to finding them "boring" in his early reading (a judgment found nowhere in his diary or letters) his complaint that the ending of *Dombey and Son* was artificially conventional (Makovitskii, *U Tolstogo*, 1:208) and the implicit example of his own practice clearly reflect his rejection of the complex Dickens plot with its strained denouements. He also objected to *Martin Chuzzlewit* on less specific grounds: "not a good work – except for one, all bad characters (ibid., 1:366–67).

25. This moment of inspiration appears not to have resulted in writing after all.

26. Ivakin, "Zapiski," 76.

27. R. F. Christian, *Tolstoy's "War and Peace": A Study* (Oxford: Clarendon Press, 1962), 148.

28. Ibid., 149.

29. Ibid., 151.

30. All page references for quotations from Dickens's novels refer to the various volumes of the Oxford Illustrated edition, except references to Tolstoy's personal copies of the novels, which are noted separately.

31. Sergeenko, "Zapisi," 557.

32. Ibid., 540.

33. According to A. E. Gruzinskii's study of the manuscript variants of *The Cossacks*, the vineyard scene of chapter 29 was written sometime between 1855 and 1858 (*PSS*, 6:286–87). Since Tolstoy did not read *Little Dorrit* until the late summer and fall of 1856 (*PSS*, 47:90, 98), the date of composition may perhaps be more precisely limited to between late 1856 and 1858. Turgenev, an avid reader of Dickens (his stylistic criticism notwithstanding), was most likely reading *Little Dorrit* at the same time as Tolstoy, since Tauchnitz issued each of four volumes serially. Their argument probably took place during late 1856 or in February–March 1856, when they were often together in St. Petersburg and Paris. In his discussion of this episode Waddington speculates that Tolstoy may have imitated Dickens's grape harvesting scene, but in *Youth* rather than *The Cossacks:* Dickens would have been "tickled to learn that Tolstoy was supposed to be his imitator, and that scenes like the grape-harvesting in Book II of *Little Dorrit* may well have had some influence on *Youth*" (Waddington, *Turgenev and England*, 138).

34. This quotation is based on Rosemary Edmond's translation (*The Cossacks* [Baltimore: Penguin, 1967]) but has been modified to restore Tolstoy's repetitions and the rhetorical emphasis of the original (*PSS*, 6:109–10). Quotations from Maude's translations of *The Death of Ivan Il'ich*, as revised by Michael Katz, and *War and Peace* have been similarly modified when they conceal Tolstoy's emphasis.

35. L. N. Tolstoi, *The Death of Ivan Ilych*, trans. Michael R. Katz, rev. trans. (New York: Norton, 1991). Hereafter, references to this work will be indicated in the text as *Ivan Ilych* with the page numbers.

36. In this same episode, the Veneering butler, as he pours the wine, is an "Analytical Chemist," a metaphor similar in kind to Anne Pavlovna as a spinning-mill foreman applying oil. Other similarities between the two scenes have been noted briefly by V. Sklovskii, "Roman tain," in *O teorii prozy* (Moscow: Federatsia, 1925), 125; Futrell, "Dickens and Three Russian Novelists," 280–81; and in an extensive analytical discussion by John

Romano, *Dickens and Reality* (New York: Columbia University Press, 1978), 8–47.

37. Similar instances abound: for example, ten repetitions of "there was" in introducing the guests at the Meagles's dinner party in *Little Dorrit* (34:377–79) and the last paragraph of the novel, which repeats "went down" as the introductory verb of five successive sentences.

38. The vacillations conveyed in Tolstoy's rhetoric are also manifested in Ivan's physical motion, as Rimgaila Salys explains in "Signs on the Road of Life: *The Death of Ivan Il'ich,*" *Slavic and East European Journal* 30 (1986): 18–28.

39. "Could Caius really" is an attempt to convey Tolstoy's insistent repetition of "*razve Kaia*" (*PSS*, 26:93), which is attenuated with synonyms in the Maude-Katz translation.

40. Philip Collins, ed., *Charles Dickens: The Public Readings* (Oxford: Oxford University Press, 1947–58), 1.

41. In his extensive analysis of temporality in *Ivan Il'ich*, William V. Spanos notes that "the temporal movement of the *'Death of Ivan Illych'* is integrally related to the degrees of Ivan's consciousness of death" ("Leo Tolstoy's *The Death of Ivan Illych*: A Temporal Interpretation," in *Restructuring the Novel: Essays in Applied Hermeneutics*, ed. Leonard Orr [Troy, N.Y.: Williston, 1982], 9).

42. Edgar Johnson, *Charles Dickens: His Tragedy and Triumph*, 2 vols. (New York: Simon and Schuster, 1952), 1:485.

43. Ivakin, "Zapiski," 76.

44. See Rogers, "A Tolstoyan Reading," 8–10.

45. The rhetoric of the passage is also a noteworthy example of Dickensian repetition: "Come night, come darkness" (and three more "comes").

46. E. Wasiolek, *Tolstoy's Major Fiction* (Chicago: University of Chicago Press, 1978), 169.

47. L. N. Tolstoi, "C. Dikkens rozdestvenskaia skazka," 226. This is Tolstoy's emendation of the Rytsen translation.

48. Ivakin, "Zapiski," 76.

49. Tolstoy underlined first with fingernail pressure, later with pencil, this passage in his copy of the Russian translation of Dickens's *Kholodnii Dom: Roman* (*Sovremennik* 92–94 [1854], 92:188).

50. Ivakin, "Zapiski," 76.

51. Dickens, *Kholodnyi Dom*, 92:153.

52. Ibid., 92:190–93.

53. Unlike Sir Leicester's paralysis, Ivan's is manifested not in an inability to move but, as Rimgaila Salys has shown ("Signs on the Road of Life," 25), in the progressive constriction of the space in which he seeks to move, culminating in the black sack. In *Bleak House* a further extension of the paralysis motif is seen in Smallweed's immobility (*Bleak House*, chap. 21); here again Trooper George's robust and innocent vulnerability is juxtaposed with malevolent power-in-paralysis. Another of Dickens's powerful and harmful paralytics is Mrs. Clennam of *Little Dorrit*.

54. He also underlined the entire paragraph beginning, "If there be any who have never known the blank that follows death" (72:545). Tolstoy's copy was in *Master Humphrey's Clock* (Dickens's periodical in which *The Old Curiosity Shop* and *Barnaby Rudge* were first published); the underlined paragraph is 1:278. In this original format, *The Old Curiosity Shop* is narrated by Master Humphrey. In Dickens's revised edition of the novel, Master Humphrey's frame narratives were separated from *Curiosity Shop* and published as *Master Humphrey's Clock*.

55. The conception of the afterlife implicit in Dickens's "Truth" is one of good deeds performed by the bereaved: the virtues, "bright creations" of the living (not Little Nell) are what "spring up" from the grave and "walk the earth." While this idea is not stressed in *The Death of Ivan Il'ich*, it is clearly analogous to Tolstoy's view of the afterlife set forth in *On Life*, chap. 31: "On the life of dead people not ceasing in the world" (*PSS*, 26:411–16). Dickens's heterodox view of the afterlife was criticized at the time. *The Christian Remembrancer* (December 1842), for example, was not taken in by Dickens's capitalized "Heaven," and complained that in the treatment of Nell's death, "not a single Christian feature is introduced."

56. For a full discussion of this passage and the importance of the death and brotherhood theme in Dickens's development, see Rogers, "The Dynamics of Time," *Nineteenth-Century Fiction* 28 (1973): 130–33, 142–43.

57. Wasiolek, *Tolstoy's Major Fiction*, 179.

58. In his public readings of *A Christmas Carol* Dickens raised his brows significantly when he came to this line (Collins, *Charles Dickens*, 7).

59. Gor'kii, "Lev Tolstoi," 2:477.

60. Sergeenko, "Zapisi," 557.

61. Tolstoi, "C. Dikkens rozdestvenskaia skazka," 226.

III  PRIMARY SOURCES

Annotations to the Text

These annotations are intended to offer explanation and discussion of passages in the novel that the editor considers either likely to be unfamiliar to the modern reader or particularly significant to understanding the themes, style, and structure of the work. The selection of passages for the latter kind of annotation, of course, is heavily dependent on the editor's own understanding and interpretation of the text. For a detailed exposition of that particular manner of approaching the text of the novel, the interested reader is referred to Gary R. Jahn, *The Death of Ivan Ilich: An Interpretation* (New York: Twayne, 1993).

The annotations provided here are linked to the text of *The Death of Ivan Ilich* as published in *Tolstoy's Short Fiction*, ed. M. Katz (New York: Norton, 1991), 123–67.

PAGE 123
"The Death of Ivan Ilych"

The Ivan Il'ich mentioned in the title is Ivan Il'ich Golovin, the novel's protagonist. Tolstoy modeled this character in part on a certain Ivan Il'ich Mechnikov, an acquaintance of his who served as prosecutor in the district court of Tula, the nearest sizable town to Tolstoy's country estate at Yasnaya Polyana. According to N. F. Golubov's commentary on *The Death of Ivan Il'ich* in volume 26 of *Complete Collected Works of Lev Tolstoi in 90 Volumes*, the circumstances attending Mechnikov's illness and untimely death in 1881 closely resembled those described by Tolstoy in the story. Shortly after Mechnikov's demise in July 1881, Tolstoy made his first recorded mention of the idea that he eventually developed into *The Death of Ivan Il'ich*.

Chapter 1

"During an interval in the Melvinsky trial"

The Melvinsky case was a celebrated court case of the 1880s.

"the members and public prosecutor"

In the 1880s both civil and criminal cases were often heard by a panel of three judges before whom matters were argued by opposing counsel. The "members" of the court were these judges. Ivan Il'ich, whose death is about to come to the attention of these gentlemen, was such a judge.

"the celebrated Krasovsky case"

The Krasovsky case was another well-known trial of the 1880s. Evidently Tolstoy is at pains to connect his narrative to the authentic realities of life in the period described.

"it was not subject to their jurisdiction"

The motifs of judge, judgment, and jurisdiction (the right or responsibility of rendering judgment) emerge immediately, frequently, and forcefully in the story. It seems clear that the theme of judgment will be important; it may be that we as readers will ourselves be implicated in the responsibility of rendering judgment on the life and death of Ivan Il'ich.

"Peter Ivanovich, not having entered into the discussion at the start, took no part in it"

Peter Ivanovich takes no part in the discussion concerning judgment here. He continues steadfast through chapter 1 (after which he more or less disappears from the novel) in his refusal to "get involved." He is concerned only to perform the superficial rituals required by the death of his colleague and then to leave the entire unpleasant situation behind him in order to spend the remainder of his evening playing cards.

"*The Gazette*"

The Gazette (*Vedomosti*) was the name shared by prominent daily newspapers in both St. Petersburg and Moscow. Most commentators believe that Tolstoy had Moscow in mind as the setting of the novel.

"Surrounded by a black border"

This is the first of many examples of images of enclosure and containment in the text of the novel. These images become a veritable leitmotiv of isolation and estrangement over the course of the story.

"Praskovya Fedorovna Golovina, with profound sorrow, informs relatives and friends of the demise of her beloved husband Ivan Ilych Golovin, Member of the Court of Justice, which occurred on February the 4th of this year 1882. The funeral will take place on Friday at one o'clock in the afternoon."

The text of the funeral announcement is typical in its formality and its use of prescribed clichés. We will soon learn, for instance, that it has in fact been many years since Praskovya Fedorovna regarded her husband as "beloved." Later on, in chapter 2, it will be said of Ivan Il'ich that one of his great strengths as an official of the court was his ability to reduce even the most complex of legal matters to a one-page summary executed in the proper form. In a manner of speaking, the funeral announcement is done in just this way.

"Ivan Ilych had been a colleague of the gentlemen present and was liked by them all."

Ivan Il'ich is a good man who is liked by all his coworkers. This motif is taken up again at the beginning of chapter 2; his story is that of an ordinary man. Neither villain nor hero, Ivan Il'ich is just such a pleasant and likable fellow as we would all prefer to have around us.

"He had been ill for several weeks with an illness said to be incurable."

The irony, of course, is that what Ivan Il'ich suffered from most was, in fact, incurable by medical means. His spiritual malaise is much more painful to him than his physical disease. The novel concludes, however, on the hopeful note that this spiritual illness can be alleviated.

"His post had been kept open for him,"

The Russian text says, literally, that "his place remained behind him." His friends' conversation will soon make it clear that, pleasant fellow though he was, his vacant place in the official world is much more important than the person who has died. There is also the clear suggestion that a person's place or position is of considerably more importance than the person himself.

"Now I must apply for my brother-in-law's transfer from Kaluga,"

Kaluga is a provincial city. Just as Ivan Il'ich's final promotion had brought him, at last, from the provinces to the capital, so here Peter Ivanovich can imagine no happier and more desirable fate for his brother-in-law.

PAGE 124
"I thought he would never leave his bed again"

The Russian text says, literally, "he wouldn't raise himself up," a somewhat peculiar way to indicate that a sick person won't recover. It may, however, serve to suggest the notion of the raising of the dead by a miracle of the spirit. So, for example, in scripture Jesus "raised" Lazarus from the dead. That Ivan Il'ich in the end did succeed in "raising himself" seems to be suggested in the last chapter of the novel.

"The doctors couldn't say – at least they could, but each of them said something different."

This is the first example of the novel's satirical attitude toward physicians. Doctors and other professionals (Ivan Il'ich's colleagues, Ivan himself) are all shown in the novel as concerned exclusively with forms or phenomena rather than with the individuals who appear before them. Of Ivan Il'ich it will be said that his great talent as an official is his ability to reduce even the most complex individual case into a properly executed one-page form.

"When last I saw him I thought he was getting better."

Here is another example of a revealing choice of words. The Russian for "was getting better" is, literally, "would right himself, would correct himself." As in the remark about "raising himself" this colloquial and metaphorical expression seems to contain a hidden, literal meaning. In the end, Ivan Il'ich does seem to "right himself" before he dies. Given the novel's eventual outcome, these examples suggest that Tolstoy is telling two stories here: one about the physical illness and death of Ivan Il'ich, the other about the spiritual condition of the protagonist. These two stories are related in that the second is, so to say, told through the first. Phrases that superficially refer to the first narrative are often also very important for the second.

"Everything's far away from your place."

The separation among people, the emotional distance separating them, is a prominent motif in the development of the novel. In a sense, the story of Ivan Il'ich's life is a history of his increasing and self-imposed isolation from those close to him.

"Then, still talking of the distances between different parts of the city, they returned to the Court."

The very serious topic of the death of a valued colleague is replaced by trivialities. The colleagues of Ivan Il'ich, like all of us, are unwilling to deal with the fact of death. They deny it, avoid it, eventually flee from it. Note that this process is reflected in detail in the behavior of Peter Ivanovich as he goes to pay a condolence call on Ivan Il'ich's widow. He wishes he could avoid it, he seeks to minimize his connection with the body of his dead friend, and he leaves the proceedings with unseemly haste so as to be able to join a game of cards in progress.

"Besides considerations as to possible transfers and promotions likely to result from Ivan Ilych's death, the mere fact of the death of a near acquaintance aroused, as usual, in all who heard of it the complacent feeling that, 'it's he who is dead and not I.'"

The thought "it's he who is dead and not I" is symptomatic of the belief in the separability of people from one another. We have already learned that the characters mentioned so far live far away from one another, and this passage is another example of the same idea: that other people, unpleasant occurrences, distressing situations can be kept at a distance, that each individual has a separate fate that can be controlled simply by avoiding all perceived threats. We will see Ivan Il'ich again and again putting this distance between himself and various forms of unpleasantness. It will turn out, however, that this distancing carries with it the necessary consequence of closing the individual off from contact with others. Thus it is that two primary sets of images in the novel – pertaining to distance and enclosure – are causally related to each other.

"his so-called friends"

"So-called," of course, because they seem to lack any concern at all for Ivan Il'ich as an individual person. Their interest in him is, one might say, functional; he is a coworker, a husband, a father, a deceased acquaintance whose funeral must be attended.

"demands of propriety"

The Russian words for "propriety" (*prilichie*); "appropriate, fitting" (*prilichno*); and "pleasant" (*priiatno*) play a very important role in the novel's description of the life of Ivan Il'ich. They function as a sort of verbal leitmotiv of his life and the life of those around him. They suggest a life ruled by adherence to a known set of standards. One gets an image of the individual comfortably surrounded by well-marked boundaries of behavior within which the individual may be confident of a pleasant and well-regulated existence. In this way the ideal life of propriety may be seen as an instance of the images of enclosure and distance. We already know that the end of such a life is the enclosure of the coffin and the distance the living seek to put between themselves and the deceased.

"a coffin-lid"; "two ladies in black"; "his colleague Schwartz"

Peter Ivanovich's arrival at the home of Ivan Il'ich is marked by rather obvious reminders of the fact that Ivan Il'ich has died: the coffin lid leaning against the wall in the foyer, the black clothing worn by two ladies who have just arrived. Also present is a character with a prominent role in chapter 1, Schwartz, whose name (in German) means "black." Thus, from one point of view, Schwartz is just one *memento mori* among several presented here.

"He winked, as though to say 'Ivan Ilych has made a mess of things – not like you and me.' Schwartz's face with his Piccadilly whiskers, and his slim figure in evening dress, as usual had an air of elegant solemnity which contrasted with the playfulness of his character and had a special piquancy here (or so it seemed to Peter Ivanovich)."

On the other hand, Schwartz is clearly presented as being somehow above and impervious to the death of Ivan Il'ich: he winks; he seems to say that Ivan Il'ich died because of his own foolishness, that Schwartz and Peter Ivanovich will not die; he has a playful character. At the same time his clothing, like his name, is all black, and his manner is superficially solemn. In short, Schwartz is a puzzle. In what follows he will be directly and significantly compared to the dead Ivan Il'ich.

PAGE 125

"where they should play bridge that evening."

Actually, Peter Ivanovich is interested in playing a card game of French origin called *vint*, which much resembles the modern game of bridge. Card playing will be a major motif in the novel. It functions throughout as a symbol of a life of propriety. We will find that as Ivan Il'ich grows older he values card playing as an activity ever more. There is often an opposition, as here, between playing cards as an attractive, pleasant activity on one side and the harsh realities of life, the funeral, an illness, on the other.

"The butler's assistant,"

This is the first mention of a character who will play an increasingly important role in the story later on. Gerasim often expresses ideas and sentiments that the other characters in the story would find unpalatable. At the end of chapter 1, for example, Gerasim reminds Peter Ivanovich that "we will all come to it one day" when asked about his feeling concerning the death of Ivan Il'ich. In Russian, Gerasim is identified as a *"bufetnyi muzhik,"* thereby linking him closely to the Russian peasant (*muzhik*), even though he is working in an urban, domestic situation.

"The expression on the face said that what was necessary had been accomplished, and accomplished rightly. Besides this there was in that expression a reproach and a warning to the living. This warning seemed out of place to Peter Ivanovich, or at least not applicable to him. He felt a certain discomfort and so he hurriedly crossed himself once more, turned and went out the door – too hurriedly and regardless of propriety, as he himself was aware."

Here we see a distinct contrast between the solemnity and certainty manifested by the face of the dead Ivan Il'ich, the hesitation shown by Peter Ivanovich, and the playfulness displayed by Schwartz. As if to highlight this contrast, the retreating Peter Ivanovich is, on leaving the room where Ivan Il'ich lies, immediately presented with the restorative sight of Schwartz. "The mere sight of that playful, well-groomed, and elegant figure restored Peter Ivanovich. He felt that Schwartz stood above all these happenings and would not surrender to any depressing influences. His very look said that this incident of a church service for Ivan Ilych could not be a sufficient reason for infringing the order of the session – in other words, that it would certainly not prevent his unwrapping a new pack of cards and shuffling them that evening while a footman placed four fresh candles on the table" (126).

PAGE 126

"a low pouffe, the springs of which yielded spasmodically under his weight."

In the extended scene between Peter Ivanovich and Praskovya Fyodorovna (Ivan Il'ich's widow) we see many further indications of the artificiality of the relationships among these characters. Another interesting motif is the uncommonly important role that material objects play in the scene. The "spasmodic springs of the *pouffe*" are mentioned several times as disturbing the ritual of the condolence visit. Later on, there is further awkwardness when Praskovya Fyodorovna catches her shawl on an elaborately carved table edge. A direct connection is made between Ivan Il'ich and the objects in this room. Still later we discover that the illness that killed him seemed to have stemmed from a fall he had while attempting to show the draper exactly how he wanted the curtains to be hung. Much in the manner of the games they play, the objects with which these characters surround themselves seem to have an unusual significance in their lives.

PAGE 127

"While lighting his cigarette Peter Ivanovich heard her inquiring very circumstantially into the prices of different plots in the cemetery and finally decide which one she would take."

The widow's evident clear-headedness in this discussion belies her claim that she is devastated by the death of her spouse. She is also not so distracted by grief that when "noticing that the table was endangered by his cigarette ash, she immediately passed him an ashtray."

"For the last three days he screamed incessantly. It was unendurable. I cannot understand how I stood it; you could hear him three rooms away. Oh, what I have suffered!"

Even the widow's description of her dead husband's final hours is given from her own point of view; her concern is with how much she suffered, with what the effect was on her of her spouse's passing away. The Russian for "three rooms away" is, literally, "behind three doors," which suggests that the widow follows the same practice as Peter Ivanovich and her deceased husband in dealing with unpleasantness: she tries to shut herself off from it by "slamming the door" on it.

PAGE 128

"The thought of the suffering of this man whom he had known so intimately, first as a cheerful little boy, then as a schoolmate, and later as a grown-up colleague, suddenly struck Peter Ivanovich with horror, despite an unpleasant consciousness of his own and this woman's dissimulation. He saw that brow again, and that nose pressing down on the lip, and he felt afraid for himself."

Despite the manner of the widow's description of the death of Ivan Il'ich, Peter Ivanovich is touched by it, takes it to heart. He thinks again of the dead face of Ivan Il'ich, and of its apparent message to the living. But he feels immediately comforted by the thought that such suffering and death "should not and could not happen to him, and that to think that it could would be yielding to depression which he ought not to do, as Schwartz's expression plainly showed." Thus again the image of the playful Schwartz is juxtaposed to that of Ivan Il'ich. Later on, Peter Ivanovich will resolve the conflicted state of his feelings by not looking at "the dead man once, [not yielding] to any depressing influence, and [being] one of the first to leave the room" (129). In this way Peter Ivanovich, a judge, seems to refuse to accept jurisdiction over the situation that has arisen following the death of Ivan Il'ich. He would rather make a hasty departure from the situation, observing the minimum propriety required. His flight leaves us as readers, who have accompanied Peter Ivanovich so far, on our own in the midst of the story. Ivan Il'ich's dead face had also held a message for us, and it has become our task to continue to interpret that message, even without the company of Peter Ivanovich.

Chapter 2

"Ivan Ilych's life had been most simple and most ordinary and therefore most terrible."

Thus begins the second chapter of the novel, with one of the most famous lines in Russian literature. A more literal translation of the Russian would be "The past history of the life of Ivan Il'ich was most simple and ordinary, and most terrible." In the paragraphs that follow, the text is at pains to show that Ivan Il'ich was an average, ordinary sort of person. He is middle-aged at his death, the middle son of three, an average family man with a medium-sized family and an entirely normal career.

PAGE 130
"Ivan Ilych was *le phenix de la famille* as people said."

Here is the first of several foreign-language expressions that occur in the text of the novel, many of which contain particular significance. This one normally means "the member of the family most likely to succeed," but it contains a reference to the phoenix, a mythological bird that was periodically reborn from the ashes of its own destruction. The paper by Professor Salys, included in this volume, offers a complete and convincing discussion of these phrases and their role in the text of the novel. It is interesting to note that some lines below the reference to the phoenix we read: "from early youth he was by nature attracted to people of high station as a fly is drawn to the light, assimilating their ways and views of life and establishing friendly relations with them." In the original this sentence contains a pun on the Russian word *svet* (light, world of high society). We might translate as follows: "he was, like a fly to the light (*svet*), drawn to the people most highly placed in society (*svet*)." In Tolstoy's day, of course, the "light" to which flies were drawn was the light of a burning flame in which the insect is immolated. It is suggested that this flame is society itself, which will burn up Ivan Il'ich, but that, like the phoenix, Ivan Il'ich will somehow transcend this fiery end.

"respice finem"

A Latin motto meaning "pay attention to the end, focus on the outcome." A good motto for a future lawyer but, like the reference to the phoenix, capable of being read in more than one way.

PAGE 131
"schismatics,"

Religious dissenters (sectarians) who represented special legal problems in the Russian Empire because the Russian Orthodox Church was the officially established national church. Thus religious differences could often lead to legal disputes or prosecutions.

"bon enfant"

French for "a good fellow, a nice guy" (literally, "a good child").

"French saying: *il faut que jeunesse se passe*."

The French excuse for "sowing wild oats"; many actions that might be thought of as shameful become permissible when they are felt to be appropriate to a particular age group or class of people. So here, as long as Ivan Il'ich's behavior remains within the established limits, his life seems to others and to himself to be completely *comme il faut* (French for "as it ought to be"). This latter French phrase has a long history in Tolstoy. Already in the 1850s he had used it to describe characters whose sincere and conscious goal was the achievement of a life of perfect conformity with the lives of the "best people in society." In this same passage it is twice repeated that Ivan Il'ich's behavior was always "pleasant" and "appropriate," and that he was "good-hearted," "witty," and "playful." All these adjectives, but particularly the last, draw our attention to the similarity between Ivan Il'ich as a young man and the character of Schwartz, the paradoxical symbol of blackness and death in chapter 1. Thus again the text suggests that the life of Ivan Il'ich, even at its liveliest, is better seen as a form of death.

"The new and reformed judicial institutions were introduced, and new men were needed. Ivan Ilych became such a new man."

The 1860s saw the institution of major governmental reforms in Russia. The most celebrated of these was the freeing of the serfs from their legal bondage in 1861. Among the most far-reaching (and the most needed) of the reforms was that which attempted to remodel the Russian judicial system, long marked by incompetence and venality. Ivan Il'ich's ability to conform himself to the properties and expectations of this new system is the secret to his continuing career success. He now begins a steady rise in the service of several years' duration.

PAGE 132

"In his work itself, especially in his examinations, he soon acquired a method of eliminating [in Russian, *priem otstraneniia ot sebia*; a device of estranging himself from] all considerations irrelevant to the legal aspect of the case, and reducing even the most complicated case to a form in which it would be presented on paper only in its externals, completely excluding his personal opinion of the matter, while above all observing every prescribed formality."

It is interesting to note that Ivan Il'ich's secret of success in his official career resembles the attitude his "friends" bring to the "prescribed formalities" of attending his funeral. Peter Ivanovich, indeed, does a remarkable job of estranging himself from the unpleasant sensations aroused by his feelings of personal connection with his deceased mentor and of the personal relevance that Ivan Il'ich's countenance and expression seemed to hold for him. Later on, the doctors whom Ivan Il'ich consults as his illness progresses will treat him very much as he treats those who come before him in court.

"And he began to play *vint*, which he found added considerably to the pleasure of life."

Like Peter Ivanovich and Schwartz in chapter 1, Ivan Il'ich becomes a devotee of card playing. The skills required to play bridge are similar to those that bring him success in his career: his good humor, his ability to calculate quickly and astutely, his knowledge of the rules of the game and the proper forms of play. The thrust here is to connect his "life" with his "official life" and to reduce both to triviality by suggesting that both involve little more than the artificial conventions of a game of cards.

PAGE 133
"The preparations for [in Russian, "process" or "process of"] marriage and the beginning of married life, with its conjugal caresses, new furniture, new crockery, and new linen were very pleasant until his wife became pregnant."

Ivan Il'ich's relationship with his wife, entered into more because it was a suitable and appropriate match than because he loved her, is portrayed as satisfactory and even pleasant as long as it involves only such material considerations as sexual relations, furniture, dishes, and tablecloths. It is disrupted, however, and becomes unpleasant when Praskovya Fyodorovna becomes pregnant, that is, when a new life enters into the situation. Thus marriage, too, as Ivan Il'ich wishes it to be, is suggested to be a form of death in which there is no place for life. By now it has already become clear that the story of the life of Ivan Il'ich is really the story of his steady approach toward death. In the midst of his successful "life," real life is already a devastating threat. Later in this same passage the pregnancy is said to introduce something "new, unexpected, unpleasant, depressing (*tiazheloe*; "heavy," "serious"), and unseemly" that came into his life, "from which there was no way to escape." All these adjectives apply equally well to the illness from which Ivan Il'ich will soon begin to suffer. This is especially true of the adjective *tiazheloe*, which is part of a familiar and standard expression when applied to disease (*tiazhelaja bolezn'*). In the same way that pregnancy seems to be an intimation of Ivan Il'ich's illness, so too does Praskovya Fyodorovna's behavior while pregnant prefigure that of her husband after he has become ill. Thus the displays of unseemliness and unpleasantness, the unreasonableness, the vulgar scenes that will mark Ivan Il'ich's behavior later on are all prefigured here in the behavior of his pregnant wife. One must conclude, it seems, that just as there is a relationship between Ivan Il'ich's official and personal life and the symbols of death, so too is there a relationship between the illness which leads to the end of that "life" and the genuine new life stirring within Praskovya Fyodorovna's womb.

"*de gaieté de coeur*"

A French phrase meaning "out of sheer wantonness" or, more vulgarly, "for the hell of it." Literally, the phrase means "from gaiety of heart" and, consequently, seems to suggest the possibility that Praskovya Fyodorovna's pregnancy and its attendant symptoms, since they represent new life, should rather be a cause of happiness than of irritation.

PAGE 134

". . . and that he must therefore entrench himself against such in-fringement. . . . His official duties were the one thing that imposed upon Praskovya Fyodorovna, and by means of his official work and the duties attached to it he began struggling with his wife to secure his own independence."

Having discovered that the pleasantness and propriety of his life has been badly injured by the behavior of his pregnant wife, Ivan Il'ich first tries to ignore her outbursts and demands; but when this fails he withdraws into his work in order to protect his "independence." Thus he turns away from his family life to the still more artificial world of his life at work. Maude's translation here does not capture the organizing metaphor of this passage. Where Maude says "entrench himself" the Russian has "barricade himself" (*ogradit' sebia*), and where Maude translates "secure his own independence" Tolstoy's text has "fence off his own independent world" (*vygorazhivaia svoi nezavisimyi mir*). Thus the Russian text suggests the motif of *voluntary* separation by walls or barriers, a process of self-enclosure, which is similar to the image created by the heavy black border of the funeral announcement and the framing edge of Ivan Il'ich's coffin in chapter 1. Some lines below the Maude translation does finally make the connection with "if he met with antagonism and querulousness he retired at once into his *separate fenced-off* (*otdel'nyi vygorozhennyi im*) world of official duties" (italics added). Even here, though, the translation refers to "his fenced-off world" whereas the Russian has "the world fenced off by him," which makes Ivan Il'ich responsible for the deliberate act of closing himself off from that which irritates him. Thus it is that in his desire to escape from the unpleasantness and fullness of his personal life he more and more embraces the relative emptiness and artificiality of his official life.

"the attitude Ivan Il'ich had adopted towards his home life rendered him almost impervious to her grumbling."

The image of being surrounded by solid walls is picked up yet again in the use of the word *impervious*. In Russian the word used is *nepronicaemyi* (impenetrable).

PAGE 135

"when obliged to be at home he tried to safeguard his position by the presence of outsiders."

Making the point yet again, Tolstoy's Russian uses the phrase "*postoronnie lica*" (literally, persons ranged along the sides, rather than in the center) to suggest once more the image of Ivan Il'ich surrounded by a protective screen. Ivan Il'ich thinks always to fence the offending behavior out, never realizing that he is also, necessarily, fencing himself in. The completeness of his isolation in his official life is mainly missed by Maude's "The whole interest of his life now centered in the official world and that *interest absorbed him*" (italics added) but is vividly suggested by Tolstoy's use of the idiomatic expression "And that *interest swallowed him*" (italics added), which Tolstoy offers as a separate, brief, and powerful sentence.

Chapter 3

". . . when an unanticipated and unpleasant occurrence quite upset the peaceful course of his life."

The unpleasant event mentioned here is Ivan Il'ich's being passed over for an expected promotion. Since the event is "unpleasant" it has no place in Ivan Il'ich's "pleasant" life and strikes him, a few lines later, as being most unjust. This unpleasant occurrence may be seen as one of several warnings Ivan Il'ich receives in the story that his "pleasant" and "seemly" and "well-ordered" life is at odds with the real life that surrounds it. In short, Ivan Il'ich's skillfully arranged pleasant life may be just as artificial as his clever one-page summaries of the complex matters that come before him in court. Real life has intervened once before, in Praskovya Fyodorovna's changed behavior when pregnant, and now even his official life (into which he had fled to escape Praskovya Fyodorovna's bad behavior) is disrupted by this failure to provide him with the promotion he believes he has earned. As before, so now, Ivan Il'ich will react to this unpleasantness by attempting to isolate himself from it, by leaving it behind and quitting his post in the Ministry of Justice. On this occasion, however, he is saved by a lucky change in the higher administration of his department. That these disruptions (later [137] referred to as "stumbles") in the pleasant flow of his life may be seen as warnings seems rather clear from a passage some paragraphs·later in which Ivan Il'ich thinks that "it was impossible to go on living this way" (136). The Russian text has the phrase *"tak zhit' nel'zia"* which may be understood to mean either that living so is "not possible" or "not permitted." The final indication that Ivan Il'ich's life works neither as he imagines it nor as he would prefer it to work is the onset of his illness, which arises from a "stumble" from a step stool (138). In the end it is his sickness which finally convinces him that his life, as he had arranged it and lived it, was false and artificial; as Tolstoy writes, was not "the real thing."

PAGE 138

"It's a good thing I'm a bit of an athlete. Another man might have been killed."

The Russian here says, literally, "I am not an athlete for nothing. Another would have killed himself [*ubilsia*]." This is a powerful indicator, once the principle of seeing the literal in the metaphorical in this story is understood, that Ivan Il'ich himself is responsible for the condition in which he will find himself. In lavishing all his attention on the pleasant and proper arrangement of his new apartment, in behaving as though his new apartment were the center and essence of his life, he has actually been killing himself. In this way, apparently casual expressions (remember here the phrase that his life "swallowed" him [135]) point the way to a method of reading the text in which the apparent and actual are at odds with each other. We begin to see metaphors as exact descriptions; we begin to understand that what seems to be a most pleasant life is actually a kind of death; we understand that apparent disasters (his wife's behavioral change in pregnancy; being passed over for promotion) are actually timely warnings of possible rescue (the advent of new life; a chance to come out of the official shell the service has created for him). At a certain point the logic becomes quite inescapable: his illness is not the cause of his death but rather the mechanism that returns him to life.

Perhaps the most direct verbal reminder of this conflation of opposites starts at the end of chapter 3 and recurs throughout the final four chapters of the novel. The last paragraph of chapter 3 begins: "Thus they lived, and all went well" (141). This is Maude's rendering of a Russian text that reads, literally: "So [*tak*] they lived. And everything went along so [*tak*]," so that Ivan Il'ich's life is identified as "just so" [*tak*]. In the last four chapters of the novel the thought that, strange as it seems, his life had been lived "wrongly" (as Maude translates it) occurs several times to Ivan Il'ich. An exact translation of these passages would be that "he lived not so [*ne tak*]" with the result that his life, which had been thought to be "just so," turns out to have been its binary opposite ("not just so") instead.

PAGE 139
". . . capacity to separate his real life from the official side of affairs and not mix the two"

Even at moments when Ivan Il'ich's life has in fact become the pleasant and easy thing he wants it to be, we are reminded that this life is not his real life. We understand the text to be referring to the distinction between Ivan Il'ich's life at home and his life at the office, but since we know that his home life is no less artificial than his office life we are struck by this oblique reminder that there is, beyond both these artificial, surrogate lives, a real life that is uniformly ignored.

Chapter 4

PAGE 141
". . . it could not be called ill health if Ivan Il'ich said that he sometimes had a queer taste in his mouth . . ." and following.

The first few paragraphs of chapter 4 present Ivan Il'ich as experiencing symptoms similar to those exhibited by Praskovya Fyodorovna when she was pregnant: the well-known "morning sickness" in pregnancy is reflected in Ivan Il'ich's difficulties with taking food; the increasing sense of pressure and weight in the abdomen is also common to both experiences. Most striking of all is the common behavioral patterns of the two: the sudden outbursts, the demands, the vulgar scenes. As though to point up these similarities the text reports that Praskovya Fyodorovna asserts that Ivan Il'ich "had always had a dreadful temper, and that it had needed all her good nature to put up with it for twenty years [i.e., since the time of her first pregnancy]. It was true that now their quarrels were started by him [thereby suggesting a comparison with those quarrels of twenty years before which were started by her!]."

". . . not even his death could save her."

This is the first of several phrases and incidents in the novel that can and have been understood as allusions to the story of Jesus' death by crucifixion as reported in the New Testament. This set of motifs in the story is discussed by various scholars, including the present author ("A Note on the Miracle Motifs in the Later Works of Lev Tolstoy," in *The Supernatural in Slavic and Baltic Literatures: Essays in Honor of Victor Terras* [Columbus, Ohio: Slavica, 1988], 191–99). The presence of these allusions in the text is challenging because the miracle of the Resurrection – that people are saved by the death and resurrection of Jesus – was explicitly denied by Tolstoy in his study of the Gospels. I will indicate these allusions as such as the text progresses but leave their interpretation to the reader. Both George Gutsche and Daniel Rancour-Laferriere, each in his own way, discuss the Christian/religious dimension of the novel in detail in articles included in the present volume.

PAGE 142

"There was the usual waiting and the important air assumed by the doctor, with which he was so familiar (resembling that which he himself assumed in court) . . ."

Here we should note the explicit comparison the text offers between the cold and impersonal treatment Ivan Il'ich receives from the doctors and that which he himself accorded to those whom he encountered in his own official capacity. A strict reading of the Russian text would say not that this behavior "resembled" that which he practiced himself but that it was "the very same as that which he knew in himself in court." A few lines later we read: "It was all just as it was in the law courts. The doctors put on just the same air towards him as he himself put on towards an accused person." The text seems so emphatic and unambiguous on this point that the reader must conclude that it is important to recognize that Ivan Il'ich's life has been just as much a sham and just as disconnected from the real life and real concerns of individual people as the doctors' lives are now shown to be.

"It was not a question of Ivan Il'ich's life or death but one between a floating kidney and appendicitis."

The Russian text has it that "there was no question about the life of Ivan Il'ich." The suggestion seems to be that the doctors are not concerned about the life of their patient, but only about the identification of his illness. The distinction between health and disease now asserts itself at the expense of the distinction between life and death. In one sense, then, the novel has two levels of concern. On one level we are offered the story of Ivan Il'ich's progress from health to disease to death; on another level we are dealing with a concern about the proper distinction between life and death. One level invites a three-part structuring of the narrative, the other a two-part structuring.

PAGE 143
". . . Ivan Il'ich still obeyed his [the doctor's] orders implicitly and at first derived some comfort from doing so."

The extensive description of Ivan Il'ich's relationship with his doctor makes it clear that the doctor is quite unequal both to the treatment of his patient's illness and to the meeting of his emotional needs. The text here states that Ivan Il'ich "still" obeyed the doctor's instructions, reminding us of the confusion and apparent incompetence of the doctor and his office described in the preceding paragraph. Even so, Ivan Il'ich attempts to continue to follow doctor's orders, apparently hoping that by going through the "proper channels" the desired result of full recovery might be assured. Thus his first attempts to come to grips with his illness resemble the efforts he made within the system to seek redress when he was, unfairly he thought, passed over for promotion. On that occasion, following the approved procedure had availed him not at all; his recovery of his appropriate (in his view) position in the service came about almost miraculously, through an entirely unexpected and, from Ivan Il'ich's point of view, extremely fortunate change in the leadership of the department. So here, in dealing with his illness, the prescribed, approved measures will fail to produce recovery; before the end, Ivan Il'ich will consider going to a religious shrine to seek a miraculous cure. This second major failure of the artificial system of life to which Ivan Il'ich is dedicated still, however, fails to lead him at once to the obvious conclusion – that his pleasant, seemly, official life is not a real life and offers no help for or protection from the vicissitudes of that real life. At this point Ivan Il'ich can still derive some comfort from the thought that he is doing what he is supposed to do and still hoping that this seemly action within the system will produce the desired results.

"He could do this so long as nothing agitated him."

The Russian text here reads, more exactly, "And he could deceive himself as long as nothing agitated him." Thus it is suggested that all his efforts to recover by taking approved steps within the limits of the life he has developed for himself are just so much self-deception, and the implication of this would naturally be that his life as a whole is just as much a self-deception as his attempts to follow his doctor's orders.

"But as soon as he had any unpleasantness with his wife, any lack of success in his official work, or held bad cards at bridge . . ."

From this passage one might well infer a connection between Ivan Il'ich's illness, the episodes of Praskovya Fyodorovna's first pregnancy, and Ivan's being passed over for promotion at work. All three reveal that Ivan Il'ich's understanding and expectations of life are entirely faulty and not congruent with life as it actually is. Life is actually not analogous to a game of cards, but Ivan Il'ich seems quite unable to understand this!

PAGE 145

"It ought to be jolly and lively. They would make a grand slam. But suddenly Ivan Il'ich was conscious of that gnawing pain, that taste in his mouth, and it seemed ridiculous that in such circumstances he should be pleased to make a grand slam."

This passage emphasizes yet again the point that the card game, the symbol of Ivan Il'ich's life as he has lived it so pleasantly until now, is ridiculously incommensurate with life as it actually is. The further implication is that the pain and the putrid taste in his mouth, the symptoms of his disease, are functioning as symbols of the call away from the false life of the card game and, by implication, toward the true life. In this sense, Ivan Il'ich's illness brings him into life as much as it leads him out of it. This apparent confusion can only be resolved by supposing that the text suggests there are two forms of life – one false, the other true. The card game stands for that false life of pleasant superficiality and the other a true life where suffering and illness are real and personal, but so, too, potentially, are joy and well-being.

Chapter 5

PAGE 147

"Don't you see it? Why, he's a dead man! Look at his eyes – there's no light in them."

The first four chapters of the novel have brought Ivan Il'ich to a point where his illness has developed so far as to be out of control. So serious is the situation that Ivan Il'ich seems already near death. His visiting brother-in-law here states that Ivan Il'ich is already a dead man. This emphasis on the extent to which Ivan's condition has already deteriorated continues throughout chapter 5, and at the end of chapter 6 he even imagines that he sees "death" looking at him from behind some flowers in the sitting room. The reader may well wonder why such emphasis is placed on Ivan's death or his nearness to death or the apparition of death at this point in the novel. After all, there are still six more chapters (half the novel, in terms of chapters) before he will in fact die. Let us note, at least, that Ivan is, in a sense, already pronounced dead in chapters 5 and 6, and that it is therefore possible that the final six chapters will do more than provide further repetition of this motif.

". . . the consciousness that he had put something aside – an important, intimate matter which he would revert to when his work was done – never left him. . . . this intimate matter was the thought of his vermiform appendix."

The text here mentions an "intimate" (*zadushevnyi*, a word derived from the root word *dusha* [soul]) matter, that is, one that pertains to a person's inner, private world rather than the exterior world of daily activities. This is made explicit by emphasizing that Ivan can turn his attention to this matter only when his official duties are completed; thus the two are mutually exclusive. And yet this "matter of the soul" turns out to be no more than giving thought to his appendix (*slepaia kishka* [blind gut]). However Ivan Il'ich may have misconstrued the etymology of the word *intimate*, the fact is that at last, and apparently for the first time in a long time, the conception of an inner life has occurred to him. In chapter 6 he will remind himself that he "lived by his official duties" (150), that he thought his official life was his life. It is perhaps not strange, then, that he thinks his inner life involves no more than the condition of his colon.

Almost at once, though, his pain drives him to the thought that it is "not a question of my appendix or my kidney, but of life . . . and death" (148); and later, on the same page: "I think of mending my appendix, and all the while here comes death!" Thus the ground is prepared for the advent, in chapter 6, of the first mention of an "inner voice," the voice of that life within, a life quite distinct from the life Ivan Il'ich has made for himself.

Chapter 6

PAGE 149
"Ivan Il'ich saw that he was dying."

Chapter 6 continues the motif of imminent death introduced in chapter 5. The chapter is devoted to Ivan's ineluctable recognition of his death and to his unavailing efforts to hide himself from this recognition by erecting various screens (again the motif of self-enclosure) to protect himself from this recognition. "I lost my life over that curtain. . . . It can't be true, but it is" (151). The last sentence of chapter 6, translated literally, says: "Only to look at it [death] and grow cold." Maude's translation offers "except to look at it and shudder." While this is a good translation, it fails to capture the rhetorical force of the original. In the Russian the interior cause of the action ("growing cold") is used to represent the exterior action itself ("shuddering"). In this way the text manages to express simultaneously the ideas (1) that there are two sorts of "life" involved in what is happening to Ivan Il'ich, an inner one and an outer one; and (2) that Ivan Il'ich is, from a certain point of view, already dead and growing cold, in the manner of a corpse.

PAGE 150
"If I had to die like Caius I should have known it. An inner voice would have told me so, but there was nothing of the sort in me."

Here the notion of an "inner voice" and, by extension, an inner life is mentioned in the text for the first time. If we follow the practice of paying exact attention to what is said we see that Ivan Il'ich here seems to admit not only that there was no inner voice in him but also no inner life. In fact, this inner voice will enter the text in chapter 9 and will reappear in each chapter thereafter. At the very end, in chapter 12, Ivan Il'ich will himself seem to become that inner voice and inner life, and to view the agonized, dying remains of his body as though from a distance. At this point in the text (i.e., chapter 6), however, the emphatic point seems to be that there is no such inner voice/inner life within Ivan Il'ich. We might say that he, and we, have discovered, at the end of chapter 6, that he has lost his inner life and that, at the end of chapter 12, he regains it again. From this point of view, the novel again seems to fall naturally into two main parts: in the first, he gradually loses his inner, personal life to his external, official life; and, in the second, through suffering and meditation, he gradually comes to acknowledge that loss and finally to regain his inner life. At the same time, the novel is relating the same series of events from a strictly external viewpoint in which the inner life refers to no more than the kidneys and the intestines. This external story is related in three stages: Ivan Il'ich former life, up to the onset of his illness (chapters 2–4); the development of his illness (chapters 5–8); and his final agony and death (chapters 9–12). We might call the first stage "health"; the second, "illness"; and the third, "death." The first stage involves years; the second, months; and the last, only days and hours.

It seems, then, that just as Ivan Il'ich has two distinct lives – an inner one and an outer one – so, too, can the story of those lives be organized in two different ways at the same time: the external life story according to a three-part division of the material (health, illness, death) and the inner life story according to a two-part division. The two-part division shows us an Ivan Il'ich who is already inwardly dead at the midpoint of the story, and another Ivan Il'ich who has regained his inner life at the end.

Chapter 7

PAGE 151

"the whole interest he had for other people was whether he would soon vacate his place, and at last release the living from the discomfort caused by his presence and be released himself from his sufferings."

Thus chapter 7 begins by reemphasizing the conclusion which, as noted above, emerges from chapter 6, namely, that Ivan Il'ich is already as good as dead, indeed that he is essentially dead and is only awaiting formal removal from the scene.

PAGE 152

"But it was just through this most unpleasant matter that Ivan Il'ich obtained some comfort."

No sooner does the text make it clear that Ivan Il'ich is virtually dead already, and so beyond help or comfort, than it presents the first of several consolations and remissions of his agony. The servant Gerasim, a young, healthy, and energetic figure, is assigned to assist Ivan Il'ich by cleaning up after evacuation. Surprisingly enough, the health and vitality of this young man does not anger Ivan Il'ich (as does the health and vitality of his daughter and her financé), but brings him comfort instead. In particular, Ivan Il'ich places a high value on Gerasim's truthfulness and ability to acknowledge that his master is not simply ill but is actually dying. His relationship to Ivan Il'ich is simple and direct. He acknowledges the terminal nature of Ivan Il'ich's illness without pretense and is willing to spend long periods of time patiently helping his master to feel better. Gerasim first appeared in chapter 1. There he had made Peter Ivanovich feel uncomfortable by reminding him that we will all die one day.

PAGE 153

"Gerasim raised his master's legs higher and Ivan Il'ich thought that in that position he did not feel any pain at all."

Gerasim's value to Ivan Il'ich is based primarily on two factors: Gerasim's truthfulness (and the salutary contrast between his truthfulness and candor, on the one hand, and the lying (*lozh'*) and convention of his wife, doctors, and acquaintances, on the other) and his willingness to spend long periods in intimate contact with Ivan Il'ich. This intimacy is emphatically physical; it involves helping Ivan Il'ich with his processes of bodily elimination and also sitting with him in such a manner so that Ivan Il'ich can place his heels on Gerasim's shoulders. The relationship with Gerasim is the first example of physical touching that is represented in Ivan Il'ich's life story. In the main, Ivan Il'ich has striven to cut himself off from other people. It has also been noted that the position in which Ivan Il'ich feels better is not dissimilar to the position in which women are placed in the process of giving birth. Thus chapter 7's antidote to the funereal gloom of chapter 6 goes so far as to raise the motif of birth to counter the motif of death, perhaps thereby introducing the possibility of rebirth into Ivan Il'ich's story.

"What tormented Ivan Il'ich most was the deception, the lie, which for some reason they all accepted, that he was not dying but was simply ill . . ."

From this point on the text makes it increasingly explicit that the spiritual pain of enduring the falseness and deception – the lies – with which he is surrounded and in which he participates is greater than the physical pain of his illness. One gets the sense that it is this moral pain that abates when he is in the company of Gerasim. As chapter 8 will make clear, however, the pain returns in full force (both physically and morally) in Gerasim's absence. Only Gerasim is able to tell Ivan Il'ich directly that he is dying. Only Gerasim seems capable of coming close to Ivan Il'ich, where "close" implies honesty, physical touch, and even the (highly inappropriate!) linguistic closeness of Gerasim's using the second-person singular, familiar, form of address in speaking to his master (154). The lie (*lozh'*) from this point on begins more and more to replace the physical illness from which Ivan Il'ich suffers; the lie, so to speak, now *becomes* his illness.

Chapter 8

PAGE 157

"Just as the doctor had adopted a certain relation to his patient which he could not abandon, so had she [Praskovya Fyodorovna] formed one towards him – that he was not doing something he ought to do and was himself to blame, and she reproached him lovingly for this – and now she could not change that attitude."

This very important passage conveys several messages simultaneously. The most obvious concerns the attitude that both the doctor and Praskovya Fyodorovna have adopted toward Ivan Il'ich and his illness. The Russian word Maude translates as "adopted" is *vyrabotal* (worked out; constructed by effort), suggesting the artificiality of their relation to him (despite their pleas of sincerity). The doctor's inability to "abandon" this attitude and Praskovya Fyodorovna's inability to "change" it are both reflections of the same Russian word *sniat* (to take down; to take off, as clothing or covers). Thus the attitude they have adopted toward him is a covering or screen they have put up between him and themselves. Once again, there is the familiar image of screens, curtains, fences, walls, and enclosures that we have seen so often in the attitudes of Ivan Il'ich himself.

A second point emerging from this passage is that her superficial attitude toward him is one of loving concern while at the same time it is clear that her actual attitude is one of hostile impatience for his death, that is, that her real attitude is the opposite of her professed attitude. A couple of paragraphs farther down, she makes the facetiously intended but nonetheless curious statement that everything she does for him is done "for my own sake" (157). The text adds this explanation: "He felt that he was surrounded and enmeshed in such a web of falsity that it was hard to unravel anything. Everything she did for him was entirely for her own sake; she told him she was doing for herself what she actually was doing for herself, as if that was so incredible he must understand the opposite" (157). From this it emerges that the truth can be known by understanding everything we observe in Ivan's everyday, physical life as its opposite. Thus when Praskovya Fyodorovna says facetiously that she is doing what she is doing only for herself, we should understand that she actually means this seriously.

Finally, since it is in fact true that Praskovya Fyodorovna really is concerned only with herself – that is, she is telling the truth here – perhaps it is possible that the other claim she makes here is also true, namely, her suggestion that Ivan Il'ich "was not doing something he ought to do and was himself to blame" for his condition. She, of course, believes herself to be speaking of her husband's physiological distress, just as, in the case of her other comment, she believes herself to be speaking facetiously. With respect to her husband's spiritual distress, however, it may be that she is unwittingly speaking the exact truth. What is required is to understand both what she says and what we as readers seem to see in reverse, the other way around, backward (*obratno*) in order to see the situation rightly. Therefore it is certain that her complaint that lying with his legs up on Gerasim's shoulders (157) is "bad for him" (since she means it seriously) is bound to be wrong. In fact, contact of this sort with Gerasim must be good for Ivan Il'ich. Following this line of thought we soon conclude that all the while we were being presented with what seemed to be an account of Ivan Il'ich's life, we were actually seeing the story of his death, and now, when we seem to be observing the increasingly rapid process of his death, we are actually seeing the beginnings of renewed life. The major idea to be grasped from this passage is that Ivan Il'ich himself by not "doing what he ought" has brought his spiritual illness and death on himself.

PAGE 158
"Sarah Bernhardt"

A famous French actress (1844–1923) who toured Russia in 1881–82. One of her most famous roles was that of Adrienne Lecouvreur in the play of that name by Scribe and Legouve. The heroine of the play is herself an actress, so we are presented here with the family's desire to hasten away from the bedside of its dying father and husband in order to be present at a play (an exercise in pretending and voluntary self-deception) in which one actress portrays the life of another actress. The distance between the family's proposed activity and the reality of life is astonishingly great. Of course, the family's ability to carry on with its plan of an evening at the theater is made possible in the first place only by pretending that Ivan Il'ich is only ill rather than dying. Ivan Il'ich resents most of all that he is required to join the family in this pretense. Only Ivan Il'ich's son is exempt from the hatred Ivan Il'ich begins to feel toward his family for their constant lying about his condition and their insistence that he, too, join them in this lie. The son, Vasya, is mentioned here (159) in the same sentence with Gerasim, the only other character who deals truthfully with Ivan Il'ich, and who touches him in a meaningful way. In chapter 12, Ivan Il'ich's moment of grace coincides with his hand being grasped by his son. In the context of this passage we might say that Gerasim and Vasya are concerned with life itself while the rest of the family and household prefers to deal with the imitation of life, both on the stage and in their own lives.

Chapter 9

PAGE 160

"It seemed to him that he and his pain were being thrust into a narrow, deep black sack, and though they were being pushed further and further in they could not be pushed to the bottom. . . . He was frightened, yet wanted to fall through the sack; he struggled, yet cooperated."

This is the first mention of the image of a narrow, black sack or bag or hole into which Ivan Il'ich feels himself being pushed. The image has played an important role in interpretations of the novel which emphasize that Ivan Il'ich, led by his sufferings, becomes spiritually reborn as his physical life ebbs away. The black bag, by its shape and color and the fact that when, in chapter 12, Ivan Il'ich feels that he has broken through the end of the bag into the light, has been seen as an effective symbol of the birth canal. In the same way, the trauma of birth seems well matched with the trauma of Ivan Il'ich's suffering and death. This interpretation, of course, fits very well with the concept that the novel privileges the method of "understanding in reverse." It seems quite natural in this context that the image of death should be tautologous with an image of life and also that Ivan Il'ich's attitude toward this image should be ambiguous: "he struggled, yet co-operated."

"He wept on account of his helplessness, his terrible loneliness, the cruelty of man, the cruelty of God, the absence of God. 'Why hast Thou done all this? Why hast Thou brought me here? Why, why dost Thou torment me so terribly?'"

Here is another reflection of the Passion narrative contained in the Gospels, specifically of Jesus' outcry "My God, my God, why hast Thou forsaken me?" (Matthew 27:46 inter alia).

"It was as though he were listening not to an audible voice, but to the voice of his soul . . ."

Here is the first indication that Ivan Il'ich does indeed have a soul, that he is more than the physiological being suffering so dreadfully from the effects of disease. We remember that in chapter 5 his "inner life" was still completely a question of the physical organs located within his body. Here the inner life and voice represent a qualitatively different kind of life. Ivan Il'ich's attention has finally been redirected from his physical life and sufferings to his spiritual life and sufferings. We note that, since chapter 7, it has seemed to him that his spiritual suffering has in fact been greater than his physical pain. At the end of chapter 9 (161) the thought occurs to him that "maybe I didn't live as I ought to have done," that is, that he is where he is by his own actions and responsibility. This thought, and the conclusion arising from it, is repeated yet again in each of the three remaining chapters.

Chapter 10

PAGE 162

"Another fortnight passed."

In chapter 7 it was noted that Ivan Il'ich's illness was in its third month. Here were learn that two more weeks have gone by. In chapter 11 weeks are mentioned again, and chapter 12 begins by mentioning days and concludes with the note that the agony of the patient lasted another two hours. Clearly the steadily diminishing units of time mentioned in the text are matched with the steadily decreasing size of the chapters in which they are mentioned. This lends a steadily accelerating rhythm to the final chapters. The text draws our attention to this in the passage: "And the example of a stone falling downwards with increasing velocity entered his mind" (163). The Russian text might be translated more exactly as: "And the image of a stone flying downward with increasing speed lodged in his soul" (literally, fell into his soul; *zapal v dushu*).

". . . loneliness . . . that could not have been more complete any-where – either at the bottom of the sea or under the earth . . ."

We note that both images supplied here suggest places of burial, providing confirmation that Ivan Il'ich is, for practical purposes, already long since dead and even buried. Thus the struggles he continues to face are suggested once more to be spiritual in kind, and to be associated with the rebirth of the spirit. From this also stems the importance Ivan Il'ich attaches to his childhood memories and his desire to be a child again and to be treated as a child (chapter 9). His preference is to move, in thought, spiritually, back from the life he has led toward the moment of his birth.

Chapter 11

PAGE 164

"It occurred to him that what had appeared perfectly impossible before, namely that he had not spent his life as he should have done, might be true after all. . . . if that's so and I'm leaving this life with the consciousness that I've lost all that was given to me . . ."

The Russian makes still clearer Ivan Il'ich's personal responsibility for the fact that his life was "wrong" (*ne to*). Maude's "I've lost all that was given to me" would be more accurately rendered as "I ruined (*pogubil*) everything that was given to me."

PAGE 165

"And to this was added a new sensation of grinding . . . pain"

The English does not capture the pun here on the word *vintit'* (to twist in, to screw in), which Maude translates as "grinding" and its homonym *vintit'* (to play *vint* [bridge]). Thus a tautology of sorts has been arranged between the pain (i.e., his illness, his death) and the card playing of which he was so fond. Not only was his life "wrong"; it was not life at all (the Russian *ne to* literally asserts that whatever has been is not at all the thing it is supposed to be). It was, in fact, not life, but death.

Chapter 12

"He was hindered from getting into it by his conviction that his life had been a good one."

This is the final appearance of the image of the black sack. We recall Ivan Il'ich's ambiguous relation to this sensation: his competing desires to resist and cooperate. Here the desire to "get into it" has supervened, and it is only his persistent desire to see his life as good that prevents him from doing so. We know with certainty from the material in the three preceding chapters that his life has not been good, has been characterized, in fact, as not having been "life" at all.

"What had happened to him was like the sensation one sometimes experiences in a railway carriage when one thinks one is going backwards while one is really going forwards and suddenly becomes aware of the real direction."

At this moment Ivan Il'ich finally realizes that his life has not been life at all in the true sense of the word, and we as readers receive our final clue that the significance of Ivan Il'ich's story can only be grasped by seeing it as the reverse of what it might appear to be: not only the story of how he died, but, more important, the story of how he returned to life.

"With a look at his wife he indicated his son and said: 'Take him away . . . sorry for him . . . and for you, too . . .'"

This is another allusion to the Passion narrative, the passage in which Jesus, near death, entrusts his mother to the care of the apostle John with the words "Mother, behold thy son; son, thy mother" (John 19:26–27).

"He tried to add 'Forgive me,' but said 'Let me through' . . ."

The confusion reflected here can be seen as a moment of coalescence between the spiritual concerns of the novel and the physiological description of Ivan Il'ich's illness and death. At the final moment the forgiveness requested for a life that was wrong becomes mixed with the passage out of that life. In this way the novel may be seen to remain true both to its account of Ivan Il'ich's physical death and to its story of his spiritual rebirth.

PAGE 167
"Suddenly it grew clear to him that what had been oppressing him and would not leave him was all dropping away at once from two sides, from ten sides, from all sides."

The entire course of the story of Ivan Il'ich's life has prepared us for this moment at which the space available to him would shrink to no space at all (his movement from the breadth of the provinces, to localization in a single city, to confinement at home rather than going to work, to a preference to remain always in his study, to his final positioning on the sofa, and then at last to a particular position on the sofa – facing into the back of it). But as this moment is reached, these confinements are transcended and Ivan Il'ich is precipitated into a region that has no limits whatsoever: "In place of death there was light" (167).

A similar phenomenon occurs with respect to the dimension of time. The steadily shortening temporal framework (from years, to months, to weeks, to days, to hours) has been leading Ivan Il'ich to the moment when his time is up, when no time at all remains. Instead, time, too, is transcended and we learn that "all this happened in a single instant, and the meaning of that instant did not change" (167). This changeless instant is described in the Russian as one that "no longer continued to change" (*uzhe ne izmenialos*).

It is also clear, however, that the ordinary course of time, despite the transcendence asserted in these passages, also continues. Although Ivan Il'ich has somehow escaped the ruin of his body, that body still continues its course toward death without interruption: "For those present, his agony continued for another two hours" (67).

"It is finished!"

This is the last of several allusions to the Passion story related in the Gospels. Tolstoy here uses the very same expression he had employed in emending the received Russian (Slavonic) translation of John 19:30. It is, besides, a final affirmation of the principle of reading in reverse which we have been pursuing through these annotations; the final note the novel sounds would seem to be not that the life of Ivan Il'ich is finished but that it has finally begun.

IV SELECT BIBLIOGRAPHY

Select Bibliography

Primary Works

Polnoe sobranie sochinenii v devianosto tomakh (*Complete collected works in ninety volumes*). Moscow: Gosudarstvennoe Izdatel'stvo Khudozhestvennoi Literatury, 1928–58.

    Called the "Jubilee edition" because its publication commenced on the hundredth anniversary of Tolstoy's birth, this is the standard scholarly edition of Tolstoy's works. It contains printed and manuscript variants, supplemented by introductions to and commentary on the texts. In addition, it contains the most complete collection of Tolstoy's letters, diaries, notebooks, and other personal papers. Text of and commentary on *The Death of Ivan Il'ich* (*Smert' Ivana Il'icha*) is in volume 26 of this edition.

The Death of Ivan Ilych. In *Tolstoy's Short Fiction*, edited and with revised translations by Michael R. Katz, 123–67. New York: Norton, 1991.

    Of the many translations of *The Death of Ivan Il'ich* currently available, this edition, originally translated by Louise and Aylmer Maude, provides the best text for study. It provides a translation of the text by persons who were closely acquainted with Tolstoy and who had the benefit of his advice with respect to the translation of difficult passages. Their work has been further improved by the editor's revisions. The annotations in part 3 of the present volume are keyed to this edition and provide further clarification of various points of translation. The Norton edition also contains a helpful supplement of scholarly materials, including extracts from Tolstoy's personal papers and letters, a selection of scholarly articles on Tolstoy's short fiction, a chronology of his life and works, and a select bibliography.

Tolstoy's Letters, edited and translated by R. F. Christian. 2 vols. New York: Scribner's, 1978.

Tolstoy's Diaries, edited and translated by R. F. Christian. 2 vols. New York: Scribner's, 1985.

Secondary Works

Barrett, William. "Existentialism as a Symptom of Man's Contemporary Crisis." In *Spiritual Problems in Contemporary Literature*, edited by Stanley Hopper, 139–52. New York: Harper, 1952.
  Brief discussion of the novel as exemplary of the spiritual emptiness of modern life.

Bartell, James. "The Trauma of Birth in *The Death of Ivan Ilych*: A Therapeutic Reading." *Psychological Review* 2 (1978): 97–117.
  The novel discussed from the vantage point of certain schemes of psychotherapy.

Borker, David. "Sentential Structure in Tolstoy's *Smert' Ivana Il'icha*." In *American Contributions to the VIal International Congress of Slavists: Linguistics and Poetics*, edited by H. Birnbaum, vol. 1, 180–95. Columbus, Ohio: Slavica, 1978.
  A linguistic analysis of the sentence structure of the novel.

Cain, T. G. S. *Tolstoy*. New York: Barnes and Noble, 1977.
  General overview of the life and works of Tolstoy; contains a chapter on the novel.

Carr, Arthur C. *The Death of Ivan Illych*. New York: Health Sciences, 1973.

Cate, Hollis L. "On Death and Dying in Tolstoy's *The Death of Ivan Ilyich*." *Hartford Studies in Literature* 7 (1975): 195–205.
  Discussion of the novel in the context of modern discussions of the stages of dying and death.

Christian, R. F. *Tolstoy: A Critical Introduction*. Cambridge: Cambridge University Press, 1969.
  The standard life and works of Tolstoy in English; contains a solid and circumspect discussion of the novel.

Clive, Geoffrey. "Tolstoy and the Varieties of the Inauthentic." In *The Broken Icon: Intuitive Existentialism in Classical Russian Fiction*, 86–127. New York: Macmillan, 1970.
  Approaches the novel as a portrait of a spiritually and emotionally empty life.

Danaher, David S. "Tolstoi's Use of Light and Dark Imagery in *The Death of Ivan Il'ich*." *Slavic and East European Journal* 39 (1995): 227–40.

Dayananda, Y. J. "The Death of Ivan Ilych: A Psychological Study on Death and Dying." *Literature and Psychology* 22 (1972): 191–98.

The most complete discussion of the novel as a fictional precursor to modern discussions of the stages of dying and death.

Donnelly, John. "Death and Ivan Ilych." In *Language, Metaphysics, and Death*, edited by J. Donnelly, 116–30. New York: Fordham University Press, 1978.

The novel is used as a point of departure for the author's own philosophical reflections.

Duncan, Robert. "Ivan Ilych's Death: Secular or Religious?" *University of Dayton Review* 15 (1981): 99–106.

Edel, Leon. "Portrait of the Artist as an Old Man." In *Aging, Death, and the Completion of Being*, edited by David D. Van Tassel, 193–214. Philadelphia: University of Pennsylvania Press, 1979.

Edgerton, William B. "Tolstoy, Immortality, and Twentieth-Century Physics." *Canadian Slavonic Papers* 21 (1979): 300 ff.

A seminal contribution to the discussion of patterns of reversal in the novel.

Eremin, M., "Podrobnosti i smysl tselogo. Iz nabljudenii nad tekstom povesti *Smert' Ivana Il'icha*." In *V mire Tolstogo*, edited by S. Mashinskii. Moscow: Sovetskii pisatel', 1978.

Glicksberg, Charles L. "Tolstoy and *The Death of Ivan Illyitch*." In his *The Ironic Vision in Modern Literature*, 81–86. Hague: Nijhoff, 1969.

Gubler, Donworth V. "A Study of Illness and Death in the Lives and Representative Works of Leo Tolstoy and Thomas Mann." Ph.D. diss., Brigham Young University. Summary in *Dissertation Abstracts International*, vol. 32, 4000A.

Gustafson, Richard F. *Leo Tolstoy: Resident and Stranger.* Princeton, N.J.: Princeton University Press, 1986.

A very important book on Tolstoy; based firmly in an extensive knowledge of Tolstoy's diaries, letters, and nonfictional writings; the most complete modern treatment of the relationship between Tolstoy and the established church.

Gustafson, Richard F. "The Three Stages of Man." *Canadian-American Slavic Studies* 12 (1978): 481–518.

Gutsche, George. *Moral Apostasy in Russian Literature.* DeKalb: Northern Illinois University Press, 1986.

Contains a chapter on the novel, which provides an excellent synthesis of previous scholarship and an original view of the novel, particularly of the moral perceptions and struggles of the protagonist.

Halperin, Irving. "The Structural Integrity of *The Death of Ivan Il'ich*." *Slavic and East European Journal* 5 (1961): 334–40.
One of the first studies to point out the significance of the novel's organization and structure.

Hirschberg, W. R. "Tolstoy's *The Death of Ivan Illych*." *Explicator* 28, no. 3 (1969): item 26.

Howe, Irving. "Leo Tolstoy: *The Death of Ivan Illych*." In *Classics of Modern Fiction*, 113–78. New York: Harcourt Brace Jovanovich, 1972.

Jahn, Gary R. "The Death of Ivan Il'ich – Chapter One." In *Studies in Nineteenth and Twentieth Century Polish and Russian Literature in Honor of Xenia Gasiorowska*, 37–43. Columbus, Ohio: Slavica, 1983.
Discussion of the placement of the first chapter in violation of the novel's predominantly chronological organization.

Jahn, Gary R. "A Note on the Miracle Motifs in the Later Works of Lev Tolstoi." In *The Supernatural in Slavic and Baltic Literatures: Essays in Honor of Victor Terras*, 191–99. Columbus, Ohio: Slavica, 1988.
Discussion of the references to the crucifixion of Jesus in the novel.

Jahn, Gary R. "The Role of the Ending in Lev Tolstoi's *The Death of Ivan Il'ich*." *Canadian Slavonic Papers* 24 (1982): 229–38.
Discussion of patterns of reversal, structural considerations, and multiple levels of significance in the novel.

Jahn, Gary R. *The Death of Ivan Il'ich: An Interpretation*. New York: Twayne, 1993.

Matual, David. "'The Confession' as Subtext in *The Death of Ivan Ilich*." *International Fiction Review* 8 (1981): 121–30.
Discussion of the connection between the novel and Tolstoy's earlier work *A Confession*.

Olney, James. "Experience, Metaphor, and Meaning: *The Death of Ivan Iliych*." *Journal of Aesthetics and Art Criticism* 31 (1972): 101–14.
An important contribution to the discussion of the use of symbol and metaphor in the novel.

Opul'skaia, L. D. *Lev Nikolaevich Tolstoi: Materialy k biografii s 1886 po 1892 god*, 7–16. Moscow: Nauka, 1979.

Pachmuss, Temira. "The Theme of Love and Death in Tolstoy's *The*

Death of Ivan Ilych." *American Slavic and East European Review* 20 (1961): 72–83.

Parthé, Kathleen. "The Metamorphosis of Death in Tolstoy." *Language and Style* 18 (1985): 205–14.

    Further discussion of Tolstoy's attempts to deal with his own deeply rooted fear of death.

Parthé, Kathleen. "Tolstoy and the Geometry of Fear." *Modern Language Studies* 15 (1985): 480–92.

    A discussion of Tolstoy's attitudes toward death as shown in the novel and in other works of Tolstoy.

Rahv, Philip. "*The Death of Ivan Illych* and Joseph K." In *Image and Idea: Twenty Essays on Literary Themes*, 121–40. Norfolk, Conn.: New Directions, 1957.

    Discussion of the comparability between the novel and Kafka's *The Trial.*

Raleigh, John Henry. "Tolstoy and Sight: The Dual Nature of Reality." *Essays in Criticism: A Quarterly Journal of Literary Criticism* 21: 170–79.

Reichbart, Richard. "Psi Phenomena and Tolstoi." *Journal of the American Society for Psychological Research* 70 (1976): 249–65.

Rogers, Philip. "Scrooge on the Neva: Dickens and Tolstoy's *Death of Ivan Il'ich.*" *Comparative Literature* 40 (1988): 193–218.

Russell, Robert. "From Individual to Universal: Tolstoy's *Smert' Ivana Il'icha.*" *Modern Language Review* 76 (1981): 629–42.

    Discussion of the means Tolstoy employed to "globalize" the experience of the protagonist.

Salys, Rimgaila. "Signs on the Road of Life: *The Death of Ivan Il'ich.*" *Slavic and East European Journal* 30 (1986): 18–28.

    An excellent, detailed study of metaphor in the novel, especially the covert significance of foreign-language phrases.

Schaarschmidt, Gunter. "Theme and Discourse Structure in *The Death of Ivan Il'ich.*" *Canadian Slavonic Papers* 21 (1979): 356–66.

    Commentary on the organization of the novel and of the interface between theme and organization.

Schefski, Harold K. "Tolstoy's Case Against Doctors." *Slavic and East European Journal* 22 (1978): 569–73.

    Information on Tolstoy's attitude toward the medical profession.

Shepherd, D. "Conversion, Reversion, and Subversion in Tolstoi's *The*

Death of Ivan Il'ich." *Slavonic and East European Review* 71 (1993): 401–16.

Shestov, Lev. *The Good in the Teaching of Tolstoy and Nietzsche: Philosophy and Preaching.* Athens: Ohio University Press, 1969.

Shestov, Lev. "The Last Judgment: Tolstoy's Last Works." In *In Job's Balances: On the Sources of the Eternal Truths,* 83–138. Athens: Ohio University Press, 1957.

    An important reading of Tolstoi by a contemporary and one of the founders of existentialist thought.

Smyrniw, Walter. "Tolstoy's Depiction of Death in the Context of Recent Studies of the Experience of Dying." *Canadian Slavonic Papers* 21 (1979): 376–79.

Sorokin, Boris. "Ivan Il'ich as Jonah: A Cruel Joke." *Canadian Slavic Studies* 5 (1971): 487–507.

    A thought-provoking analysis of certain aspects of the symbolism of the novel.

Spanos, William V. "Leo Tolstoy's *The Death of Ivan Ilych:* A Temporal Interpretation." In *De-Structing the Novel: Essays in Applied Postmodern Hermeneutics,* 1–64. Troy, N.Y.: Whitston, 1982.

Speirs, Logan. "Tolstoy and Chekhov: *The Death of Ivan Ilych* and *A Dreary Story.*" *Oxford Review* 8 (1968): 81–93.

Tarasov, B. "Analiz burzhuaznogo soznaniia v povesti L. N. Tolstogo, *Smert' Ivana Il'icha.*" *Voprosy literatury* 3 (1982): 156–76.

Turner, C. J. G. "The Language of Fiction: Word Cluster in Tolstoy's *The Death of Ivan Ilych.*" *Modern Language Review* 65 (1970): 116–21.

    Discussion of the placement of the first chapter of the novel.

Wasiolek, Edward. *Tolstoy's Major Fiction.* Chicago: University of Chicago Press, 1978.

    Discussion of Tolstoy's most important works; contains a chapter on the novel.

Wasiolek, Edward. "Tolstoy's *The Death of Ivan Ilych* and Jamesian Fictional Imperatives." *Modern Fiction Studies* 6 (1960): 314–24.

    A discussion of the possible strategies that might be followed in reading the novel.

Wexelblatt, Robert. "The Higher Parody: Ivan Ilych's Metamorphosis and the Death of Gregor Samsa." *Massachusetts Review* 21 (1980): 601–28.

    Comparison of the novel with Kafka's story "The Metamorphosis."

Zhdanov, Vladimir Aleksandrovich. *Ot Anny Kareninoi k Voskreseniiu.* Moscow: Kniga, 1967.

Contributors

George J. Gutsche is a professor of Russian and the head of the Department of Russian and Slavic Languages at the University of Arizona. From 1989 to 1996 he served as executive director of the American Association of Teachers of Slavic and East European Languages. He has published numerous articles on nineteenth- and twentieth-century Russian literature. His books include *Moral Apostasy in Russian Literature, New Perspectives on Nineteenth-Century Russian Prose* (coedited with Lauren Leighton), and a volume of the *Modern Encyclopedia of Russian and Soviet Literature.* He is currently writing a monograph on Alexander Pushkin.

Gary R. Jahn is a professor of Russian at the University of Minnesota. He is the author of numerous essays on Tolstoy and other Russian authors and of a monograph on *The Death of Ivan Il'ich.*

Daniel Rancour-Laferriere is a professor of Russian and the director of the Russian Program at the University of California, Davis. He has published numerous articles on psychoanalysis and Russian literature. His most recent book is *Tolstoy on the Couch: Misogyny, Masochism, and the Absent Mother.* Rancour-Laferriere's current research is on Russian ethnonational identity.

Philip Rogers is an associate professor of English at SUNY Binghamton, specializing in the English Victorian period, with secondary interests in English-Russian literary relations. His writings include essays on Dickens and Tolstoy and Zamyatin, and a book dealing with Charlotte Brontë's politics.

Rimgaila Salys is an associate professor of Russian at the University of Colorado at Boulder and specializes in twentieth-century literature and culture. She is the author of a catalogue raisonné and study of the artist Leonid Osipovich Pasternak and *Olesha's Envy* (Northwestern University Press, 1999).

Chris (C. J. G.) Turner studied at Cambridge, Munich, and Oxford Universities, has taught Russian at McMaster University and the University of British Columbia, and has written books on Lermontov, Tolstoy, and Chekov and articles on Byzantine and Russian topics.